Arms Proliferation Policy

Support to the Presidential Advisory Board

Marcy Agmon

James L. Bonomo

Michael Kennedy

Maren Leed

Kenneth Watman

Katharine Webb

Charles Wolf, Jr.

Prepared for the
Office of the Secretary of Defense

National Defense Research Institute

RAND

Title XVI, Section 1601 of the National Defense Authorization Act for Fiscal Year 1994 mandated the creation of the President's Advisory Board on Arms Proliferation Policy to conduct a study of (1) the factors that contribute to the proliferation of strategic and advanced conventional military weapons and related equipment and technologies, and (2) the policy options that are available to the United States to inhibit such proliferation. The five-member Board, established by Executive Order 12946 on January 20, 1995, was tasked to advise the President on implementation of United States conventional arms transfer policy, other issues related to arms proliferation policy, and other matters deemed appropriate by the President. Areas specified for study in the Board's Terms of Reference include trends in the international arms market, instruments of restraint, export financing facilities, and the relationship between arms exports and the defense industrial base.

In April 1995, RAND was asked to provide analytical and documentation support to the President's Advisory Board. The research reported here was performed for the project, "RAND Support for the President's Advisory Board on Arms Proliferation Policy," conducted within the International Security and Defense Policy Center of RAND's National Defense Research Institute (NDRI), a federally funded research and development center sponsored by the Office of the Secretary of Defense and the Joint Staff. The study was supported by the Under Secretary of Defense for Policy.

The report should be of interest to U.S. government agencies, nongovernment agencies, Congress, and private organizations interested in issues related to conventional arms transfer and control. Those in the defense industry and political scientists concerned with national security affairs should also find the report useful.

CONTENTS

TABLE

This project provided the President's Advisory Board on Arms Proliferation Policy with background information and research on a number of topics, including a review of trends in the international arms market, instruments of restraint for use with weapons and weapons-related technologies, the economics of arms exports, and the implementation of arms and technology export-control regulations. This report documents the RAND research provided to the Board. As the document supporting the *Report of the Presidential Advisory Board on Arms Proliferation Policy*, this study does not contain overarching recommendations concerning arms proliferation policy. It does contain some analytical conclusions pertaining to the above issues.

The Board neither endorses nor rejects the detailed aspects of the RAND study that follows below. In key areas of both policy and process, however, the RAND approach is consistent with the Board's thinking and findings.

OVERVIEW

The control of conventional arms and technology transfers must become a more important and integral element of United States foreign and defense policy if the overall goals of nonproliferation are to succeed. Through improvements in precision, conventional weapons have attained degrees of military effectiveness previously associated only with nuclear weapons. Moreover, these conventional weapons can destroy military targets without the massive collateral casualties and damage that would result from use of weapons of mass destruction, making their military use less constrained by political factors.

Arms transfers can be expected to remain a central element of America's national security strategy. To mitigate their potential significant risks, however, policy decisions on trade in strategic technologies and advanced conventional weapons will continue to require an artful reconciliation of complex competing national priorities. Foreign policy, national security, and economic interests that are served by the approval or denial of particular weapons sales can be compelling, but often pull in different directions. Striking the right balance among cross-cutting priorities is the key to an effective weapons transfer policy. What makes this task particularly difficult is the need for consensus among the major weapons suppliers; in the absence of consensus, unilateral U.S. restraint in weapons transfers can be circumvented to the profit of other suppliers. This means that solutions must be found that accommodate the national security, foreign policy, and economic interests of other key supplier states as well.

The major suppliers remain in economic competition for the sales of conventional weapons, and this economic competition is perhaps the greatest remaining obstacle to developing a cooperative control regime among suppliers. Although the end of the cold war has brought the potential for increased cooperation among states, there is also a dampening of enthusiasm for restraint. In major supplier nations, shrinking federal budgets have increased the perceived importance of exports as a means of sustaining the financial viability of defense firms. Exports are similarly being viewed as a mechanism to maintain the defense industrial base, a rising concern as domestic weapons procurement is falling.[1] The heart of the problem is striking a balance between the preservation of advanced conventional military production capabilities and a healthy industrial base, on the one hand, and restraining exports that imprudently accelerate the diffusion of advanced conventional weapons and associated technologies.

TRENDS

U.S. conventional arms exports have averaged around $10 billion for the past eight years, although U.S. sales as a proportion of the world's total arms exports have increased from 25 percent in 1987 to a predicted share of almost 60 percent by the end of the century. During the same period, major European producers nearly doubled their arms sales, almost 24 percent of the world total in 1995. Some 60 percent of these sales were to countries outside Europe. The expansion of the U.S. and European nations' market share has displaced some of Russia's weapons exports (or deliveries), which have dropped dramatically in the past several years, although Russia's actual earnings from weapons transfers have remained relatively stable. Russia has recently become more aggressive in pursuing increased sales, particularly in Asia. In contrast to the United States and Europe, Chinese defense spending per person has remained at about the same level for the past decade. During this period China has displayed a willingness to sell to countries in unstable regions or to countries that have been identified as pariahs by other producers.

The result of the widespread decline in national weapons acquisition is substantial excess capacity for weapons production, which in turn has led to increased competition among the major suppliers. Not only is there competition in pricing but there is increased pressure to offer state-of-the-art equipment previously reserved for national or allied forces. Not all buyers can afford to buy new platforms, so some countries have pursued upgrades to improve their stocks.

The Middle East accounts for the majority of arms purchases, with Saudi Arabia expected to remain the largest single weapons buyer in the world for the remainder of the decade. The Europeans have also been major importers in the 1990s, although

---

[1]U.S. Department of Defense, Office of the Under Secretary of Defense (Acquisition and Technology), *World-Wide Conventional Arms Trade (1994-2000): A Forecast and Analysis,* Washington, DC, Department of Defense, December 1994.

purchases are likely to tail off toward the end of the decade. Although arms exports to East Asia have been in relative decline since 1987, the region is expected to overtake Europe by the year 2000. This is a region where the indigenous arms industry has grown and where interest in collaboration with European and U.S. firms is on the rise. Arms exports in South Asia have declined since 1989; however both India and Pakistan plan major purchases in the next several years. Improved economic circumstances in South America are facilitating the purchase of arms, although U.S. transfer decisions are complicated by internal policy disputes.

Collaborative R&D and procurement programs are also on the rise in response to cuts in defense budgets. Coproduction agreements, or other offsets transferring production knowledge, can create potential new producers and may result in a loss of jobs at home. While industry's self-interest provides some check on the transfer of particularly sensitive processes or technologies, and foreign trade generally has a positive impact on employment, the government review process must continue to examine transfer agreements closely.

The emergence of new suppliers is a trend fueled by regional conflicts and an increased demand for items such as antitank weapons and artillery, which many less-industrialized countries can produce. Israel, South Africa, many East European countries, and states that were part of the Soviet Union are among the new suppliers competing for markets.

One result of the proliferation of producers and buyers is that concerns and interests are focused on particular regions rather than on global conventional proliferation. To gain support for global conventional nonproliferation goals may require greater cooperation on the part of the major suppliers to accommodate their respective national security concerns. An area of common concern is the need to control or prevent arms trade with so-called "rogue states" such as Iran, Iraq, Libya, and North Korea.

With greater leverage than in the past, buyers have been seeking and finding lower prices and other special-purchase arrangements. More worrisome, suppliers' pressing economic incentives to export are enabling regional arms buyers to acquire front-line, state-of-the-art military equipment and technologies that previously were not available to them. The value and effectiveness of high-technology weapons systems in the Persian Gulf War were clear and dramatic, and the desire to acquire these types of systems has sharply increased. Few such systems have actually been transferred thus far, but pressures are growing to do so. Thus, despite the worldwide quantitative reduction in the level of production and acquisition of conventional weapons in recent years, there is reason for renewed attention to the dangers of conventional weapons and technology proliferation. And there is opportunity in the momentum of new international initiatives, such as the Wassenaar Arrangement.

DOMESTIC AND INTERNATIONAL ARMS TRANSFER REGIMES AND REGULATIONS CURRENTLY IN PLACE

The two primary U.S. acts that include general restrictions related to conventional arms transfers are the Arms Export Control Act (AECA) of 1976, as amended, and the Export Administration Act (EAA) of 1979, as amended. With antecedents dating to the Battle Act of 1954, the AECA outlines eligibility guidelines for arms recipients, and limits the sale (and resale) of military equipment. The Export Administration Act restricts the export of dual-use goods or technologies that could be used either for weapons of mass destruction or for conventional arms.

International arrangements relating to conventional weapons transfers include the Missile Technology Control Regime (MTCR), a voluntary regime created in 1987 to control the proliferation of missiles and related technologies; the UN Transparency in Armaments Initiative (TIA), also known as the UN Register of Conventional Arms, established in 1991 to promote "openness" or "transparency" in the transfer of arms; the Wassenaar Arrangement on Export Controls for Conventional Arms and Dual-Use Goods and Technologies, which aims to control the export of both conventional weapons and dual-use technologies; and the Convention on Conventional Weapons (also known as the Inhumane Weapons Convention), which aims to restrict the wartime use of weapons fragments not detectable by x-ray, of land mines and booby traps, and of incendiary weapons.

A REGIME TO CONTROL THE TRANSFER OF CONVENTIONAL WEAPONS

Transparency is one approach to regulating the transfer of weapons, although such regimes do not bind participants to refrain from selling whenever and whatever they wish. A second approach is to specify formal and explicit limits on transfers on particular types or amounts of weapons. While formal agreements are more binding than transparency regimes, they are also more difficult to achieve. Successful implementation of an international regime to control conventional weapons will require recognition by the key suppliers that the benefits of accepting controls outweigh the benefits of continued sales. One set of criteria designed to increase the benefits of controls and decrease the costs would control only those weapons that have (1) high military effectiveness, (2) low substitutability, and (3) low opportunity cost.

Highly effective weapons are those that can threaten targets of value and for which there are few, if any, counters even when in the hands of a relatively unsophisticated user. Weapons that function autonomously can perform as well for unsophisticated as for sophisticated militaries, thereby offsetting inadequacies in training and organization. While some advanced systems require a few trained individuals to operate them, these capabilities are within the reach of most nations. Autonomous weapons that also have precision capabilities, such as long range and stealth, can attack targets with high confidence of success and resist defenses and other countermeasures. Some examples of weapons with these characteristics are submarines, stealth aircraft, advanced sea and land mines, advanced missiles and munitions, tactical ballistic missiles and cruise missiles with advanced conventional warheads, and directed-energy weapons.

Many types of autonomous, precise weapons currently have few, or no, substitutes. A related consideration is the speed with which states could develop substitutes to circumvent the controls. In both cases, the autonomous functioning characteristic is critical—it is what makes highly effective weapons useful to less capable armies, and the technical expertise needed to make such weapons is considerable.

Controlling highly advanced munitions and missiles rather than weapons platforms greatly reduces the costs of participating in a control regime. In the example of transfers to the Middle East, 85 to 90 percent of total revenues generated by first-tier suppliers to the region came from major end items such as tanks, aircraft, and ships. Missiles, munitions, and other highly effective weapons account for only a small portion of the revenues generated by arms sales.

Pressure to sell such highly effective weapons is increasing. Several types of autonomous, precise weapons are on the verge of being marketed. The Gulf War provided a powerful demonstration of the effectiveness of advanced weapons, and as existing arms stocks become obsolete countries will seek to replace them with these more modern weapons. Many of the advanced weapons soon to be available from the major suppliers are attractive to regional powers, including antiship and antitank missiles. Therefore, the time available to control some of these weapons before they are widely disseminated is decreasing.

Another approach to stimulating conventional arms control is to emphasize restraint in the sale of weapons that raise international concerns because of the risks they pose to noncombatants or because of their perceived repugnance, even when used on the battlefield. Examples of these "weapons of ill repute" include dumdum, exploding, or poisoned bullets, chemical and biological weapons, some fragmentation weapons, and some incendiary weapons and land mines. The advantage of focusing on these weapons is that the international opprobrium associated with their use may make efforts to discuss their control easier.

REGIMES FOR CONTROLLING TECHNOLOGY TRANSFERS

It has long been recognized that controlling the technologies critical to the manufacture and functioning of weapons is an important component of controlling proliferation. Technology controls implemented during the cold war are no longer in place, and even before their demise, were under pressure from those wishing to loosen the rules on commercial trade. Increasing reliance on commercial technology for military applications has increased the number of dual-use technologies and the growing number of multinational corporations, with technological capabilities located in many nations, makes control of technology diffusion difficult. Political, economic, and technical developments have erased many of the lines separating commercial and military technologies, have increased the incentives to transfer technologies or develop them indigenously, and have decreased the sense of common threat that sustained controls in the past.

As with arms transfers, control of technology transfers must be based on an acceptable balance on effectiveness and opportunity costs. Controls of single-use technologies, such as the traveling-wave tubes (TWTs) used in the Advanced Medium Range Air-to-Air Missile (AMRAAM), can be based on straightforward export prohibitions, because they have no significant commercial applications. In addition to the monitoring and re-export restrictions that might be included in an export prohibition regime, control of related design skills might also be limited. Such knowledge-based technologies are generally transferred through joint programs. Such technologies are clearly transferred in codevelopment efforts, but some are even transferred in coproduction programs through the inevitable testing and rework involved.

Controlling dual-use technologies is more complex and should focus on the application of the technology to weaponry rather than on simple prohibitions on exports. The task is to devise a control regime that permits both increased trade in the commercial applications of a technology and effective limitations on military end users. Focusing controls on the application of a technology requires a general principle of full disclosure of the application in return for freer trade. This in turn requires confidence in the buyer's statements of intended application.

Assessing a buyer's performance may be done by nonintrusive or intrusive means. Nonintrusive verification would include memoranda of understanding and agreements, national technical means of verification, limitations designed into the transferred technologies, and transparency measures. Intrusive measures would include inspections and tagging, perhaps with the use of "smart" tags which report information back on the items' position or use. Controlling dual-use design skills becomes even more difficult as these may be transferred in the context of a commercial transaction. Because particular firms in industry are in the best position to identify the importance of the dual-use technologies they are "giving up," the government should work in partnership with industry to reinforce the coincidence of proprietary and military interests in restraint. Finally, no system of overseeing the applications of dual-use technologies is useful unless violations are punished.

Logically, the technologies to control first are the ones associated with the critical weapons characteristics discussed earlier—autonomous operation, precision, stealth, and long range. Industry should be involved in efforts to classify technologies by their relationship to these characteristics.

Technologies so early in development they have no immediate specific application are not covered by the system described here, yet they may be used to make weapons in the longer term. Where a concept of operations can be defined by which technology could be used in a putative weapon, for example, antisatellite weapons, the key systems and subsystems can be identified and regulated appropriately. In fact, because such systems are not yet deployed, it may be easier to forge an international agreement on limits. The harder case is technologies with many potential applications but with no particular application yet evident. An example might be those technologies having a sweeping effect on the world, such as telecommunications and computing technologies or emerging biotechnologies. It is unclear how these technologies could be identified as candidates for limits, at least until their military applications become more sharply defined.

IMPLEMENTATION: INTERNATIONAL INSTRUMENTS AND POLICY PROPOSALS

Effective control over exports of key, high-leverage weapons and components requires multinational participation. The Board was presented with several proposals involving the participation of other key countries; only one proposal, the Wassenaar Arrangement, is currently being implemented. The proposals included: (1) a concept of an "Inner Circle" with "Concentric Circles" of participating countries, (2) a successor to the Coordinating Committee on Multilateral Exports (CoCom) regime—the Wassenaar Arrangement, (3) a computer-based registry system, and (4) a Market Stabilizing Mechanism.

Five criteria were used to evaluate these alternatives: (1) their consistency with U.S. foreign and defense policies; (2) their effectiveness in inhibiting proliferation of key, high-leverage weapons; (3) incentive effects on suppliers and buyers; (4) their general economic effects on U.S. defense industry (e.g., in forgone revenues); and (5) their administrative practicability.

The Inner Circle concept would provide U.S. allies with access to U.S. technology as an incentive for cooperation in the control of weapons and technology proliferation. Other countries would compose the Concentric Circles. The degree of restraint imposed on them would depend on a number of criteria, including the closeness of their alliance to the United States and the reliability of their own controls over re-exports.

The 28-member Wassenaar Arrangement is very different from the CoCom regime it nominally replaced. It is global in scope, and aims to implement restraint in dealing with current problems and to use transparency to address future ones. It encompasses both conventional arms and dual-use technologies. A small group, made up of the P-5[2] (minus China) plus Germany and Italy—all of the major weapons exporters—will deal exclusively with conventional arms sales. The potential for multilateral restraint is greater in this small group than anywhere else.

The computer-based registry is a disclosure-based regulatory system that would reduce or eliminate the information asymmetry between government regulators and industry suppliers of advanced and advancing technology. Currently, the pace of technological change enables industry suppliers and prospective arms buyers to negate a regime's effectiveness by decomposing proscribed systems or finding substitutes for them. The computer-based registry would require all companies involved in the exports of weapons or dual-use technologies to register and tag each item throughout its product cycle with essential information concerning its specifications,

---

[2]The five permanent members of the UN Security Council: the United States, United Kingdom, France, Russia, and China.

destination, recipient, and end use. By monitoring this information the government could interrupt transfers that failed to meet prescribed requirements.

A Market Stabilizing Mechanism (MSM) would operate under the aegis of an MSM Council consisting of both a suppliers' group and a buyers' group. The MSM Council would focus on prohibiting or severely limiting those weapons systems that tend to destabilize interregional or intraregional arms balances.

The types of control regimes described here differ widely from one another, but this does not imply mutual incompatibility. Linking the Wassenaar Arrangement with the computer-based registry and the MSM could be quite useful, although it would require a degree of attention in the policy community that is not easy to envisage in the near future.

THE ECONOMIC IMPACT OF CONVENTIONAL ARMS EXPORTS

The economic and defense industrial base effects of arms sales are often raised in discussions of arms export policy. Three important issues are:

- What is the evidence on the quantitative economic and industrial impact of arms exports?

- What are the pros and cons of including economic considerations in decisions concerning arms exports?

- What are the pros and cons of other policy options concerning arms exports, such as export financing and R&D recoupment charges?

The findings of this report on these issues can be summarized as follows:

1. The post–cold war reduction in arms production (over 50 percent) has had major negative economic effects on workers and localities associated with defense industries. The arms export market is small relative to this reduction, however, and is not a potential source for major alleviation of these negative impacts. Other policies must be brought to bear.

2. Whereas arms exports cannot alleviate the economic and industrial problems associated with the downsizing of the arms industry after the cold war, these exports can have strong positive local and regional economic impacts, as well as substantial industrial benefits for the U.S. Defense Department. Therefore, political pressures to approve arms exports to achieve these benefits are strong. However, there are also strong arguments for not permitting economic or industrial base considerations to override national security considerations in arms export decisions, especially when the arms export in question is governed by an international agreement.

3. Changes in public policy toward arms exports are under way or are being considered. One recent change will permit the federal government to provide export finance guarantees for defense sales; another would repeal the recoupment charge for R&D expenditure currently assessed on foreign military sales (FMS) of

major defense equipment. There are two arguments for these changes. The first is that, *once it is determined that an arms sale is in the U.S. national security and foreign policy interest,* these sales should have no additional burden put on them. Since other exports are eligible for export finance and free of any government-imposed R&D recoupment charge, this argument implies that arms exports should be accorded the same treatment. The second argument is that other arms-exporting nations financially support their industries' sales, and, therefore, current U.S. policy does not result in a neutral playing ground for U.S. exporters. There are several arguments against such changes, however. The first is that extending export financing to arms sales would provide politically unwise encouragement of such trade at a time when weapons proliferation poses detrimental security risks. (This argument presumably implies that the foreign policy and national security review of the sales is inadequate.) The second is that foreign arms purchasers should pay a fair share of U.S. government-financed R&D expenses. Other arguments in opposition are that U.S. exporters have been successful in the market and do not need an improved playing field, and that current U.S. budget stringency makes it unwise to risk any revenue losses or to incur any unnecessary new outlays.

U.S. GOVERNMENT ARMS EXPORT-CONTROL PROCESS

Weapons and dual-use export controls are a means of preventing the acquisition of threatening capabilities by our enemies and are tools of foreign policy. For as long as these controls have been in existence there has been a tension between industry desires to export and foreign policy or national security desires to control.

Weapons exports are administered and controlled by the State Department, whereas exports of dual-use items are administered and controlled by the Commerce Department. Weapons are controlled through the International Transfer in Arms Regulation, which lists proscribed export destinations, regulated weapons (the Munitions List), procedures for applying for export licenses, and penalties for failure to comply with the regulations. The Munitions List is compiled by the State Department with the concurrence of the Department of Defense. Weapons or munitions export-control implementation guidance is handled by several different offices in the State Department, depending on whether the export item is controlled through an international regime or simply according to U.S. interests. Criteria considered in making decisions are the potential impact of the transfer on regional stability, the military and other needs of the procuring country, and concerns over activities that might support terrorists and drug trafficking. Considerations of foreign availability of substitute weapons plays a role in these decisions, but it is not a decisive criterion.

Dual-use technology controls are administered by the Commerce Department through regulations that identify the commodities to be controlled (the Commodity Control List), countries for which certain items are controlled, and the justification for the control. The Commodity Control List is based on the Military Critical Technologies List, updated annually by the Defense Department in a process that includes industry and other agency representation. It also incorporates controls in accordance with various international regimes, such as the MTCR. In contrast, the Nuclear Referral List is updated only on an ad hoc basis. Unlike the Munitions List, the Commodity Control List is intended to be as limited as possible while still supportive of U.S. policy objectives.

The process for controlling dual-use technologies is in general perceived to be weaker than that for weapons because control of nonmilitary items is the exception rather than the rule and the criteria for denial of a dual-use technology export license are more narrowly defined than those for denying an arms export license.

Interagency groups meet frequently to discuss contentious cases in both the arms and dual-use categories; however, licensing decisions are left to the lead agency, with others able to appeal decisions with which they do not agree. Enforcement of the laws relating to exports of arms and dual-use technologies is also split among a number of agencies, with several of them having their own investigative branches.

As with many governmental processes, the output and outcomes of the export-control laws have both intended and unintended consequences. The decision to separate arms export controls from those on dual-use items made sense in the immediate postwar period when it was relatively easy to distinguish between the two and the United States was the world's technological leader and could single-handedly control technology proliferation. The increasing use of commercially developed technologies for military applications, the dissolution of a monolithic enemy (the Soviet Union), and the proliferation of capable technology competitors have fundamentally changed the environment in which the export-control process functions.

The separate interagency groups convened to discuss matters related to particular regimes will be ineffective in the future increasing need for cross-cutting analyses of trends and capabilities. Interagency groups will need to focus on linkages between civilian technologies and weapons and are likely to find that items previously associated with only one type of weapon now apply across the board. As the lines between civilian and military uses of technologies are blurred, the interagency process may become more contentious. The fact that agency roles for advocacy, review, and decisionmaking are often inseparable contributes to confusion over priorities and makes it difficult to achieve consistent decisions.

The problems outlined above are compounded by administrative inefficiencies. Lack of a common database leads to numerous inefficiencies in the use of staff time and impedes the establishment of historical case files to support license applications. With the increasing globalization of the arms industry, analyzing trends and sales is more complex than ever. Lack of information about allied and non-aligned nations' equipment and capabilities continues to hamper intelligence evaluations, and technical expertise has been difficult to recruit and retain in the government.

Among the steps that could be taken to improve the implementation of policies and streamline the process, the most critical may be the establishment of a common database, accessible by all in the community. Another important step would be to integrate technology and weapons controls into one legal and regulatory framework. This would help focus attention on the points of convergence between technologies and weapons and should ease jurisdictional disputes between arms and dual-use items. More aggressive attention on the part of the National Security Council (NSC) staff, and the establishment of a senior NSC official to guide the implementation of consistent conventional arms and dual-use technology export-control decisions are important features in creating a successful export-control process.

Arguments have been made in other reports about the need for a central administrator or even a central organization to manage arms and dual-use technology export controls. It is important to distinguish between a single administrator who would be responsible for assigning cases and moving them along to a decision, and a central organization that would be responsible for making the decisions, with interagency consultations as necessary. Strong arguments can be advanced for locating either role in any of several agencies. The choice of a location for either centralized function will require both further analysis and political judgment.

ACDA	Arms Control and Disarmament Agency
ACRS	Arms Control and Regional Security
AECA	Arms Export Control Act
AMRAAM	Advanced medium range air-to-air missile
APC	Armored personnel carrier
ARF	Asian Regional Forum
ASEAN	Association of Southeast Asian Nations
ASW	Antisubmarine warfare
BASIC	British American Security Information Council
BVR	Beyond visual range
BW	Biological weapons
CAT	Conventional arms transfers
CCL	Commodity Control List
CIA	Central Intelligence Agency
CoCom	Coordinating Committee for Multilateral Export Control
CRS	Congressional Research Service
CW	Chemical weapons
DCS	Direct commercial sales
DEFP	Defense Export Financing Program
DIA	Defense Intelligence Agency
DoD	U.S. Department of Defense
DSAA	Defense Security Assistance Agency
DTAG	Defense Trade Advisory Group
EAA	Export Administration Act
FAA	Foreign Assistance Act
FAR	Federal Acquisition Regulation
FMF	Foreign Military Financing
FMS	Foreign Military Sales
GAO	General Accounting Office
GDP	Gross Domestic Product
GPO	Government Printing Office
IC/CC	Inner Circle/Concentric Circle
IEEPA	International Emergency Economic Powers Act
IR	Infrared
ITAR	International Transfer in Arms Regulation
MCTL	Military Critical Technologies List

MFN	Most Favored Nation
MSM	Market Stabilizing Mechanism
MTCR	Missile Technology Control Regime
NATO	North Atlantic Treaty Organization
NRL	Nuclear Referral List
NSC	National Security Council
OAS	Organization of American States
OMB	Office of Management and Budget
P-5	The five permanent members of the UN Security Council: U.S., UK, France, Russia, and China
PDD	Presidential Decision Directive
PRC	People's Republic of China
R&D	Research and Development
SAM	Surface-to-air missile
STAR 21	Strategic Technologies for the Army for the 21st Century
TIA	Transparency in Armaments, UN Register of Conventional Arms
TWT	Traveling-wave tube
UAV	Unmanned aerial vehicle
UK	United Kingdom
UN	United Nations
WAECCADUT (WA)	Wassenaar Arrangement on Export Controls for Conventional Arms and Dual-Use Technologies
WMD	Weapons of mass destruction

Chapter One

INTRODUCTION

MANDATE AND BACKGROUND OF THE STUDY

Title XVI, Section 1601 of the National Defense Authorization Act for Fiscal Year 1994 mandated the creation of the President's Advisory Board on Arms Proliferation Policy to conduct a study of (1) the factors that contribute to the proliferation of strategic and advanced conventional military weapons and related equipment and technologies, and (2) the policy options that are available to the United States to inhibit such proliferation. The five-member Board was established by Executive Order 12946 on January 20, 1995, and tasked to advise the President on implementation of U.S. conventional arms transfer policy, other issues related to arms proliferation policy, and other matters deemed appropriate by the President. Areas specified for study in the Board's Terms of Reference include trends in the international arms market, instruments of restraint, export financing facilities, and the relationship between arms exports and the defense industrial base.

In its initial conception, the Board was envisioned by Congress as a participant in the development of the Clinton Administration's conventional arms transfer policy, which was finalized in February 1995 in a Presidential Decision Directive (PDD). In fact, timing of the Board's appointment was such that the PDD had been released before the Board began its deliberations. The Board accordingly undertook to examine the policy and to recommend how to proceed with next steps.

SCOPE OF THE BOARD'S WORK

In executing its mandate, the Board met frequently throughout 1995 and into 1996. It was assisted by two groups. Within the government, the Defense Security Assistance Agency provided staff support, administrative services, and coordination of several meetings and presentations. The Board was supported in its analysis and in its research for data and alternative policy and process approaches by RAND. The RAND team worked closely with the Board to produce the study documented here, an effort that addresses many of the issues brought to the Board in the course of its deliberations.

Meetings of the Board provided representatives from government agencies, industry, and nongovernmental organizations the opportunity to share insights and perspectives with the Board members. Among the governmental organizations represented at the meetings were the National Security Council (NSC), Departments of State, Commerce, Treasury, and Defense, the Arms Control and Disarmament Agency (ACDA), the Central Intelligence Agency (CIA) and the Defense Intelligence Agency (DIA), Sandia National Laboratories, and the Defense Trade Advisory Group. Private groups included Business Executives for National Security, the Arms Project/Human Rights Watch, the National Commission on Economic Conversion and Disarmament, the British American Security Information Council (BASIC), Aerospace Industries Association, Lockheed-Martin, IBM, IPAC Inc., the Federation of American Scientists, and the Council for a Livable World. Individuals from the Brookings Institution, MITRE, the Carnegie Endowment for International Peace, Pacific Sierra Research, and the Henry L. Stimson Center also provided briefings. A list of briefers and contributors to the Board's deliberations and to RAND's research can be found in Appendix A.

The topics addressed by the Board in these meetings included the following:

- **Current conventional arms transfer policies and objectives for a post-CoCom (Coordinating Committee for Multilateral Export Control) regime**

  The Board paid considerable attention to understanding the intent and implementation of the Presidential Decision Directive (PDD) on Conventional Arms Transfer Policy of February 1995. Discussions with government staff explored the roles of various agencies in implementing that directive. The Board was also briefed on current government positions and strategies with regard to the establishment of a post-CoCom regime, as well as other efforts to limit the proliferation of advanced conventional weapons. Staff members from the NSC, Department of State, Department of Defense, and ACDA were helpful in keeping the Board abreast of new developments. The numerous discussions held with government representatives highlighted the government's serious commitment to conventional arms control, as well as the range of other objectives expected to be served by an arms transfer policy. The objectives sought by arms and technology exports, often in tension with one another, were commented upon by a variety of nongovernmental and industry representatives.

- **International conventional arms control regimes (supplier and consumer perspectives on incentives for participation)**

  A number of presentations offered for discussion and evaluation alternative approaches to conventional arms control and the incentives or penalties associated with them. Discussions focused not only on the supplier side of the issue but also explored incentives for consumer nation cooperation and restraint. The issues of transparency and incentives for accurate reporting of transfers were discussed.

- **Non-U.S. views of conventional arms control issues**

  The Board heard from several speakers on the views of other supplier and consumer nations toward conventional arms control. While presentations focused largely on European producers and Middle Eastern consumers, the discussions also included reference to East Asia, Central Europe, South Asia, and South America as regions of interest and concern.

- **The relationship between arms exports and the defense industrial base, domestically and for foreign suppliers**

  Issues relating to the defense industrial base, both within the United States and in other arms-producing states, were set forth by government representatives, by representatives from U.S. industry, and by several nongovernmental organizations. Discussions addressed the health of the arms industry in the United States and abroad, the relative macroeconomic contribution of arms sales to the economy, the impact of arms exports on individual firms and specific weapons production lines, the downsizing of defense industry here and abroad, and the impact of excess capacity on political support for arms transfer restraint.

- **The role of government financing and the administration of arms transfers and their relation to conventional arms control efforts**

  Presentations on export credit financing, Commerce Department approaches for cooperation to ensure a secure industrial base, and the Foreign Military Sales program administrative surcharge were provided to the Board.

- **The role of the intelligence community in conventional arms transfer policy implementation**

  Representatives from the Defense Intelligence Agency and the Central Intelligence Agency were invited to discuss their roles in the arms control process. Government agency representatives, nongovernmental organizations, and industry were consulted for their views on the role of the intelligence community. Discussion of intelligence capabilities was supported by additional presentations on methods for end-use monitoring and enforcement, including a session on tagging technologies. The coordination of end-use monitoring by the various regulatory agencies—the State Department for weapons and the Commerce Department for dual-use technologies—was discussed.

- **The export-control implementation process in the federal government**

  The Board consulted extensively with government representatives on the U.S. licensing process for arms and technology exports and gathered perspectives on the topic from industry representatives and several nongovernmental organizations.

- **Control of "weapons of ill repute"**

  The Board addressed so-called weapons of ill repute—weapons that can pose a high risk to noncombatants and cause indiscriminate effects, and heard presentations on prospective measures to limit the transfer of these weapons.

ORGANIZATION OF THE REPORT

The report that follows postulates a number of concepts and specific approaches to new restraint regimes for advanced conventional weapons, dual-use technologies, and so-called weapons of ill repute. The report also treats in some depth three other areas of interest and concern to the Board:

- The economics of arms exports, a subject used selectively by both proponents and opponents of arms sales in making their respective cases;

- The characteristics of various specific control regimes presented in one form or another to the Board during its deliberations, along with RAND analysis and evaluation of those proposals; and

- A discussion and series of observations and recommendations regarding various aspects of the U.S. government policy and administration process, looking at potential ways to improve those processes.

The Board neither endorses nor rejects the detailed aspects of the RAND study that follows below. In key areas of both policy and process, however, the RAND approach is consistent with the Board's thinking.

Chapter Two reviews domestic and international policy and practice in arms transfers, past and present, and surveys the broad trends in the international arms market. Chapter Three proposes criteria for determining which conventional weapons systems should be controlled and identifies candidate end items for control. It also addresses issues relating to the control of weapons of ill repute—those weapons whose use produces intense international opprobrium. Chapter Four addresses the control of technologies associated with the critical capabilities of the end items identified in Chapter Three, as well as "strategic technologies" that could lead to the development of future weapons systems and pose risks to regional and international stability.

Chapter Five assesses the utility and prospects of international policy instruments intended to control undesirable arms transfers or to facilitate those that are not, and Chapter Six evaluates the economic and industrial base impacts of arms exports and the relative importance of these factors in influencing decisions about individual arms transfers. Finally, Chapter Seven evaluates the adequacy of existing domestic institutional arrangements to implement current and prospective U.S. policy on conventional arms transfers.

Chapter Two

OVERVIEW AND TRENDS

Arms transfers can be expected to remain a central element of America's national security strategy. To mitigate their potential significant risks, however, policy decisions on trade in strategic technologies and advanced conventional weapons will continue to require an artful reconciliation of complex competing national priorities. Foreign policy, national security, and economic interests that are served by the approval or denial of particular weapons sales can be compelling, but often pull in different directions. For example, weapons transfers may improve regional military stability by augmenting states' self-defense capabilities, but they may also foster regional tensions leading to wasteful and dangerous arms races. Weapons transfers may provide valuable contributions to the nation's trade balance and additional cash flow to domestic defense industries, but they may also create sharp economic competition among suppliers that, in turn, may lead to disharmony on matters of greater interest and the fueling of international proliferation.

Weapons transfers can enhance regional alliance relations and increase U.S. access and influence, but they can also adversely affect the economic, political, or social priorities of a recipient country, which may damage U.S. national interests. Arms transfer approvals can be used to reward allies, and denials to punish or pressure.

Striking the right balance among cross-cutting priorities is the key to an effective weapons transfer policy. What makes this task particularly difficult is the need for consensus among the major weapons suppliers; in the absence of consensus, unilateral U.S. restraint in weapons transfers can be circumvented to the profit of other suppliers. Solutions must be found that accommodate the national security, foreign policy, and economic interests of other key supplier states as well. Experience has shown that this is a formidable task, and progress must begin with efforts to obtain greater agreement on "rules of the road" and restraint that furthers the interests of all.

During the cold war, such cooperation was not possible. Conventional arms transfer decisions by the United States and the Soviet Union were driven by the conflicting strategic and ideological objectives of the two sides. The end of the cold war has fundamentally altered this situation. East-West strategic and ideological conflicts have been reduced in many cases and eliminated in others. The six major suppliers of conventional weapons—the United States, the United Kingdom, Germany, France, China, and Russia—are not currently pursuing sharply conflicting policy objectives in most regions of the world. While the six may differ in the degree of urgency they feel about discouraging conflict in specific regions, none has an interest in actively fomenting it.

On the other hand, the absence of cold war concerns has removed a rationale for restraint in regions where, in the past, the fear of superpower confrontation forced some degree of tacit caution in the transfer of certain systems to regions of extreme tension. Moreover, because of the political flux in the states of the former Soviet Union, in U.S. relations with China, and, to a much lesser extent, in U.S. relations with Europe and Japan, one cannot be sure that the current greater congruence of strategic interests will endure. There are serious divisions in North-South perspectives, as well as differences among the major suppliers about how to think about arms and technology transfers.

The major suppliers remain in economic competition for the sales of conventional weapons, and this economic competition is perhaps the greatest remaining obstacle to developing a cooperative control regime among suppliers. The magnitude of this hurdle should not be underestimated. In a period of contracting defense budgets, conflicting economic interests are a major impediment to controlling the international arms market. In major supplier nations, shrinking federal budgets have increased the perceived importance of exports as a means of sustaining defense firms' financial viability. Exports are also being increasingly viewed as a mechanism to maintain the defense industrial base, a rising concern as domestic weapons procurement is falling.[1]

However, economic interests can be negotiated; compromises may be possible given the proper economic "sticks" and "carrots." Vital strategic and ideological objectives are much less tractable. There is room for optimism that some economic obstacles to controlling conventional arms transfers can be surmounted, because there are important strategic benefits to be gained from doing so. As Operation Desert Shield/Storm demonstrated, the United States, Great Britain, France, and, to a lesser extent, Russia, have a strong interest in preserving stability in important regions, such as the Persian Gulf.

CONVENTIONAL WEAPONS CHALLENGE

Among the many reasons why control of conventional arms and technology transfers must become a more important and integral element of United States foreign and defense policy if the overall goals of nonproliferation are to succeed, three stand out. First, "conventional" weapons—that is, those with destructive mechanisms that are not nuclear, chemical, or biological—have, through improvements in precision, attained degrees of military effectiveness previously associated only with nuclear weapons. Moreover, these conventional weapons can destroy military targets without the massive collateral casualties and damage that would result from use of

---

[1]U.S. Department of Defense, Office of the Under Secretary of Defense (Acquisition and Technology), *World-Wide Conventional Arms Trade (1994–2000): A Forecast and Analysis*, Department of Defense, Washington, DC, December 1994.

weapons of mass destruction, making their military use less constrained by political factors. Further, certain advanced systems can be used to deliver weapons of mass destruction.

Second, as the world's economies develop technologically, the current and potential future sources of conventional weapons are steadily expanding beyond the handful of nations previously designing and building such systems. This changing and increasingly diffuse character of the international technology market further complicates the effective application of international controls.

The third reason stems from the sum of the economic stresses and discontinuities brought on by the fall of the former USSR and the Communist governments in key East European states, the decline in U.S. defense procurement budgets, and the downsizing of military force structures throughout the world. These events have caused both governments and their defense industrial bases to become more aggressive in trying to sell products abroad which they had previously been able to buy for or sell only to their own armed forces.

In the face of the economic forces detailed above, alliances and individual nations that have been counted upon historically to take conservative and restrictive approaches to sales of state-of-the-art conventional weaponry today show much less, if any, inclination to do so. The demise of CoCom, with its structured and reasonably disciplined approach to the control of conventional arms and related technologies, leaves a major gap in the international coordination of national export-control policies.

The control of conventional arms and technology exports has always been less important than other forms of military trade regulation. The nuclear nonproliferation regime owes its genesis to the years-long monopoly on nuclear capabilities maintained by the five declared nuclear powers and is held together by a widespread consensus about the unique dangers of nuclear weapons. In the case of chemical and biological weapons, eliciting multinational support for a restraint regime is possible in large measure because of the less-than-compelling military utility of these weapons among the advanced powers and the opprobrium raised by the grave risks they pose to noncombatants.

In contrast, the proliferation of conventional technologies shares few of these attributes: the monopoly among a few suppliers for all but the most advanced armaments is already shattered; the dangers of proliferation are disputed by many; and the perceptions of utility tend to overwhelm any moral opprobrium. Conventional weapons transfers have been seen as a benign alternative to nuclear proliferation and remain the most common instrument of dissuasion in efforts to stop new states from acquiring nuclear weapons. The principal formal conventional arms restraint regime, the Missile Technology Control Regime (MTCR), restricts the sale of ballistic and cruise missiles, largely because of their association with nuclear, chemical, or biological weapons delivery.

The problem is made more difficult by the absence of internationally accepted criteria for determining what kinds of arms and technology exports are undesirable. It is impossible as a practical matter to classify most weapons and technologies as either offensive or defensive. Nor is it easy to target particular technologies for delegitimization, as the line between weapons used for self-defense and for provocation must be drawn in context and is therefore extremely hard to judge.

The experience of the U.S.-led coalition war against Iraq indicates the dangers of a *laissez-faire* approach to the international trade in conventional arms and technologies. Western militaries confronted an Iraqi arsenal made up largely of weapons and technologies provided by the industrialized countries, prompting recognition that the political will to control military technology trade was far too weak. Since then, however, the predominant focus of policy innovation has remained on nuclear, chemical, biological, and missile technologies. The real challenge yet to be addressed in the United States or other advanced countries is how to preserve superior conventional military capabilities and a healthy industrial base without a chronic dependency on exports of the kind that may accelerate diffusion of weapons and technology beyond what is prudent.

Three factors must be taken into account. First, the effects of this diffusion are diverse and profound. Supplier instruments, like the missile technology cartel, work only in proportion to the clout of the members and their relative monopoly of the products they are trying to control. Over thirty-five countries are able to export conventional weapons[2] (admittedly of widely varying levels of capability) and many suppliers have indicated they would not support a restraint regime until they have a more equal share of revenues from the arms market. In areas of weaponry where domestic procurement needs have fallen sharply, such as fighter aircraft and naval vessels, the consensus in favor of controls is even weaker.

Second, trends in the technology market presage declining control by governments over the disposition of defense-related innovations. Critical technologies vital to defense, from supercomputers to biotechnologies to fiber optics, are increasingly commercial in origin. As developing countries establish their own weapon industries, they too are increasingly capable of tapping into new sources of commercial and dual-use goods without reference to constraints imposed by larger powers. In the future, an ever-shrinking percentage of technology will be subject to direct government controls, testing the viability of supplier cartels or trade restrictions for all but a select number of the most advanced technologies.

Third, certain transfers have a particular adverse effect on U.S. national security policy and on the security of U.S. personnel deployed overseas, especially if an American military presence is maintained in key regions such as Asia and the Persian Gulf. Heavily armed, politically unstable countries could pose a direct threat to the security of deployed U.S. personnel or America's allies. The proliferation of advanced weaponry could constrain U.S. policy options in many contingencies by making the human and material risks and costs associated with forward deployment prohibitively high. An example is the recent test firing of a Chinese-exported C-802 anti-

---

[2] *World Military Expenditures and Arms Transfers, 1993–94,* U.S. Arms Control and Disarmament Agency, Washington, DC, 1994.

ship cruise missile in Iran. Export of this missile has significantly increased the threat posed by Iran in the Gulf, and it will increase the costs to the United States to maintain an appropriate counterforce. The military services have tended not to promote advanced technology exports to politically unstable developing areas, fearing that the same types of weapons they use themselves could be captured by hostile forces. Technology compromise typically occurs when a well-defended client is transformed into an aggressively armed adversary. This is not an uncommon development in volatile regions of the developing world and, perhaps, among states in the former Soviet bloc.

TRENDS[3]

The general decline in defense spending worldwide since the late 1980s, particularly in the developed world, has been one of several by-products of the end of the cold war. Not only has our need and that of our NATO allies to procure new weapons dropped significantly, but the global dollar value of conventional arms exports has been in decline as well.[4] This situation reflects the quantitative reduction in the level of production and acquisition of conventional weapons. Qualitatively, the trend is not so salutary. Incentives for increased proliferation of *advanced* conventional weapons systems and technologies appear to be increasing, for reasons discussed below.

Since the end of the cold war the constant dollar value of conventional weapons exported by the six major suppliers has dropped by more than half, from $54 billion in 1988 to $22 billion in 1993, as illustrated in Figure 1.[5] Estimates indicate that national earnings from defense exports have declined more sharply for some arms suppliers than for others.

Supplier Export Patterns

U.S. arms export revenues have averaged around $10 billion, and U.S. arms transfers are expected to remain at about the same level in the future. The stability of demand for U.S. arms in the midst of huge reductions in the overall market has meant that the U.S. *share* of world sales has steadily increased. 1994 totals indicate that the United States accounted for one third of the world's arms agreements and over half of all weapons deliveries, up from 25 percent of global totals in 1987. This trend is expected to continue, with the United States projected to account for up to 59 percent of world arms sales by the end of the century.

---

[3]Much of the data and analysis of trends that follows are supported by or drawn from *World-Wide Conventional Arms Trade (1994–2000)*; from conversations with Richard Grimmett and from his annual report to the Congress, *Conventional Arms Transfers to Developing Nations, 1987–1994*, Congressional Research Service, Washington, DC, August 4, 1995; and from U.S. Arms Control and Disarmament Agency, *World Military Expenditures and Arms Transfers 1993–94*, U.S. GPO, Washington, DC, February 1995 (hereafter referred to as WMEAT).

[4]Deliveries of military items. Unless specified otherwise, data are based on U.S. Arms Control and Disarmament Agency, *World Military Expenditures and Arms Transfers 1993–94*.

[5]Ibid.

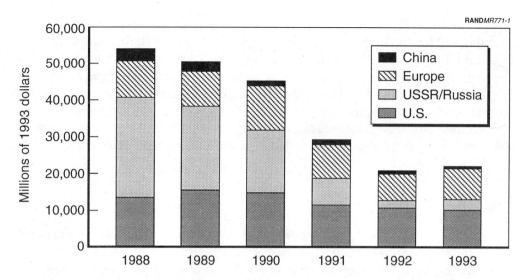

SOURCE: U.S. Arms Control and Disarmament Agency, *World Military Expenditures and Arms Transfers, 1993–1994*, U.S. Government Printing Office, Washington, DC, February 1995.

Figure 1—Export Deliveries of Conventional Weapons, 1988–1993

One third of U.S. arms transfers between 1991 and 1993 went to the Middle East (to Saudi Arabia in particular, but also to Egypt, Israel, and Kuwait). Another fifth of U.S. weapons sales were to East Asia, primarily Japan, South Korea, and Taiwan, and accounted for more than half of all sales to that area of the world. Looking further back, between 1987 and 1994 the United States was the largest supplier to the Middle East (39 percent of all weapons sold there), and accounted for 30 percent of Asian arms purchases and 15 percent of sales to Latin America.[6]

European arms suppliers have also increased their relative market share, both in agreements and deliveries. The "Big Four"—France, the United Kingdom, Italy, and Germany—more than doubled their arms sales between 1987 and 1993, and deliveries of European weapons last year represented almost 24 percent of the world total. Although this was a decline from peaks at the beginning of the decade, it was an increase from 18 percent of global deliveries in 1987.

From 1987 to 1994, West European countries sold primarily to Asia, the Near East, and Africa, accounting for 19 percent, 32 percent, and 8 percent of total regional sales, respectively. Western Europe's overall growth in weapons sales is dominated from year to year by different countries; the relative positions of France, Germany, and the United Kingdom change almost annually, typically because of a few large contracts. The United Kingdom's share of West European sales fell from 51 percent in 1992 to 43 percent in 1993; France's increased from 16 percent in 1992 to 37 percent the following year; and Germany dropped from 13 percent of the West European total to 11 percent. From 1991 to 1993, three quarters of the United Kingdom's

---

[6]See Grimmett, *Conventional Arms Transfers to Developing Nations, 1987–1994*.

weapons deliveries went to Saudi Arabia, which bought almost twice as many weapons from London as it did from Washington.[7] France relies heavily on sales to the Middle East; transfers to the region are expected to remain an important but decreasing percentage of French exports. French sales to the Far East and Europe have been expanding, however, and France is expected to remain in stiff competition worldwide with the United States for sales of tactical missiles, electronics, and naval equipment. Germany is also expected to become one of the leading arms exporters, primarily of helicopters and ships.[8]

It is projected that other European arms exporters will continue about the same level of foreign sales. Italy is focusing on agreements for transport aircraft and smaller naval vessels, and has been courting customers in South America, Asia, and Oceania. Sweden and Spain are also expected to maintain their niche positions in the global arms market, Sweden with sales of submarines, naval combat systems, and infantry fighting vehicles, and Spain through transport aircraft and minor combatant naval vessel sales.

The rise in U.S. and European shares has come largely at the expense of Russia. Long the world's largest weapons supplier, the value of agreements for Soviet (then Russian) arms dropped from $31 billion in 1987 to $5 billion in 1994, down from 43 percent to 13 percent of the world total. Actual deliveries of Russian arms from 1987 to 1993 declined by an order of magnitude.[9]

However, the implications of this sharp decline in Russian weapons transfers, in terms of actual sales and cash earned, are not what they appear. A relatively small proportion of Soviet arms exports historically were direct cash transactions; most arms transfers were for credit, and much was never repaid. In fact, recent Russian cash earnings from weapons transfers may not be significantly different from actual Soviet earnings during the 1980s.[10]

---

[7]WMEAT, pp. 139–141.

[8]*World-Wide Conventional Arms Trade (1994–2000)*, p. 29.

[9]*World-Wide Conventional Arms Trade (1994–2000)*.

[10]See Kevin P. O'Prey, *The Arms Export Challenge: Cooperative Approaches to Export Management and Defense Conversion*, The Brookings Institution, Washington, DC, 1995. In a recent interview, Marshal of Aviation Yevgeniy Ivanovich Shaposhnikov, Russian Federation presidential representative in Rosvooruzheniye Company, responded to the assertion that Russia had lost markets in which it had traded successfully in weapons.

> You can say anything you like, but the facts indicate differently. As a matter of fact, it was believed that in past times the Soviet Union sold weapons and military equipment abroad for around $15 billion (approximately as much as the United States did). But in reality almost all weapons sent gratis to so-called "brothers in the socialist idea," according to the principle: Do you respect me and my socialism? If you do, ask what you want! We had such partners in Africa, the Near East and certain other places. Except for assurances of eternal love and support of its course, the USSR received a few bananas, oranges, lemons and sometimes sour wine. On the whole, our "profit" never exceeded two billion dollars, and in the final account that went to support the international communist movement. At any rate, I was unable to find any "remainders" of money earned for arms . . . And what is the case today? Russia sold weapons abroad in 1993 for a little over two billion dollars, and last year [1994] for a little under two billion.

> Aleksandr Protsenko, "How It Is Done: Weapons Abroad," *Obshchaya Gazeta*, 6–12 July 1995, p. 5.

Russia's decline reflects in part the departure of many of its traditional customers, because they cannot meet Russia's need for cash payments, are under international arms embargoes, or have turned to more stable and reliable suppliers. The Russian government has become more aggressive in hopes of recovering some of its lost sales and is looking at the Asian market in particular for expansion. Russian sellers are targeting countries such as Taiwan, Malaysia, the Philippines, Vietnam, and Thailand, and hope for upgrades and maintenance contracts with Central and East European countries that rely primarily on Russian-made equipment. Russia is pursuing South American defense markets as well.

Russia's main customers are now China and India, as opposed to their past cold war clients, such as Afghanistan, Cuba, Iraq, Syria and Vietnam. Sales of weapons systems to Iran, including submarines, surface-to-air missiles, and high-performance aircraft, have been of considerable concern to the United States, as have agreements on the transfer of nuclear technology. On a positive note, Russia recently became an official member of the Wassenaar Arrangement and agreed not to enter into any additional arms transfer agreements with Iran.

China's arms exports continue to be problematic. While its overall percentage of the world arms market remains small (only 4 percent in 1993), China has displayed an apparent willingness to sell weapons to countries in unstable regions, posing concerns for the international community. During the Iran-Iraq war, China sold weapons to both participants, and throughout the decade China made significant arms transfers throughout the developing world. It does not offer a large technological advantage to its clients, but emphasizes less expensive major systems such as the F-7 fighter to cash-strapped or isolated countries like Iran, Pakistan, and Burma. While other countries' military expenditures have been falling, defense spending per person in China has remained at about the same level over the last ten years.[11] China is not a participant in the Wassenaar Arrangement and has recently been sanctioned for violations of missile transfer agreements.[12]

---

[11]Based on data from the Arms Control and Disarmament Agency, in *World Military Expenditures and Arms Transfers, 1990* and *1995*. Estimates of Chinese military spending vary widely: 1994 figures range from $20–$140 billion. For a more complete explanation of the difficulties in obtaining more widely accepted, convergent and accurate data on China's military expenditures, see *The Military Balance 1995–96*, IISS, London, 1995, pp. 270–275, and *1994–95*, pp. 278-281.

[12]Although China has expressed an interest in joining the CoCom successor regime, the United States maintains that it has not yet met the necessary requirements for membership, which include a system of viable domestic export controls and adherence to international nonproliferation regimes. See *The Arms Control Reporter 1995*, "Plan for the CoCom Successor Organization," Institute for Defense and Disarmament Studies, Cambridge, MA, p. 250.B.43, October 1995. China's missile sales have been a continuing sticking point in U.S.-China relations. In 1991, the U.S. objected to Chinese sales of M-11 ballistic missile technologies to Pakistan. After the United States imposed sanctions restricting some technology exports to China, the Chinese agreed to observe the Missile Technology Control Regime guidelines. The sanctions were lifted in 1992, but they were reimposed in August 1993 when evidence arose indicating continuing sales. China denied having violated the agreement, but it renewed its commitments to MTCR requirements in early 1994, after which the sanctions were first waived and then removed. Concerns persist about possible transfers to both Iran and Pakistan, and the U.S. government continues to monitor the situation. See *The Arms Control Reporter 1995*, pp. 706.A.1–706.B.193, and Henry Sokolski, "U.S. Satellites to China," *International Defense Review*, April 1994, pp. 23–26, and *Arms Sales Monitor*, Federation of American Scientists, Washington, DC, 15 February 1995.

General Decline in Domestic Procurement

Accompanying the overall decline in exports, domestic arms procurement in supplier countries also has dropped precipitously, leaving excess weapons production capacity worldwide. As Figure 2 shows, the exports of all six major suppliers combined would have to triple in value to equal the $60 billion decline in the level of U.S. procurement alone.

Facing a tighter market, many firms and states have adjusted by undertaking downsizing, consolidation, product diversification, and defense conversion. However, the pace of adjustment has been slow in some areas, and there remains considerable excess capacity in certain sectors.

Defense conversion is costly. In Russia, for example, funds available to finance conversion have been inadequate, and the national need for hard currency earnings, including that from arms exports, has been high. Because influential Russians continue to believe that an increased market share for Russian arms exports will revive the Russian military-industrial complex and contribute to the health of the national economy, enthusiasm for defense conversion is limited. Even those who do acknowledge a need to convert defense industries propose arms exports as a way to fund those efforts, as well as to raise hard currency, buy debt relief, and cushion unemployment shocks.[13] The priority conversion apparently accorded in 1991 and

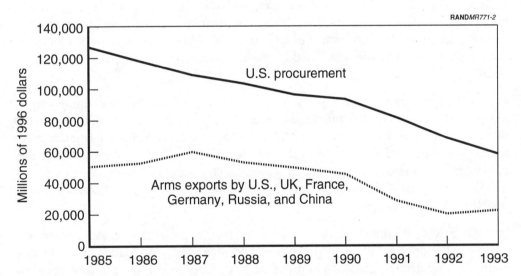

SOURCES: U.S. Arms Control and Disarmament Agency, *World Military Expenditures and Arms Transfers, 1993–1994*, U.S. Government Printing Office, Washington, DC, February 1995; and Office of the Secretary of Defense (Comptroller), *National Defense Budget Estimates, FY96*, March 1995.

Figure 2—U.S. Procurement and Global Exports

---

[13]See Igor Khripunov, "Russia's Arms Trade in the Post–Cold War Period," *The Washington Quarterly*, Vol. 17, No. 4, 1994, p. 81.

1992 had diminished substantially by 1993; this resistance is characteristic of many more countries than Russia alone.

Risks of Increased Export Competition

A more constrained domestic and inter-allied market, coupled with excess capacity, has increased competition among the major suppliers for other available outlets, both in pricing and in the quality of weapons offered for purchase. More competition has meant more leverage for regional arms purchasers—buyers are asking for and getting lower prices, offset agreements, and coproduction and special financing arrangements, as will be discussed further below. Most worrisome, the incentives to sell front-line, state-of-the-art equipment are now more powerful than they were before, and, coupled with increased demand for such systems (due in part to the impressive demonstration of U.S. weaponry during the Persian Gulf War), evidence is mounting that such systems are now being sold far more liberally.

The trend toward transfer of more advanced conventional systems is difficult to evaluate precisely. A new generation of systems is only now making its way into the international market and, because of the political sensitivity of these systems, information about their actual sale and transfer is often closely held. We do know that many restrictions on the export of advanced systems and technology have been lifted in Russia. The December 1995 announcement of the first-ever export sale of SA-11 air defense missiles to Finland may be a manifestation of this phenomenon. In a further departure from past practices, products are being transferred by the Russians even before they are fully absorbed in the Russian military (e.g., the Ka-50 Black Shark attack helicopter and the Su-30MK air superiority fighter).[14]

Regional buyers are taking advantage of the buyers' market. Thailand, for example, has publicly conditioned its purchase of U.S. F/A-18s on U.S. release of the AIM-120 Advanced Medium Range Air-to-Air Missile (AMRAAM).[15] Similar demands were made by Finland and the United Arab Emirates (UAE).[16] The Thai government also considered the purchase of the French Mirage 2000-5, equipped with the Mica air-to-air missile, and the Russian Su-27 and MiG-29 fighters, both of which could be armed with the AA-12 Adder.

In today's tighter budgetary environments, the fact that new aircraft systems, on average, cost about four times as much as modernizing existing planes has led some countries to pursue upgrades to improve current weapons stocks or to buy more advanced operating systems to increase the effectiveness of other new arms purchases. Significantly, countries other than the original producers can provide the upgrades. This trend too is likely to continue, with system upgrades becoming increasingly common. Among the capabilities most widely sought are command, control, com-

---

[14]Ibid., pp. 79–94.

[15]See John Glashow and Theresa Hitchens, "Thailand to Get AMRAAMs in F/A-18 Fighter Package," *Defense News*, 8–14 January 1996, p. 5.

[16]See Theresa Hitchens, "Thais Use AMRAAM as U.S. Fighter Buy Lever," *Defense News*, 4–10 September, 1995, p. 3.

munication and intelligence systems, surveillance equipment, and early warning capabilities.

Coproduction, Collaboration, and Offsets

Another response to domestic defense cuts has been an increased focus on cooperative and collaborative R&D and procurement programs for new weaponry. Collaborative arms production first became popular in the 1950s in Europe. Pooling resources was seen as a way for the smaller European nations to continue development of the widest possible range of modern weaponry and to advance political ties. In the 1970s, Europe began to see continental consolidation as necessary to balance competition from America; the European Union process has further facilitated this trend. France and Germany are the primary drivers; in fact, this industrial alliance now essentially dominates most major European programs in missiles, space, helicopters, future large aircraft, and armored vehicles. In the United States, proponents of codevelopment have stressed its operational (e.g., better interoperability and standardization) as well as political benefits. More recently, as economic pressures have increased, collaboration has become increasingly important: visible efforts include the Eurofighter-2000 and, between Japan and the United States, the F-2.

Cooperative programs have spread far beyond the United States and its closest allies, another manifestation of the degree to which greater competition for arms sales has resulted in greater leverage for arms buyers. Many purchasers are increasing their demands for coproduction agreements, technology transfer, offsets, and other "deal sweeteners."

Two types of offsets are typically offered with arms sales: "direct" and "indirect." Direct offsets provide buyers the opportunity to undertake licensed production of U.S. weapons systems or components. Indirect offsets are agreements by the arms selling company to import other goods from the arms buyer, to invest in the buying country, or to transfer commercial technology.

Concern about offset provisions as a part of arms sales generally has taken two forms. First, elements of direct offset—setting up the buyer to be able to build or assemble parts or all of the weapon involved—could represent a potentially problematic diffusion of technological capabilities in the *de facto* creation by U.S. firms of potential new producers. Industry's own healthy self-interest provides some real restraint as to how much knowledge and technology should be included as direct offset. The government review process must continue to look closely at this matter. Major direct offset approvals in the past—examples include the F-16 European Production Group, the Japanese F-15 Coproduction agreement, and the Republic of Korea K-1 tank development and production contract—should continue to be reviewed to ensure that long-term security interests are adequately taken into account.

There is also legitimate concern about the loss of jobs if and when work content is transferred abroad through offset agreements. On the other hand, the overall economic and employment impact of foreign trade is highly positive, and any nation's attempt to dictate or curtail pricing, workshare, or "countertrade" agreements between buyer and seller would be counterproductive. Offsets are, of course, just one subset of such overall negotiations. Currently, offsets are increasingly being demanded by buyers, are in turn more often agreed to by U.S. companies, and tend to be viewed as a competitive necessity by the arms industry.

New Suppliers

While existing major arms suppliers seek ways to adjust to new realities, the change in the kinds of arms countries want to buy, together with the redistribution of traditional market shares caused by the cold war's end, has helped to fuel the emergence of new suppliers. Regional conflicts, no longer constrained by the bipolar system, have flared, and have increased demand for items such as antitank weapons and artillery, which many less industrialized countries can produce. These factors have helped to create an environment conducive to the emergence of new or strengthened supplier states.

At the higher end of the technology spectrum, Israel may gain most from recent market shifts. In addition to its proficiency in aircraft production and armor upgrades, Israel has become a world-class supplier of electronics and tactical missiles. It is particularly skilled in aircraft upgrades of both U.S. and Russian equipment, and has found willing customers for high-quality improvements to inventories in the former Eastern bloc, South America, and Asia. Its arms exports are projected to remain at about $1.6 billion annually, with rising sales to the Far East and Central Europe. Romania has been buying avionics and night-vision subsystems, Hungary has been interested in satellites, and the Baltic states have purchased some advanced technologies. Israel also offers advanced unmanned aerial vehicle (UAV) technologies, which it hopes to sell in Europe and elsewhere.

Among other minor suppliers, South Africa has been increasing its weapons sales, and arms transfers increased by a factor of ten between 1984 and 1993. A particular area of expertise is mine-resistant armored vehicles, which were developed in response to heavy mining along the Namibian border; Sri Lanka has been among recent customers. South Africa has also had success with artillery systems and tank upgrades, which have been sold primarily in the Persian Gulf, and is hoping for large sales of the "Rooivalk" combat helicopter.

Among the former Warsaw Pact states, the Czech Republic's indigenous advanced technology infrastructure has provided strong capabilities for system upgrades and other improvements. Poland is focusing on the helicopter market, and has entered into cooperative agreements to develop transport helicopters.

After the breakup of the Soviet Union, Russia housed some 80 percent of the USSR's military industrial complex. Following the collapse, many small arms were shipped throughout the world, including hundreds of thousands of AK-47s to Yemen, Nigeria, and the UAE.[17] With Russia's drawdown, large quantities of excess equipment were placed on the market, including fighter aircraft, bombers, and tanks, as well as older surplus equipment.

Ukraine inherited a large military industrial base with high-technology and aircraft engineering capabilities. Initially, arms exports were de-emphasized, in part because the Ukrainian government was trying to curry favor with the West, and in part because it was heavily reliant on Russian spare parts. More recently, Ukraine has signed cooperation agreements with Russia for aircraft production, rocket and space technology, electronics, and aircraft motors, and with Belgium for small arms, sighting systems, and infantry weapons. It is now aiming to become a producer in space technology, and is increasingly looking toward arms sales, including spare parts for Russian aircraft in India, for armored personnel carriers (APCs), and for combat helicopters.

Regional Considerations

All of these suppliers—the traditional major sellers and the emerging, smaller countries looking for market niches—are competing vigorously for fewer sales. Of the major conventional weapon suppliers, however, none fully shares U.S. concerns about the implications of intensified global conventional proliferation. To the degree they worry about proliferation, China focuses on its periphery, including East Asia, South Asia, and Russia. Europe is concerned about Central Europe and the Middle East—with French attention to parts of Africa and British concern about the South American cone. Russia watches its periphery. A focus on broader, more global conventional nonproliferation goals may require greater cooperation by first-tier suppliers to mutually accommodate their respective national security concerns.

Middle East. As the global arms market has shrunk, all regions of the world have decreased their military imports. But within this smaller overall total, the largest purchasing region in the developing world since 1987 has been the Near East,[18] accounting for almost 60 percent of all sales. The Middle East accounts for the majority of these purchases, and represented 43 percent of the world total in 1993.[19] Saudi Arabia alone purchased $76 billion in weapons from 1987–1994, 29 percent of all sales to developing nations; it is expected to remain the largest single weapons buyer in the world for the remainder of the decade. See Figure 3.

Because of the ongoing embargo on Iraq, Iran and Egypt have overtaken Baghdad to become the second and third largest regional arms importers. They have, however, decreased their overall levels of weapons purchases in recent years. While Israel's purchases fell between 1988 and 1991, their imports now appear to be moving upward. The Department of Defense projects that while demand for weapons in the

---

[17]National Security Planning Associates and Institute for Foreign Policy Analysis, *Defense Conversion and Arms Transfers: The Legacy of the Soviet-Era Arms Industry,* National Security Planning Associates, Inc. and Institute for Foreign Policy Analysis, Inc., Washington, DC and Cambridge, MA, June 1993, p. 17.

[18]The "Near East," as used by Richard Grimmett, includes the Middle East and all of North Africa.

[19]Grimmett, *Conventional Arms Transfers to Developing Nations, 1987–1994.*

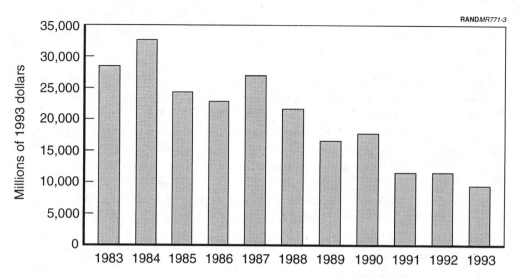

SOURCE: U.S. Arms Control and Disarmament Agency, *World Military Expenditures and Arms Transfers, 1993–1994*, U.S. Government Printing Office, Washington, DC, 1995.

Figure 3—Middle East Arms Imports, 1983–1993

Middle East is likely to decline from 1980s levels, through the turn of the century the region will absorb about one third of all arms sold worldwide.[20]

Europe. In this decade, Europe has emerged as the second largest arms importing region. Looking ahead, however, European countries are expected to drop to third position among importers, behind the Near East and East Asia. Over the past decade, the ratio between Central and West European arms purchasers changed significantly; in the early 1980s, European purchases were evenly divided between East and West, but by 1993 Western Europe accounted for three-quarters of the region's purchases. Most were from the United States; the remainder came from other West European nations. Imports by Central European countries are expected to continue falling by more than 50 percent from the $55 billion they spent during the 1980s. Most of the weapons they do acquire are likely to be Russian systems, in exchange for debt relief. See Figure 4.

East Asia. East Asia is a region of vital economic interest to the United States, as it is to other major weapons supplier states. In this region there are three zones of tension, within which conventional arms balances are of interest and concern: In Northeast Asia, relations between the two Koreas remain strained, and there is tension among China, Korea, and Japan. Also in Northeast Asia, China and Taiwan are highly sensitive to potential changes in their military balance. In Southeast Asia, the

---

[20] *World-Wide Conventional Arms Trade (1994–2000)*, pp. 20–21.

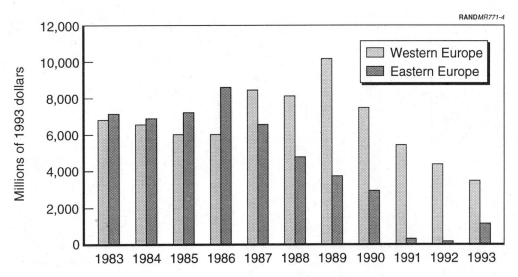

SOURCE: U.S. Arms Control and Disarmament Agency, *World Military Expenditures and Arms Transfers, 1993–1994*, U.S. Government Printing Office, Washington, DC, 1995.

Figure 4—European Arms Imports, 1983–1993

Association of Southeast Asian Nations (ASEAN) countries and their neighbors are uneasy about China's objectives in the South China Sea.

Southeast Asia is an example of how an increase in regional tensions can lead nations to change their perceptions of the threats to their security and seek to acquire new weapons to meet emerging challenges. In this region, for example, internal security risks were the primary concern before concern about external threats emerged over the past decade. Areas of potential conflict have become water- rather than land-focused (e.g., issues of maritime boundaries, sovereignty of islands, etc.). This shift, in turn, has been reflected in weapons purchases, which now include fighter aircraft, precision-guided missiles, more advanced naval craft, and submarines.[21]

Even though arms imports to East Asia have been in relative decline since 1987, East Asia is now the third largest regional market and likely will become the second largest by the year 2000. See Figure 5. The distribution of purchases has shifted in recent years, with Japan, Vietnam, North Korea, and Cambodia accounting for smaller percentages of the East Asian total than they did in 1989, and South Korea, Taiwan, and China buying more. East Asia's highly successful economies are facilitating rapid modernization of the region's militaries. As observed by the U.S. Director of Naval Intelligence, "[M]any countries could dramatically increase their military acquisition budgets without significant economic repercussions."[22] Taiwan, for example, has

---

[21]See Brian Cloughley, "ASEAN at Arms: A Defense Profile," *International Defense Review,* December 1995, pp. 22–33; and Michael Richardson, "Asian Navies Lean to Submarines," *International Herald Tribune,* 29 November 1995, p. 4.

[22]Director of Naval Intelligence, *Posture Statement,* 1994.

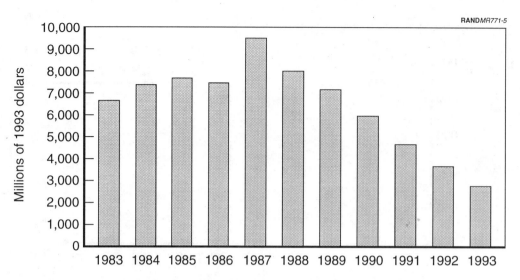

SOURCE: U.S. Arms Control and Disarmament Agency, *World Military Expenditures and Arms Transfers, 1993–1994*, U.S. Government Printing Office, Washington, DC, 1995.

Figure 5—East Asian Arms Imports, 1983–1993

the world's largest cash reserves and is viewed by international arms industrialists as a growth market.

A major growth area may be in submarines. China is both upgrading its domestic submarine fleet and purchasing additional boats from Russia; Taiwan, Thailand, and Malaysia are reportedly interested in buys; Indonesia is purchasing submarines from Germany; Australia is building six new submarines based on a Swedish design; and South Korea is expected to construct four German-designed submarines by the turn of the century. Japan does not appear to be pursuing additional submarine purchases, but is shielding its current submarine fleet from planned defense cuts. From 1991 to 1993, Japan was the largest weapons importer, followed by South Korea, China, and Taiwan; together, these countries bought almost three-quarters of all regional arms imports.

A decline in overall East Asian arms *imports* since 1987, notwithstanding, total *defense spending* in the region has generally risen. For many states, this may reflect the gradual buildup of an indigenous arms industry. China and Japan already have major domestic arms industries, and Taiwan's and South Korea's industries are growing. Facing hard times, European and U.S. firms may seek more defense collaboration in this region. As a result, future conventional proliferation in East Asia may not be as transparent to international observers.

South Asia. South Asia is perceived by the U.S. Department of Defense as an increasingly important area for U.S. national security interests; good relations in the region are thought to be supportive of a number of U.S. objectives, including nonproliferation. The conventional force relationships in this region are particularly important because of the presence of nuclear capabilities; conventional provocation could lead to nuclear use between adversaries on the subcontinent. On the other hand, influential members of the U.S. government are convinced that conventional arms embargoes, such as that imposed on Pakistan, may prompt countries to pursue nuclear weapons with additional vigor.

Arms imports in South Asia have declined rapidly from a peak of over $9 billion in 1989, as can be seen in Figure 6. Both India and Afghanistan cut their weapons purchases dramatically early in the decade, although India is expected to resume higher import levels. In 1993, Pakistan accounted for over 90 percent of regional imports, but its purchases totaled only $430 million. In the remainder of the decade, this share should rise; India and Pakistan are expected to make up about 5 percent of the global arms market, and both are planning purchases of tanks, artillery, helicopters, fighters, and air defense systems.[23]

Continued interest in South Asian arms purchases will likely be driven by the region's economic growth. Estimates by the World Bank, the International Monetary Fund, and a recent RAND study[24] suggest that India will be the world's fourth largest economy in the early part of the 21st century. China will watch that growth with concern, and conventional arms transfers to India will be closely monitored. Growth of India's conventional capabilities is likely to increase China's involvement and influence in the region through Pakistan.

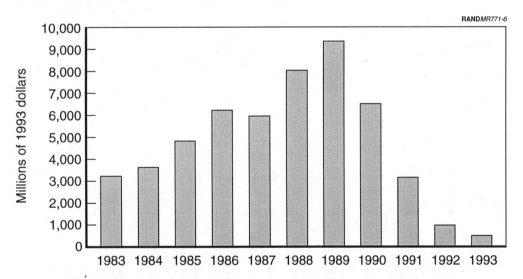

SOURCE: U.S. Arms Control and Disarmament Agency, *World Military Expenditures and Arms Transfers, 1993–1994*, U.S. Government Printing Office, Washington, DC, 1995.

Figure 6—South Asian Arms Imports, 1983–1993

---

[23]*World-Wide Conventional Arms Trade (1994–2000)*, p. 24.

[24]See Charles Wolf, Jr., K. C. Yeh, Anil Bamezai, Donald Henry, and Michael Kennedy, *Long-Term Economic and Military Trends, 1994–2015: The United States and Asia*, RAND, MR-627-OSD, 1994.

South America. South American markets for arms, particularly in Venezuela, Brazil, Argentina, and Chile, are opening because of improved economic and political circumstances, such as the movement toward democracy in Chile and the easing of trade restrictions on Argentina. Although the region's stability may create a more open arms transfer environment, transfer decisions in some sectors remain complex. These tensions are apparent in current debates on U.S. policy toward the region. U.S. defense contractors have requested that previously restrictive policies be reviewed in light of recent trends, which has resulted in disagreements between the State Department, which favors continuing a cautious approach, and the Joint Staff, who reportedly advocate loosening current restraints.[25] Despite the region's progress, some fear that the export of major conventional weapons systems to Chile, for example, could lead to requests for offsetting transfers from Argentina, where the United Kingdom has political and security concerns. See Figure 7.

Africa. African nations are not expected to increase their arms imports much beyond their current one percent share of the global market.

Rogue States. While global concerns have given way to a regionally based perspective in some aspects of U.S. policy, certain nations present a disproportionately large challenge to international security. So-called "rogue states," as presently defined, include Iran, Iraq, Libya, and North Korea. Prior to the Persian Gulf War, Iraq had been supplied with British tanks, U.S. commercial helicopters, French fighters and missiles, and Russian MiGs; since the War, however, it has been subject to an international arms embargo. Baghdad did not receive six Italian frigates it had already pur-

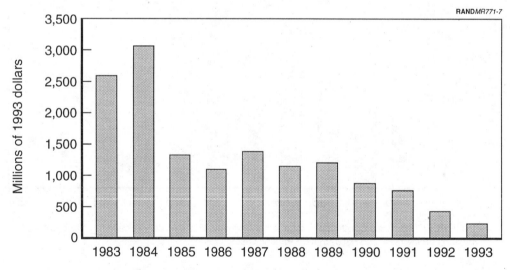

SOURCE: U.S. Arms Control and Disarmament Agency, *World Military Expenditures and Arms Transfers, 1993–1994*, U.S. Government Printing Office, Washington, DC, 1995.

Figure 7—South American Arms Imports, 1983–1993

---

[25]"South American Policy Decision 'Delayed'," *Arms Trade News,* November 1995, p. 1.

chased or many weapons-related technologies for which contracts were pending before Iraq's invasion of Kuwait.

Iran is subject to a less widely accepted embargo. Russia has recently agreed not to enter into new arms contracts with Tehran, although Moscow supplied 62 percent of all Iranian arms imports from 1991–1994, including Kilo-class submarines, T-72 tanks, mines, and advanced fighter and fighter/bomber aircraft. Iran had also reportedly been in the market for Ukrainian Backfire bombers. Previously the second-largest exporter of weapons to Iran, China is likely to assume the major supplier role; the two countries recently agreed to the transfer of patrol craft armed with cruise missiles, and may conclude deals for additional missiles, air defense systems, and rocket-propelled mines. Additionally, Pakistan has reportedly contributed to Iran's project to assemble and produce military aircraft indigenously; in 1994, the two countries held joint naval maneuvers in the Indian Ocean.

Most of Libya's weaponry is of former Eastern bloc origin, including Frog and Scud missiles and T-54 tanks. However, it does count a British frigate and some French Mirage fighters in its inventory, and some Thai companies have been sanctioned for material contributions to Libyan chemical weapons capabilities. In addition, Libya and Iran may be cooperating on a missile modernization project. North Korea has also relied heavily on the East, and Russia in particular; earlier in this decade, Russia provided 95 percent of all North Korean arms imports. This is no longer true, however, and the Pyongyang government is believed to be working hard to develop indigenous weapons manufacture capabilities, building in part upon Chinese technologies from previous missile sales. These capabilities may support increased North Korean arms exports, including missile transfers similar to past sales to Iran, Syria, and Libya.

CONVENTIONAL ARMS TRANSFERS AND CONTROLS, AND THE U.S. NATIONAL INTEREST SINCE WORLD WAR II[26]

Arms Exports as a Tool of U.S. Foreign and National Security Policy

Trade in arms is not a new practice, but arms transfers in support of national security policy objectives are a fairly recent phenomenon for the United States. The initial impetus for American military aid—to create a collective security apparatus in Western Europe in support of the policy of containment—evolved after the Korean War to include bilateral security assistance arrangements to countries beyond the Western Hemisphere, such as South Korea, Japan, Thailand, and Pakistan. Throughout the 1950s and early 1960s, the types and quantities of arms transferred to non-NATO recipients consisted predominantly of surplus or obsolescent equipment, most of which was exported as part of grant aid or highly concessionary programs.

---

[26]For a more detailed discussion of the evolution of U.S. policy on export control, see Mitchel B. Wallerstein, with William W. Snyder, Jr., "Appendix G: The Evolution of U.S. Export Control Policy: 1949–1989," in National Academy of Sciences, *Finding Common Ground: U.S. Export Controls in a Changed Global Environment*, National Academy Press, Washington, DC, 1991, pp. 308–320.

But fundamental structural changes in the international environment beginning in the late 1960s imposed a far more complex political-military calculus on the use of this instrument for advancing the national interest. Foremost among these changes was the growing competitiveness of the arms market, which was a natural outgrowth of the European nations' economic recovery, the growth of a robust Soviet arms industry, and the ascendant economic capabilities of former colonial states. A virtual U.S. and Soviet monopoly of the arms market throughout the 1950s and 1960s had given way by the late 1970s and early 1980s to intense competition among all the industrial countries and some newly industrial countries, such as South Korea and Israel, to sell armaments to an ever larger number of countries.

The advent of the Nixon Doctrine in 1969 marked a watershed in U.S. arms transfer policy that coincided with a metamorphosis of the international defense technology market. The declared objectives of the policy—to promote self-reliance in defense among friendly countries in place of continued dependence on U.S. interventionary forces—rendered explicit a growing requirement to accommodate developing countries' demand for greater independence in their own defense. It also lent formal recognition to the decline of traditional instruments of diplomacy. Arms shipments were once only one of several manifestations of a U.S. security commitment, usually accompanied by more tangible indicators such as formal security alliances, U.S. troop deployments, and clear consonance of political and military objectives between supplier and recipient.

Arms transfers evolved in the 1970s as a leading instrument of U.S. and Soviet security relations with a wide range of developing countries. Increasingly, many of the countries receiving liberalized access to advanced military technology seemed remote from traditional superpower security perimeters—in some cases exhibiting little ideological or political compatibility. Arms sales were a manifestation of U.S.-Soviet rivalry for international influence, but by the end of the 1970s, many countries were being equipped by both the rivals.

The new dynamic of interdependence among developed and developing countries over the decade changed the nature and volume of arms supplied. A larger number of commercially competitive arms industries in advanced countries, accompanied by growing numbers of newly independent states with the financial resources to choose among suppliers, helped promote a rapid escalation in the volume and sophistication of arms supplied globally. In the 1960s, the types of weapons transferred to the developing world consisted of limited quantities of relatively unsophisticated items such as MiG-17 or A-4 aircraft. By the mid-1970s, suppliers were competing among each other for lucrative contracts with developing nations based on the provision of front-line, state-of-the-art technologies, including manufacturing technology and equipment diverted for export from the supplying countries' own forces.

The shift in developing countries' dependency for imported goods from equipment to components over the last three decades also has helped hasten the pace of technology diffusion, giving emerging producers more stature in the international technology market. The commercial availability of dual-use components and systems, including guidance and telemetry equipment, satellites, and computer technology, has contributed to many developing countries' capacity for independent or quasi-independent weapon production programs, which in turn has provided them with an export capability. As summarized by one analyst, "Today's advanced technology is tomorrow's intermediate-level weapon system, and through a network of licenses, offsets, and joint ventures, today's buyer is often tomorrow's producer."[27]

Control of Arms Exports as a Tool of Foreign and National Security Policy

The need to restrain some exports was first recognized as a wartime necessity during World War I, but a formal arms export control regime was not established until 1935, in response to fears that the United States might be dragged into war. Early post–World War II U.S. export control policy was influenced more by continuing shortages of critical materials, including chemicals, raw materials, and food, than by strategic, ideological, or other national security considerations. Implementation of the Marshall Plan kept demand for these goods high, and policy did not yet address a potential Soviet national security threat. Indeed, the United States continued to offer to include the Soviet Union in the Marshall Plan as late as 1947. By 1948, as the cold war took hold with the beginning of the policy of containment, that situation changed. Late that year, export licensing requirements were imposed on the Soviets and their satellites, giving the President broad and relatively unquestioned authority to restrict the export of items critical to U.S. national security. By 1949, the cooperation of the allies was enlisted with the establishment of the Coordinating Committee for Multilateral Export Controls (CoCom) in Paris to deny the transfer of critical dual-use technology (that which can be used for either civilian or military purposes) to the Communist bloc.

At the same time, the North Atlantic Treaty Organization (NATO) was forming. Arms and technology transfers were important tools in solidifying the alliance and ensuring its military effectiveness. With NATO's decision in the early 1950s to rely on maintaining a qualitative edge—a "force multiplier" strategy—to balance the Warsaw Pact's quantitative superiority and maintain NATO's technology lead gave further impetus to the strategy of denial of technology to the Warsaw Pact.

The détente of the late 1960s and early 1970s brought a congressional reexamination of export control policies to give greater consideration to the promotion of commercial and dual-use trade. The Nixon Administration, however, chose to tie relaxation of export controls on the Soviet Union to positive changes in Soviet behavior. This strategy was formalized by Congress through the Jackson-Vanik amendment to the 1974 Trade Reform Act, which conditioned the granting of most favored nation status (MFN) on issues of human rights. This linkage prevented significant relaxation of export controls during this period. Détente weakened in the late 1970s and ended with the Soviet invasion of Afghanistan. The invasion, coupled with growing concern that the Soviets had in fact been able to exploit détente to gain access to critical de-

---

[27]Stephanie G. Neuman, "Third World Arms Production and the Global Arms Transfer System," in James Katz (ed.), *Arms Production in Developing Countries: An Analysis of Decision Making*, Lexington Books, Lexington, MA, 1984, p. 27.

fense technologies and weapons systems, created an environment in which export controls were both broadened and made more strict.

President Carter's announcement of ambitious policies for unilateral and multilateral restraint, encapsulated in his statement in May of 1977 that arms transfers were "an exceptional foreign policy implement, to be used only in instances where it can be clearly demonstrated that the transfer contributes to our national security interests," at first found some political support. The Carter initiative imposed several specific controls on sales of advanced armaments to developing countries, excluding NATO and the ANZUS (Australia, New Zealand, and the United States) allies from any restrictions. While providing for exceptions to policy in the event of "extraordinary circumstances," the controls were intended to impose more careful scrutiny on pending arms requests.[28]

In structural terms, however, increased domestic pressures to restrain arms sales coincided with a growing dependence on this instrument to effect foreign policy objectives traditionally fulfilled by other means. The inherent conflict between efforts to appease domestic opposition to arms sales at the beginning of the Administration and the subsequent pressures that arose from the dependence of the United States on arms exports created a chronic tension in the policies which led to their constant revision. Damaged by the overblown rhetoric of early Administration statements, the Carter policy was destined to incite opponents and disappoint proponents.

The first Reagan Administration tightened technology denial policies as U.S.-Soviet tensions continued to rise and in response to events such as the imposition of martial law in Poland. U.S. efforts to extend these restrictions to U.S. foreign subsidiaries and to foreign companies contractually subject to U.S. policy met with substantial resistance from a number of members of CoCom. Many close allies resented the imposition of U.S. foreign policy objectives on the multilateral institution, and national legislation was enacted to prevent the United States from extending its law and regulatory authority to the territory of other NATO countries.

By President Reagan's second term, however, there was growing U.S. domestic pressure for change in technology export policy. It was becoming increasingly clear that the allies were less willing to forgo sales than was the United States. Suggestions were circulating that U.S. industry was losing market share to other major suppliers, and many controlled items appeared to be available from non-CoCom suppliers. Pressure to loosen controls again began to mount, but it was essentially deflated by the Reagan Administration with revelations about the "Toshiba-Kongsberg affair"— the illegal sale of controlled technology to the Soviet Union by Japanese and Norwegian corporations. With the dramatic end of the cold war during the Bush

---

[28]The Carter policy for unilateral restraints on U.S. arms sales included a pledge not to be the first to introduce an advanced weapon system into the region; on the development of weapons solely for export; on retransferring weapons from one recipient to a third country; and on coproduction agreements. See Statement by the President on Conventional Arms Policy, 19 May 1977, reprinted in Congressional Research Service (CRS), *Changing Perspectives on U.S. Arms Transfer Policy*, CRS, Washington, DC, September 25, 1981, Appendix II.

Administration, U.S. policy on arms and technology exports was clearly in need of reconsideration.

The Clinton Administration made its attempt to loosen the statutory restrictions on dual-use exports with its proposed revision of the Export Administration Act. Revisions were submitted to Congress in 1993, but the bill remains contentious and no resolution has yet been achieved. In addition to these efforts, the Administration has made a number of changes to export policies through executive order, twice easing the limits on the capabilities of computers permitted for export and relaxing restrictions on certain cryptographic software exports.

Current U.S. Policy

The Clinton Administration has developed an explicit policy not just for dual-use goods but for the sale of conventional arms. This policy emphasizes regional security and stability, helping allies to deter potential threats, promoting interoperability with U.S. defense equipment, and preserving the U.S. defense industrial base. It pledges government support in implementing sales once exports are approved, and it acknowledges the continuation of the policy of case-by-case licensing decisions. Features that distinguish current policy from that of prior Administrations are the following:

Regional focus: The Clinton Administration policy weighs arms transfer decisions primarily in their regional, rather than global, security and stability context.

Efforts to promote inter-allied cooperation: Current policy highlights the importance of multilateral consensus and cooperation in limiting arms sales, and reserves unilateral efforts for the smallest possible number of cases. To this end, the Administration continues to negotiate the final form of the recently agreed to, multilateral Wassenaar Arrangement, which replaces the expired CoCom regime. The goals of the Arrangement are to increase transparency and promote responsibility in sales of both conventional arms and dual-use technologies, again concentrating on regional security threats. The Administration also has attempted to address sales of particular concern on an individual basis.

Rogue states prohibitions: A key component of the Wassenaar Arrangement is its focus on preventing sales of arms and sensitive technologies to "countries of concern" (Iran, Iraq, Libya, and North Korea), rather than to the Communist bloc countries.

Decontrol of dual-use technologies: The Clinton Administration has taken an aggressive stance toward removing controls on dual-use technologies it believes are outdated or ineffective. The current policy attempts to tighten export restrictions on "chokehold" technologies—technologies that would make a critical difference in the capability of the recipient to produce or deliver weapons of mass destruction. Simultaneously, the Administration has sought to loosen controls on items that are widely available on the international market.

More explicit recognition of economic contributions of arms exports: The Clinton Administration's conventional arms transfer policy accords a more explicit level of recognition of the preservation of the defense industrial base and to domestic economic considerations associated with arms exports than has been the case in the past.

This policy was developed as both a response to, and a strategy for, a changing world. These changes already have been immense, but outlining the major trends underscores the uncertain future that U.S. policy confronts.

EXISTING DOMESTIC AND INTERNATIONAL ARMS TRANSFER REGIMES AND REGULATIONS

Domestic

The challenge for U.S. policy and practice is to recognize and, to the extent possible, reconcile the competing national security, foreign policy, and economic interests.

U.S. Statutory and Substantive Restrictions on Arms Sales

A broad array of laws restrict the sale of military goods and technologies, but many are directed toward weapons of mass destruction. These laws are supplemented by extensive statutory language that grants authority for sanctions and other punitive measures if illegal arms or technology transfers do in fact occur. Most establish some system of review for licensing decisions on specific items, rather than prohibiting their sale outright. The statutes with the largest effect on the transfer of conventional arms and technologies are discussed below.

The Arms Export Control Act (AECA) of 1976, as amended, and the Export Administration Act (EAA) of 1979, as amended have general restrictions related to conventional arms transfers. With antecedents dating to the Battle Act of 1954, the AECA outlines eligibility guidelines for arms recipients, and limits the sale (and resale) of military equipment. The AECA authorizes the President to control the export and import of defense articles and services, which are licensed through the International Transfer in Arms Regulation (ITAR). The ITAR lists proscribed export destinations, regulated weapons (the Munitions List), procedures for applying for export licenses, and penalties for failure to comply with the regulations.[29]

The Export Administration Act restricts the export of dual-use goods or technologies that could be used either for weapons of mass destruction or for conventional arms. Exports may be restricted for one of three basic reasons: national security, foreign

---

[29]For further readings on this topic, see Ian Anthony (ed.), *Arms Export Regulations*, Oxford University Press, Oxford, 1991; Glennon J. Harrison, *Export Controls: Background and Issues,* CRS Report for Congress, 94-30E, Library of Congress, Congressional Research Service, Washington, DC, 12 January 1994; National Academy of Sciences, *Finding Common Ground: U.S. Export Controls in a Changed Global Environment,* National Academy Press, Washington, DC, 1991; U.S. Congress, Office of Technology Assessment, *Export Controls and Nonproliferation Policy*, OTA-ISS-596, US Government Printing Office, Washington, DC, May 1994; U.S. General Accounting Office, *Export Controls: Issues in Removing Militarily Sensitive Exports from the Munitions List,* GAO/NSIAD 93-67, General Accounting Office, Washington, DC, March 1993.

policy, or "short supply." The EAA also establishes an interagency review process for license applications.

Numerous more specific restrictions on items relating to weapons of mass destruction can be found in the Foreign Assistance Act (FAA), The Nuclear Non-Proliferation Act, The Atomic Energy Act, and the Chemical and Biological Weapons Control Act.

In the conventional realm, there are additional restraints on specific countries, regions, technologies, and behaviors. Amendments to the EAA and AECA restrict sales of ballistic and cruise missiles to countries that do not adhere to the international Missile Technology Control Regime guidelines. Other statutory provisions limit transfers to Southwest Asia: sales of shoulder-launched Stinger missiles to countries around the Persian Gulf (except Bahrain) are prohibited, as is the transfer of depleted uranium ammunition for tanks to countries other than NATO, major non-NATO allies, and Taiwan (although either restriction can be waived by the President). A 1990 law limits exports of satellites and nuclear-related goods to China. Sales to Iran or Iraq of anything the Commerce Department controls for national security reasons are outlawed by the Iran-Iraq Non-Proliferation Act. The "Pressler Amendment" to the FAA prohibits sales to Pakistan of military equipment or technology unless the President certifies that Pakistan does not possess a nuclear weapon.[30] Finally, sections of the Foreign Assistance Act (FAA) prohibit security assistance to countries where governments engage in consistent human rights violations, while the Anti-Terrorism Act addresses sales of goods and technologies that could contribute to the military capabilities of any country that has repeatedly provided support for terrorism.

Principal Vehicles for U.S. Arms Transfers

U.S. arms exports are made through two channels: government-to-government, or foreign military sales (FMS) (the channel essentially required for Foreign Military Financing [FMF] recipients); and producer-to-government, or direct commercial sales (DCS). In recent years, both the ratio of FMS to DCS and the content of DCS sales have shifted. FMS was the primary channel of U.S. arms transfers until the 1980s, when limits on the size of permitted commercial sales were reduced and then removed. After those limitations were lifted, DCS almost quadrupled from their total over the previous four decades. This trend peaked in fiscal year 1989, when more weapons were delivered through DCS than through FMS; this is attributable to the perception that the DCS system is typically faster than FMS, less costly, less transparent, and involves less government oversight.

However, the Persian Gulf War and its aftermath produced a substantial increase in FMS orders. By fiscal years 1992–1993, DCS had dropped to about one fifth of total

---

[30]Included in the FY96 Foreign Operations Appropriations bill (PL 104-107) is an amendment that would modify restrictions on U.S. arms sales and assistance to Pakistan. The Brown Amendment (Sec. 559) permits certain forms of military aid, such as for international narcotics control and antiterrorism. Additionally, it allows the return of Pakistani military equipment, which was in the United States for repairs when the Pressler Amendment was imposed in 1990, and permits the President to release the Pakistani government from its obligation to pay for equipment storage costs assessed since that time.

U.S. arms deliveries. What was sold through DCS changed as well; traditionally, DCS provided spare parts, follow-on sales, light weapons, and other small equipment. But less regulation, combined with technological innovation, has resulted in DCS sales now routinely including major weapons systems.

International

Many U.S. limitations on weapons exports are tied to international agreements with the same objectives, a tacit recognition that the problem of proliferation must be tackled multilaterally. International arms control regimes generally do not address underlying political motivations for conflict and arms proliferation. They can, however, make military balances among the regional states more stable by reducing access by unstable states to technologies that could add to incentives to undertake offensive action against neighbors. They can also make international military intervention less costly, if the need for such intervention occurs.

Restraint regimes have tended to focus, for a variety of reasons, on Weapons of Mass Destruction (WMD). International as well as domestic arrangements relating to conventional weapons transfers are few.

The Missile Technology Control Regime (MTCR) is a voluntary regime created in 1987 to control the proliferation of missiles and related technologies. Originally formed by Canada, West Germany, France, Italy, Japan, the United Kingdom, and the United States, the MTCR has expanded to 28 members, of which Russia, South Africa, and Brazil are the most recent.   In addition, while not members, China, Israel, and Ukraine have agreed to abide by MTCR guidelines.

The initial agreement called on member states to coordinate domestic export policies to restrict sales of ballistic and cruise missiles (and related technologies) that could deliver nuclear weapons, defined as those missiles with ranges greater than 300 kilometers and payloads over 500 kilograms. The regime's guidelines divided missile-related exports into two categories—one with a "strong presumption of denial" (complete rocket systems and UAVs, major subsystems, and critical production equipment), and another comprised of dual-use items that may or may not be intended for use in missile systems. The regime was modified in 1993 to include missiles capable of carrying chemical or biological weapons (CW/BW) as well. Because CW/BW payloads are lighter than nuclear warheads, the missile payload requirements were removed. At its most recent meeting in October 1995, MTCR members updated the guidelines to accommodate technological advances.

The MTCR is not a treaty, and is not binding under international law. Further, penalties for violations vary between members, and the lack of an agreed-upon enforcement mechanism has led to internal disagreements. However, the MTCR has proven successful in blocking some sales of potentially destabilizing and threatening missile systems or components, and has slowed the pace of missile proliferation worldwide.

The UN Transparency in Armaments Initiative (TIA), also known as the UN Register of Conventional Arms, was established in 1991 to promote "openness" or "transparency" in the transfer of arms. As such, it is not an arms control regime, but it does permit the review of the potential impact of those arms transfers that are reported. The idea of such an international accounting of major arms exports can be traced back to attempts by the League of Nations and its efforts to operate a similar record during the 1920s and 1930s. The concept was revived by the United Nations at the end of the cold war, in the hopes that the international atmosphere would finally be conducive to such an account. The current UN Register was endorsed in 1991 from a draft proposal drawn up by the United Kingdom, and the first report was issued in 1993.

The TIA is a compilation of data and background information on annual arms imports and exports voluntarily submitted by UN member states. It tracks seven categories of weapons: battle tanks, armored combat vehicles, large caliber artillery systems, combat aircraft, attack helicopters, warships, missiles, and missile launchers. Since its first appearance, the Register has been criticized on numerous fronts. The most common complaint has been that the TIA falls far short of its main objective, "transparency," because many sellers and buyers have refused to supply data about some transfers of weapons. For example, roughly three-fifths of the trade in missiles and missile launchers is not reported each year.[31] Critics point out that in the three years the report has been issued, participation by UN member states has been wanting: by November 1995, 92, 90, and 87 countries (from 1992–1994, respectively) chose to submit information on their trade in arms. However, a total of 121 countries have participated overall, a difference attributable to the fact that the same countries did not submit data each year. (Conspicuous absences include Iran, which did not submit data in 1994, and other importers such as Saudi Arabia, Kuwait, and Algeria.) Lack of near-total participation makes it difficult to achieve one of the TIA's major functions: to provide long-term data on trends and patterns of the weapons trade.

A 1994 committee to review the TIA's progress was unable to reach agreement on categorical revisions or additions, or on a proposal to request participants to provide qualitative, as well as quantitative, information. These issues, as well as complaints about lack of verification measures and the limited scope of weapons covered, are expected to be addressed in the 1997 assessment of the TIA's progress.

The Wassenaar Arrangement on Export Controls for Conventional Arms and Dual-Use Goods and Technologies (previously known as the "New Forum") will become the follow-on regime to CoCom. Provisionally known as the New Forum during its negotiation, the Arrangement aims to control the export of both conventional weapons and dual-use technologies. The meeting of New Forum negotiators in October 1995 concluded initial elements of the Wassenaar Arrangement, which will be reviewed by the governments of the 28 founding members[32] before the first plenary in April 1996.

---

[31]This estimate is based on two methods of comparison: examination of other publicly available information and cross-referencing between the submissions of exporting and importing states. See National Security Planning Associates, *UN Transparency in Armaments: A Current Assessment and Future Prospects,* January 1995, pp. 20–23.

[32]Australia, Austria, Belgium, Canada, the Czech Republic, Denmark, Finland, France, Germany, Greece, Hungary, Ireland, Italy, Japan, Luxembourg, the Netherlands, New Zealand, Norway, Poland, Portugal, the

First proposed by President Clinton two years ago, the Administration advocated two major goals for the regime: "to prevent destabilizing buildups of weapons in regions of tension, such as South Asia and the Middle East, by establishing a formal process of transparency, consultation, and, where appropriate, adopting common policies of restraint and to deal firmly with states whose behavior is today a cause of concern—such as Iraq, Iran, North Korea, and Libya—through restraint in the export of weapons and weapons-related and other sensitive, dual-use technologies."[33] The United States expressed its the desire to push the December 1995 Arrangement further in these areas and its intent to seek expansion in future negotiations.

The Arrangement will be based on "national controls" and "common understandings" with partners, and membership criteria will include "adequate export controls, adherence to the major non-proliferation regimes, and responsible export policies toward the pariah countries." [34]

The Convention on Conventional Weapons (also known as the Inhumane Weapons Convention) is based on humanitarian concerns rather than on arms control objectives. Inspired by the horrors of the Vietnam War, the treaty and its protocols aim to restrict the wartime use of weapons fragments not detectable by x-ray, of land mines and booby traps, and of incendiary weapons. The United States signed the Convention in 1982, but delayed ratification due to concerns about protocol III's limitations on incendiary weapons. The United States finally ratified the Treaty in March 1995, but not protocol III, which prohibits the use of napalm; parties to the treaty must agree to be bound by at least two of the protocols in force.

In a review conference in September and October of 1995, a new protocol restricting the use of blinding laser weapons was adopted. However, conference participants were unable to agree on amendments to protocol II, which limits the use of land mines in wartime. Negotiations will begin again on this and other issues in April, 1996.

P-5 Talks

In the wake of the Persian Gulf War, the P-5 (the five permanent members of the Security Council: United States, United Kingdom, France, Russia, and China) decided to take a closer look at the global proliferation of conventional arms. President Bush announced his Middle East Arms Control Initiative on May 29, 1991; two days later France called for a broader look at the worldwide spread of arms.

The first meeting was held in July 1991 in Paris. The P-5 largely reiterated existing commitments, pledging to show national restraint in the transfer of arms and to support the UN Arms Register. They also stated their strong support for "the objective of

---

Russian Federation, the Slovak Republic, Spain, Sweden, Switzerland, Turkey, the United Kingdom, and the United States.

[33]Thomas E. McNamara, Assistant Secretary of State for Political-Military Affairs, *Statement Before the Subcommittee on International Finance and Monetary Policy of the Senate Banking, Housing, and Urban Affairs Committee*, Washington, DC, September 21, 1995.

[34]Ibid.

establishing a weapons of mass destruction-free zone in the Middle East,"[35] and called for a regional freeze and eventual elimination of ground-to-ground missiles, regional acceptance of nuclear safeguards monitored by the International Atomic Energy Agency, a ban on imports of materials that can be used in nuclear weapons by all Middle Eastern states, and regional accession to the chemical weapons convention.

In October 1991, the second meeting took place in London. The P-5 agreed to share information about seven categories of weapons sales to the Middle East and developed a set of draft guidelines pertaining to all transfers. The resulting communiqué identified a number of factors the P-5 agreed to weigh heavily in determining whether to make conventional arms sales, and pledged to consider whether arms would be used for self-defense, were appropriate to the security threats in the region, and would "enhance the capability of the recipient to participate in regional or other collective arrangements."[36]

Washington hosted the third and final round of the talks in May 1992. The parties agreed to a set of guidelines for weapons of mass destruction, but failed to resolve issues of advance notification of weapons sales (including the categories and destinations of sales to be covered and how much advance notification would be required) and restraint of missiles and missile technologies (the United States argued for their inclusion, but the Chinese were opposed, contending missiles were delivery systems as opposed to actual weapons).

The Chinese pulled out of the talks at the end of 1992, in response to the U.S. sale of F-16 fighters to Taiwan. Although the remaining P-5 members discussed the possibility of continuing the discussions without China, the Clinton Administration chose to pursue further restraint through the New Forum negotiations for a replacement of the CoCom regime.

Regional Initiatives

In May 1991, President Bush announced his Middle East Arms Control Initiative, which was largely carried forward by the P-5 discussions in the ensuing two years. The proposal had four major objectives: a regional nuclear weapons-free zone, a ban on ground-to-ground missiles, prohibitions on chemical and biological weapons, and the establishment of guidelines for restraint in sales by the five major suppliers. Although these principles were embraced by the P-5 in their first meeting in July 1991, the process failed to produce meaningful agreements for implementation. More recent discussions among weapons suppliers have taken place largely through the New Forum negotiations, and the resulting Wassenaar Arrangement has a "pariah state," as opposed to a regional, orientation.

---

[35] *Communiqué Issued Following the Meeting of the Five on Arms Transfers and Non-Proliferation*, July 9, 1991.

[36] *Communiqué Issued Following the Meeting of the Five: Guidelines for Conventional Arms Transfers*, October 18, 1991.

While the P-5 talks gave way to the Wassenaar Arrangement, parts of Bush's Middle East initiative continue. Within the region, arms control efforts have been hampered by the *de facto* nuclear status of Israel, whose neighbors maintain that any limitations on conventional arms cannot be separated from discussions of Israel's nuclear program. These concerns are being discussed by the Arms Control and Regional Security (ACRS) working group in the ongoing peace process, which began in 1992.[37]

South Asia remains another area of strong concern. On the supplier side, the Wassenaar Arrangement again omits mention of regional restraint. After U.S. Defense Secretary Perry's visit to Pakistan early in 1994, the U.S.-Pakistani Consultative Group was revived to provide an annual forum for discussion of issues relating to the bilateral security relationship. It is not aimed specifically at limiting arms transfers, nor are there other discussions between the two states to limit the acquisition of conventional arms, although there are a number of confidence-building measures in place.

Elsewhere in Asia, the Association of Southeast Asian Nations has developed the Asian Regional Forum (ARF) to discuss regional security issues generally. Although the ARF has not addressed the conventional arms trade directly, it may provide a venue for future initiatives and to continue efforts such as the 1993 Asian Export Control Seminar. The same promise may hold for the small weapons market in Africa through initiatives in the Organization of African Unity, which has addressed post-conflict demobilization, or through a possible "Africanized" Helsinki process.

In Latin America, relationships like the ones developed through negotiations for the Treaty of Tlatelolco (establishing a Latin American nuclear-weapons free zone) and the Argentinean/Brazilian denuclearization process hold the potential for broadening arms control efforts. The Organization of American States (OAS) has taken a leading role in furthering regional arms control, pushing forward agreements on confidence-building measures such as data exchanges on conventional arms transfers and resolutions on proliferation dangers. At a November 1995 conference on regional confidence- and security-building measures, the OAS issued the Santiago Declaration recommending a series of additional confidence-building steps, indicating further momentum on which future efforts might build.

Shrinking domestic arms procurement has increased competition among the major suppliers for other available outlets, both in pricing and in the quality of weapons offered for purchase. With greater leverage than in the past, buyers have been seeking and finding lower prices and other special purchase arrangements. More worrisome, suppliers' pressing economic incentives to export are enabling regional arms buyers to acquire front-line, state-of-the-art military equipment and technologies that previously were not available to them. The value and effectiveness of high-technology weapons systems in the Persian Gulf War were clear and dramatic, and the desire to acquire these types of systems has sharply increased. Few of them have actually been transferred thus far, but pressures are growing to do so. Thus, despite

---

[37] "Confidence Building in the Middle East: Regional Developments," *The Henry L. Stimson Center*, Washington, DC, 5 October 1995.

the worldwide quantitative reduction in the level of production and acquisition of conventional weapons in recent years, there is reason for renewed attention to the dangers of conventional weapons and technology proliferation. And there is opportunity in the momentum of new international initiatives such as the Wassenaar Arrangement.

Chapter Three

A REGIME FOR CONTROLLING THE TRANSFER OF CONVENTIONAL WEAPONS

INTRODUCTION

This chapter will propose the establishment of an international regime to control selectively the transfer of specific weapons systems and technologies. The intent is not to offer a blueprint for such a regime, but rather to illustrate the constraints on, and opportunities for, conventional arms transfer restraint in the current environment. Successful implementation of an international regime will require recognition by the key suppliers that the benefits of accepting controls outweigh the benefits of continued sales. Controls must therefore be carefully and selectively crafted. The discussion below will identify criteria that can be used by an existing or future international control regime for determining which conventional weapons systems and strategic technologies should be controlled, and it will identify candidate end items and strategic technologies for control.

There are two principal ways to regulate the transfer of conventional weapons. The first, transparency, relies on the voluntary disclosure of information to inhibit potentially hazardous transfers. Examples include the UN Arms Register and information-sharing among members of the Wassenaar Arrangement. The effectiveness of transparency depends on the willingness of states to agree—at least tacitly—on criteria for approving or disapproving proposed transfers. In principle, sellers or buyers would refrain from transfers that are inconsistent with the criteria. This discretionary or cooperative feature of transparency is both its strength and its weakness. States may agree to transparency measures because they impose relatively minor encumbrance. By the same token, such measures may have limited effectiveness in stemming undesirable arms transfers.

The second regulatory approach is to specify formal and explicit limits on transfers of particular types or amounts of weapons. The strengths and weaknesses of this approach are mirror images of the transparency measures. Formal limits bind the parties, and the discretion that characterizes transparency is largely removed. This binding character is the reason why formal compacts have been difficult to achieve. Sellers' and buyers' motivations to buy and sell are powerful. For this reason, verification is critical to the success of formal limits. But reliable monitoring of conventional arms transfers can be very difficult.

Typically, most proposals of formal limits focus on deep reductions in the transfer of all major conventional weapons. For example, the Congressional Budget Office's analysis[1] takes this approach, although indirectly, by proposing to limit the dollar volume of weapons sales ($ amount). Proposals of this sort appear regularly in the defense analysis and academic literature, but none has been implemented. One difficulty has been the high strategic and financial opportunity costs such limits would impose on buyers and sellers—even if the result might be improved regional stability. Even if a regime with such severe limits were adopted, the opportunity costs involved could raise the likelihood of defections or violations.

CRITERIA FOR ESTABLISHING FORMAL LIMITS

One way to resolve the problems surrounding formal regulatory mechanisms would be to control the sales of only those weapons that meet three specific criteria: high military effectiveness, low substitutability, and low opportunity cost.

High military effectiveness. Candidate systems for controls should affect battlefield outcomes to a degree significantly out of proportion to their relative numbers and costs (e.g., technologies that are likely to be "force multipliers" for regional militaries).

Low substitutability. Substitutes for the controlled systems should be either nonexistent or available only at prohibitive costs. This means that buyers should not be able to circumvent the control regime by acquiring a comparable system from a supplier who is not part of the regime. Similarly, buyers should not be able to substitute for the proscribed system by acquiring a less advanced system that can perform the same missions with roughly comparable effectiveness. If these conditions are not met, buyers could easily defeat the purposes of the control regime, while members of the control regime could be expected to defect as they observe other suppliers benefiting from their own restraint.

Low opportunity cost. At least at the outset of the regime, limits on conventional arms transfers should be designed to minimize perceived economic losses to participating states. Since a major obstacle to successful control of conventional arms transfer is concern about the revenues from lost sales, the lower the financial impact, the better the chance that key supplier states will be willing to join and abide by such a regime.[2]

---

[1] Limiting Conventional Arms Exports to the Middle East, Congressional Budget Office, 1992.

[2] Elsewhere in this study, we point out that in a purely economic sense, the benefits of conventional arms sales are, in fact, small, at least in the United States and Western Europe. However, given the contentiousness of this argument, we should strive to achieve agreements in which this issue is minimized.

We recognize that the dollar value of forgone sales may not be the only way to think about opportunity costs. For example, a lost sale may affect a critical company or industry out of proportion to its dollar value, if it means that important domestic capabilities or competencies might be lost. Similarly, the political opportunity cost may be great in cases of forgone sales to an important client state.

In sum, the list of weapons that are the best candidates for both strategically benefi-cial and politically feasible limits may be derived from the answers to the following questions:

- What weapons are the most highly effective weapons for the regions in question?

- What subset of these weapons has no substitutes?

- What subset of these weapons, if limits on transfers were imposed, would result at the outset in relatively low opportunity costs to suppliers in terms of lost sales?

The remainder of this chapter consists of two parts. The first is a description of a hy-pothetical control regime designed to limit transfers of conventional weapons that meet the above three criteria. The second is a description of a complementary regime for controlling the sale of weapons of ill repute. Much of this discussion is based on RAND research for the Under Secretary of Defense for Policy in the early 1990s.[3] In a significant departure from arms transfer control proposals of the past, the approach presented here does not initially attempt to control major platforms. It is important that the reasons for their omission be clear. It is emphatically *not* the position of the authors that the sale of these weapons platforms is nonproblematic, and the fact that they are not on the list of candidates for control does *not* signal in-difference to their sale. Unquestionably, advanced platforms confer important and potentially destabilizing capabilities of concern to the United States. However, the intrinsic political difficulty of controlling conventional arms transfers necessitates a strict focus that begins with those weapons most readily identified with high military effectiveness, low substitutability, and low opportunity cost. Restricting the transfer of major weapons platforms produces less military leverage, can be more easily evaded by substitutes, and imposes high opportunity costs that may preclude the prospect of even modest agreements.

DETERMINING WHICH WEAPONS SHOULD BE CONTROLLED

High Military Effectiveness

The operational definition of high military effectiveness depends on the characteris-tics of the regional balance to be affected by controls. Many end items may qualify, especially in areas in which military balances are brittle. Given the inherent difficulty of enacting controls on arms transfers in the current environment, it is important to identify the weapons with the highest effectiveness.

In general, such weapons can be defined as those that can threaten crucial targets effectively and for which there are few, if any, counters even when employed against the forces of advanced states by relatively unsophisticated military forces. Several capabilities can contribute dramatically to a weapon's military effectiveness.

---

[3] *Controlling Conventional Arms Transfers: A New Approach with Application to the Persian Gulf,* Kenneth Watman, Marcy Agmon, Charles Wolf, Jr., RAND, MR-369-USDP, 1994.

The first is autonomous functioning, which can enable military organizations with limited sophistication to offset some of their disadvantages. Such weapons incorporate technologies capable of performing many of the tasks that are currently most difficult for unsophisticated military forces—surveillance, target acquisition, maneuver, and striking the target with accuracy. Very high levels of individual and organizational training and competence are required to operate and maintain advanced weapons such as modern armored fighting vehicles and tactical aircraft. Even if successfully operated and maintained, these advanced platforms usually need to be skillfully integrated with other supporting and complementary systems and organizations. Relatively few military organizations can attain the individual and organizational levels of performance needed to employ these advanced weapons platforms effectively. Autonomously functioning weapons can provide a way to escape this qualitative deficit by reducing the demands on personnel and infrastructure through technological substitutes, thus enabling less sophisticated regional militaries to more closely match the capabilities of the United States, Western Europe, and Russia.

The second capability that contributes significantly to a weapon's military effectiveness is precision, which helps ensure that an adversary can attack crucial targets with high confidence. The third and fourth capabilities are long range and stealth, which help make weapons resistant to defenses and other countermeasures. Long range increases the area that can be attacked, as well as the area from which an attack can be launched, while stealth makes weapons difficult to detect and intercept.

The following are examples of weapons and supporting systems that possess these characteristics:

- Submarines

- Stealth aircraft

- Advanced sea and land mines

- Advanced missiles and munitions

- Tactical ballistic missiles and cruise missiles with advanced conventional warheads

- Directed-energy weapons (e.g., long-range lasers and microwave weapons).

Two platforms—submarines and stealth aircraft—are included because they are difficult to counter, can inflict costly losses, do not require large, highly complex organizations to be effective, and can vitiate the technological edge of more advanced countries. The Argentinean use of a submarine in the Falkland Islands War provides an example. Argentina's armed forces were not models of organizational effectiveness, yet they were able to maintain at sea for the duration of the conflict a relatively crude submarine that menaced the Royal Navy in the area, notwithstanding Britain's sophisticated antisubmarine warfare (ASW).

Stealth aircraft fall into a similar category. A second or third world air force, incapable of large-scale operations against advanced military forces such as those of the

United States, could compensate for some of its difficulties by using stealth technology.[4]

Advanced missiles and directed-energy weapons embody some or all the characteristics discussed above. Missile systems can strike from long range, and thus make suppression difficult. Once launched, they can travel to and strike their targets autonomously and precisely. Land and sea mines have analogous performance characteristics.

It is not necessary that a control regime include all the categories of weapons identified above. An initial agreement need not try to tackle air-to-air, air-to-ground, ground-to-air, and antiship missiles simultaneously. Agreements to regulate the diffusion of any one of these categories might be a useful first step toward a more comprehensive regime.

The list of candidate systems for control is likely to expand or contract as new systems are introduced and as countermeasures are developed against older systems. For example, the original EXOCET antiship missile is less dangerous now to the U.S. Navy than it was when it was originally deployed, since tactics and systems have been developed to counter it (and similar systems). However, EXOCET would have been on a control list developed in the 1970s or early 1980s.

If a new substitute system with comparable capability becomes available—one that a supplier refuses to include in the regime—circumvention of the agreement is virtually assured, at least for the category of weapon in question. Given this situation, it is likely that all suppliers would then be permitted to sell their systems in that category—a consequence that might discourage a supplier from developing the substitute in the first place.

Any list of candidate systems for controls should thus be seen as dynamic. In some cases, controls on trade may do no more than buy time before substitutes can be developed. Buying time is not an insignificant benefit, however, in the world of defense planning. Preventing diffusion of advanced systems for several years may be all that is necessary until countermeasures can be developed, or conflicts driving the demand for weapons resolved.

Discussed below are specific missile systems that might be included in a control regime on the basis of the criterion of military effectiveness. The list should be considered exemplary and not exhaustive.

Air-to-air missiles. Of particular interest is the new generation of medium-range, active radar-guided missiles. These systems could exert higher leverage than existing radar- and IR-guided missiles (such as Sparrow and Sidewinder) for two reasons. First, existing systems have much shorter ranges, so considerable piloting skill is necessary to use them. Second, to be used effectively, the aircraft launching Sparrow

---

[4]The submarine and stealth aircraft platforms depend upon the skills of their crews, and so are not as autonomous as some of the other high-effectiveness weapons discussed here. Nevertheless, though most nations cannot field large, organizationally effective forces, they can develop effective and skilled individuals and teams. Hence, they may be able to operate a submarine or a few specialized aircraft effectively.

must illuminate the targeted aircraft with radar for the duration of the missile's flight, which requires considerable skill and subjects the aircraft to counterfire. In contrast, more advanced missiles have sufficiently long range so that relatively less maneuver or penetration of defenses is required. These missiles function autonomously to a great extent, allowing launching aircraft to take evasive action almost as soon as the missile is fired.

The following missile systems are candidates for potential inclusion in an advanced control regime:

- AIM-120, AMRAAM (United States)
- Active Sky Flash (Great Britain)
- MICA-Active (France)
- RVV-AE/R-77 (Russia)
- AAM-12 (Russia)

Relatively few states manufacture these missiles, primarily because of the sophistication of the active radar guidance needed for their operation. This would facilitate the prospects for control, since only a small number of supplier states would have to agree.[5]

Antitank missiles. Many types of antitank missiles are marketed today. As with air-to-air missiles, however, a new and more capable type of antitank missile is emerging, with enhanced and potentially more problematic capabilities. Existing antitank missiles require manual operation to guide the missile, usually by holding a laser or some other sighting device on the targeted vehicle. Since the speed of antitank missiles is relatively low to permit effective guidance, the operator must expose himself to countermeasures (usually suppressive fire) during the missile flight.

The new type of antitank missile is autonomous. Once fixed on the target, it is self-guided, reducing risks to the operator.

The specific candidates for consideration in a control regime include:

- Antiarmor Weapon System—heavy and medium (United States)
- Trigat—long and medium range (Belgium, Britain, France, Germany)

As in the case of the advanced air-to-air missiles discussed above, the small number of current producers enhances prospects for an agreement to control the diffusion of these systems.

Air-to-surface missiles. The most advanced and potentially problematic examples of these systems are those that have both long-range capability and autonomous functioning.

---

[5]Possible sales of such systems to such states as Thailand and the UAE could undermine the viability of an agreement to control further diffusion, lending urgency to these pending decisions.

The following systems are candidates for possible inclusion in a control regime:

- Joint Stand-Off Weapon (United States)

- Stand-Off Land Attack Missile upgrade (United States)

- Maverick upgrades (United States)

- Popeye upgrades (United States, Israel)

- Apache (France, Germany)

- KH-65SE (Russia)

Only a few states are currently developing systems in this category, a factor favorable to prospects for control. The foreign developers also happen to be states with close relationships with the United States. Although in the past this has not precluded aggressive competition for sales, a history of relatively common interest could further increase the likelihood of successful controls.

Man-portable surface-to-air missiles. Unlike the previous categories, this type of system contains many candidates:

- Stinger upgrades (United States)

- SA-16, 18 (Russia)

- Javelin, Starburst, Starstreak (Great Britain)

- Mistral SATCP (France)

- CPMIEC (PRC)

- Bofors RBS 70 (Sweden)

- CSIST (Taiwan)

- Keiko (Japan)

- MSA-3.1 (Brazil)

The large number of producers of man-portable surface-to-air missiles (SAMs) indicates that the needed technology and know-how is within the reach of less-advanced producers and that the demand is substantial. Man-portable SAMs are perfect examples of how technology that permits autonomous functioning can be an "equalizer" between advanced and developing states. Unlike man-portable SAMs, more advanced, radar-directed air defense systems are more complex to operate and are vulnerable to countermeasures. They require the effective integration of target detection, data processing, and command and control technologies and organizations. For this reason, examples of these more complex systems, such as the PATRIOT, are not included here. Their absence from the list should not be construed as indifference to the implications of their diffusion. The priority given to man-portable systems reflects, instead, the judgment that they currently pose a more urgent threat not only to regional military stability, but also to civilian aircraft.

Antiship missiles. Advanced antiship missiles are among the most worrisome systems available for purchase today. Unlike the weapons already discussed, many antiship missiles already operate autonomously and from considerable range. For that reason, the widespread sales of these weapons by the United States, France, and the former Soviet Union seem particularly detrimental to U.S. interests. This point is underscored by examples such as the EXOCET missile, which was used effectively against the United States during escort operations in the Persian Gulf and against British vessels in the Falkland Islands, and also by the risks generated by Iran's Styx/Silkworm missiles. In retrospect, it would have been preferable if none of these weapons had been sold to conflict-prone regions. Obviously, it is impossible to recover the missiles already in circulation. However, it is not too late to control the sale of the latest versions of this weapon, which generally have increased range, speed, and survivability.

The following systems are potential candidates for controls:

- HARPOON II (United States)

- EXOCET upgrades (France)

- ANF (France)

- KORMORAN 2 (Germany)

- SEA EAGLE (Britain, France)

- OTOMAT upgrades (France, Italy)

- RBS-15 upgrades (Sweden)

- KH-35 (Russia)

- KH-411SS-N-22 (Russia)

- ASM-MSS (Russia)

- HSIUNG FENG 2 (Taiwan)

- C-101, C301 (PRC)

Like man-portable surface-to-air missiles, antiship missiles are in development by a large number of states, again presumably because of the relative accessibility of the technology and high recipient demand.

Low Substitutability

Many weapons that have a high degree of military effectiveness have few or no substitutes. The autonomous functioning of these weapons makes them particularly useful for less-advanced militaries, and the gap between these weapons and non-autonomous substitutes can be large indeed.

The speed with which states could independently develop versions of the proscribed weapons, either for sale or for indigenous use, is germane to the substitutability criterion. Here too the autonomous functioning of these weapons is key, and considerable technical prowess is needed to develop autonomous capability. For example, the development of medium-range, active radar, air-to-air missiles and autonomous, long-range antiarmor missiles poses substantial technical problems to all but a handful of producers. In contrast, the barriers to production are lower for antiship cruise missiles and shoulder-fired surface-to-air missiles, both of which are produced by several second-tier suppliers.

Although the potential for substitutability is low for advanced missile systems, adequate substitutes are readily available for the most advanced major weapons platforms, such as tactical aircraft, armored fighting vehicles, and ships. Many states produce these weapons, others possess large stocks for sale, and still others market sophisticated kits to upgrade older versions. For example, a state unable to purchase the latest tactical aircraft from a first-tier supplier has many alternatives for substitution. While the latest aircraft are no doubt superior to the last generation's, the gap between them is usually less pronounced than that between autonomous and non-autonomous weapons, especially with the available upgrades and the reality that many pilots are unable to exploit the full potential of even older aircraft.

Low Opportunity Cost

Controlling the transfer of highly advanced munitions and missiles rather than weapons platforms would impose fewer economic (and thus political) challenges. Opportunity costs for arms transfers to the Middle East have been calculated as an example. As Figure 8 shows, between 1984 and 1991, sales to the Middle East of such major end items as armored fighting vehicles, advanced combat aircraft, and surface combat ships amounted to between 85 and 90 percent of the total revenues generated by the sales of the first-tier suppliers to that region. Thus, even if all missiles, missile systems, and submarines had been completely proscribed for transfer to the Middle East during this period, the suppliers' loss of income would have totaled only about $16 billion, or $2 billion per year—a fraction of the overall global market. Narrowing the focus to the Persian Gulf subregion, lost revenue would be even lower, approximately $1 billion annually.

Absent any agreed-upon controls, however, there are several reasons why sales of weapons on the high-leverage list are likely to increase. First, the existing stocks of missiles and other advanced weapons in the Persian Gulf states are becoming obsolete, and states may seek to replace them with more modern weapons. Second, the Persian Gulf War provided a powerful demonstration of the effectiveness of advanced weapons, a lesson not lost on Persian Gulf and other regional powers. Third, several advanced weapons may become available from the major suppliers in the next five years that may be very attractive to regional powers, including antiship and antitank missiles and air-to-ground stand-off weapons.

As Figure 9 shows, total sales of advanced weapons (missiles and submarines) to Persian Gulf states between 1994 and 2001 are estimated to be between $12.1 and

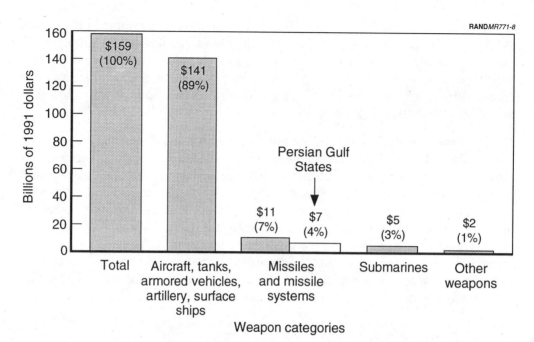

Figure 8—Categories of Arms Sales to the Middle East, 1984–1991

$18.6[6] billion—or between $1.7 and $2.7 billion per year, spread among the suppliers. The $10 billion figure for missiles reflects the cost of inventory replacement of existing stocks of missiles and advanced conventional weapons that are becoming obsolete. Because of cost growth, straightforward one-for-one replacement could force Persian Gulf users to pay significantly more than they paid to acquire their now-obsolete systems.[7] The high-estimate figure of $15 billion was computed by assuming that the Persian Gulf buyers might seek to increase their stocks of advanced conventional weapons by 50 percent (in dollar value) above current levels, if they have the resources.[8] The submarine estimates were calculated in a comparable way, based on announced and anticipated submarine purchases. Obviously, these cost figures are somewhat uncertain. Russian pricing policies are difficult to predict and the resources allocated to weapons acquisition by the Persian Gulf states will depend on a myriad of circumstances, foreign and domestic.

---

[6]This range represents low and high estimates of the sum of missiles and submarine sales for the years 1994–2001.

[7]The inventory replacement cost was calculated using data from the Defense Marketing Service surveys: Forecast International/DMS: Missiles, 22 Commerce Road, Newton, CT, 1993.

[8]An increase of this magnitude was based on the projected production schedules contained in the Defense Marketing Service (see above footnote).

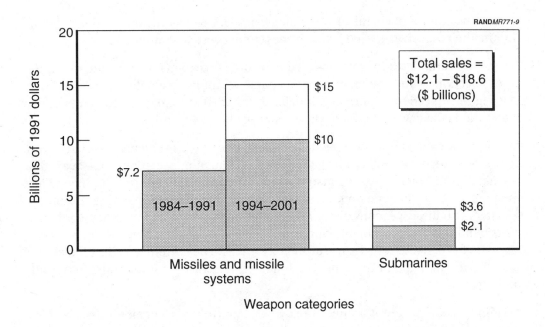

Figure 9—Anticipated Sales of Advanced Weapons and Submarines to the Persian Gulf States, 1994–2001

CONTROLLING WEAPONS OF ILL REPUTE

Thus far, the discussion of controls has focused on a small group of particularly effective conventional weapons and their associated technologies. Another approach that could help stimulate early consultations on conventional arms control would be to emphasize restraint in the sale of weapons that raise international concerns because of the risks they pose to noncombatants or because of their perceived repugnance, even when used on the battlefield.

Examples of such weapons, known by some as "weapons of ill repute," are dumdum, exploding, or poisoned bullets, and chemical and biological weapons. The 1980 Convention on Conventional Weapons (also known as the Inhumane Weapons Convention) prohibits weapons designed to produce fragments not detectable by x-rays, as well as some incendiary weapons and land mines. The United States signed the Convention in 1982, but it was not ratified until 1995. One current example of weapons regarded as particularly repugnant are antipersonnel land mines. Congress has imposed a moratorium on the U.S. export of these weapons, and a number of other states have promised to do the same.

The advantage of focusing on weapons of ill repute is that the international opprobrium associated with their use may make efforts to discuss their control easier, as has proven the case with nuclear, biological, and chemical weapons. Nuclear weapons have not been banned *per se*, but the abhorrence associated with their potential use has provided significant impetus for the controls that have been placed on them. The control of chemical and biological weapons has advanced, albeit slowly, despite their perceived military effectiveness under certain conditions.

Additional candidates for international controls as weapons of ill repute might include incendiary and fragmentation weapons, weapons easily diverted to terrorist use (e.g., advanced man-portable air defense systems) and weapons currently under international review (e.g., blinding lasers and antipersonnel mines).[9]

Incendiary weapons provide a good example of one of the problems associated with controlling weapons of ill repute—the ease with which they can be made available. Napalm, for instance, is easy to manufacture. The success of controls for incendiary weapons will thus depend on the degree to which the international opprobrium associated with these weapons discourages states from using them. In other words, the costs of international condemnation would have to be seen as higher than any military benefits derived from the use of such weapons. The current U.S. position on the sale of napalm, napalm thickeners, dispensers, and fuses is to discourage but not prohibit sales.

Blinding lasers represent another area where control may become possible. The most likely obstacle to control may be their military value. Blinding lasers are intended as countermeasures against precision weapons that home on targets designated by lasers or other electro-optical means. The objective is to disable the individual directing the designator, so that the precision weapon cannot find its target. Clearly, direction is an important function on the modern battlefield, though lasers are not the only means for performing it. The Department of Defense has registered its opposition to a draft protocol by Sweden and the Red Cross calling for control of blinding weapons.

At this time, antipersonnel mines seem the likeliest prospect for international controls because of the great toll they have taken (and continue to take) on civilian populations even long after military operations have ceased. Indeed, antipersonnel mines are now the subject of serious international scrutiny. In spite of this scrutiny, however, a number of problems stand between rhetoric and truly effective controls. First, millions of these weapons already exist in the world's inventories. Second, they are sold by many suppliers, both government and private.   Third, they are easy to manufacture indigenously in less-developed states. Fourth, and perhaps most important, their military value in certain situations is perceived to be high by many states.

These points suggest that the likeliest path to strong controls on antipersonnel mines (and perhaps other weapons viewed with opprobrium yet valued for their military effectiveness) may involve incremental steps resembling the process of nuclear arms control. This process of "successive approximations" is valuable even though it might be regarded with frustration by those eager for faster progress. Even steps that

---

[9]See "Inhumane Weapons Conference Breaks Down," *Arms Sales Monitor,* 5 December 1995; Senator Patrick Leahy, "The CCW Review Conference: An Opportunity for U.S. Leadership," *Arms Control Today,* September 1995; *Arms Trade News,* October 1995; and "Inhumane Weapons Convention," *Arms Control Reporter,* 15 November 1995.

cannot be expected to result immediately in substantial changes in international behavior can help to build a diplomatic infrastructure, mechanisms and habits of consultation, a common vocabulary, and most important, common expectations about military behavior. The significance of such controls would initially be far more political than military. Achieving agreement even on broad principles or codes of conduct for the sales of such weapons, however, could serve as a foundation for more ambitious undertakings.

SUMMARY

1. There are two approaches to controlling the transfer of conventional weapons. Transparency is attractive because many states will agree to disclose at least some information about transfers. However, transparency alone may not be effective at reducing or shaping weapons transfers.

2. Quantitative or qualitative controls are attractive because they reduce or shape transfers. However, states have been reluctant to agree to such limits because of their opportunity costs.

3. An approach to controls that may escape this difficulty is to control the sales only of weapons that satisfy three criteria: high military effectiveness, low substitutability, and low opportunity cost in terms of forgone sales. Long-range, autonomous, precision weapons such as cruise missiles and AMRAAM meet these criteria.

4. A second and complementary approach is to focus on weapons of ill repute. The repugnance with which these weapons tend to be regarded by the international community can be useful in stimulating efforts at their control.

Chapter Four

REGIMES FOR CONTROLLING TECHNOLOGY TRANSFERS

Thus far, the discussion has been on controlling the proliferation of advanced conventional weapons. The importance of also controlling the technologies critical to the manufacture and functioning of these weapons has long been recognized, although political, economic, and technical developments over the last thirty years have made such controls increasingly difficult to formulate and enforce.

During the cold war, the United States and its allies pursued a policy intended to deny the Soviet Union and its allies access to Western technology that could be used to upgrade Soviet military capabilities. The strategic objective of this policy was to compel the Soviets either to use less sophisticated weapons or to commit large amounts of precious resources to develop the withheld technologies indigenously.

Several cold war conditions permitted these technology transfer controls to function relatively effectively. First, the United States exercised a virtual monopoly on the most important advanced technologies, especially those with military applications. Second, the U.S. economy was strong enough to bear the opportunity costs of withholding these technologies from sale. Third, the West Europeans and Japanese were content to focus their energies on rebuilding their civilian economies. Fourth, in this period, the level of technology and pace of innovation in the commercial sector lagged several years behind that of the defense sector. The greater sophistication of the defense sector meant that defense and commercial technologies were essentially different and separate. Commercial technology transfers thus were usually not in tension with strict controls on the transfer of technologies with military applications. Fifth, the technically advanced nations shared a political consensus as to the identity and magnitude of the common threat.

All these conditions have been changed by the collapse of the Soviet Union. Indeed, even before that event, pressure to loosen the cold war technology transfer controls had begun to build. During the 1970s, the sophistication of commercial electronics, computing, materials, and propulsion technologies grew explosively, thereby reducing or even reversing the earlier disparity between the defense and commercial sectors. By the end of the 1970s, the most advanced microelectronics, communications, and information processing were entering commercial production and finding commercial applications well before their incorporation into defense products. At the same time, the costs of developing military technology increased sharply, and defense budgets fell. These developments produced strong incentives to use commercial technologies for military applications. As a result, the number and availability of "dual-use technologies"—technologies with both commercial and military applications—grew substantially during this decade.

In the post–cold war period, these and other trends have continued to weaken the incentives for technology transfer controls. First, the structure of the global economy increasingly encourages diffusion of advanced technologies. Multinational corporations have located technology research, development, and production facilities in many nations, and technologies, know-how, and data are routinely communicated among them across national borders. For this reason, it can be difficult to assign a national identity to a technology. Ironically, the decentralization of technology itself has been made possible by advanced communications and information processing technologies.

Second, the virtual monopoly enjoyed by the United States on advanced technology vanished long ago in most areas. Not only do all the first-tier industrial nations develop advanced technologies with military applications, but so do second-tier producers such as China, Israel, India, Korea, and Brazil. At the same time, no shared sense of threat exists that might encourage these nations with disparate interests to join in a common policy on technology transfers.

Third, the defense industrial bases of all the first-tier weapons producers have been weakened by reductions in defense spending, which has amplified the degree to which defense innovation has to depend upon technology originating in the commercial sector. Moreover, not only is U.S. defense production increasingly dependent on U.S. commercial technologies, it is increasingly dependent on foreign commercial technologies, as well.

Finally, the United States and other advanced industrialized nations have had to rely on exports for sustained economic vitality, especially to "upwardly mobile" developing nations. These exports tend to be technologically advanced end items, basic technologies, and technical know-how. Indeed, importing nations are more and more likely to make technology transfers a condition of doing business.

In sum, political, economic, and technical developments have erased many of the lines separating commercial and military technologies, increased the incentives of advanced nations to transfer technologies and of less-advanced nations to develop their own, and decreased a common sense of threat helpful for a consensus on controls. Yet control of technology transfers remains at least as important as control of arms transfers. Perhaps controlling the former is even of greater importance, since, unlike arms transfers, the transfer of technologies provides nations the means of indigenous production.

As with the control of arms transfers, the control of technology transfers must be based on an acceptable balance of effectiveness and opportunity costs. Indeed, the problem of the opportunity costs of technology controls is particularly vexing. Not only can important technology developers and producers be injured, but so can the economic growth of less-developed nations. Slower global economic growth would not be in the U.S. national interest, and might produce a more dangerous world than the one in which controls had not been attempted.

CONTROLLING SINGLE-USE TECHNOLOGIES

Familiar examples of single-use technologies would be shaped-charge warheads or dense, long-rod penetrators of antiarmor weapons; the small traveling-wave tubes used in the Advanced Medium Range Air-to-Air Missile; or radar-absorbing coatings suitable for use near the hot sections of jet engines. Such technologies have no significant commercial applications, so their use is tied to the related weaponry.

Fortunately for any regime, many large subsystems of a weapon system are specific to weaponry. This allows such subsystems to be controlled as single-use items. For example, sensors for military applications, whether for surveillance, targeting, or guiding a weapon directly, are very different from sensors for air traffic control, remote sensing, or pollution monitoring. The sensors related to weapons need some measure of resistance to countermeasures, and often have tight constraints on their packaging.

Controls of single-use technologies can be based on straightforward export prohibitions. Since they have no commercial use, there would be little need for detailed end-use controls. Only monitoring for re-export control might be needed, depending on how re-exports of controlled weapons were restricted.

Additionally, a regime might want to control the design skills that are directly related to the technologies or weapons limited by the regime. Design skills are the epitome of knowledge-based technologies. Simple purchase of a complex system, such as a weapon or related subsystem, does not immediately confer the ability to design or produce the object. In practice, these skills are usually transferred through joint programs that provide extensive interaction with the supplier. Obviously, the most intense concern about transferring such technologies comes in joint developments, and was a concern in the national debate that surrounded the F-2 (formerly FS-X) joint development between the United States and Japan. In practice, some level of these skills is transferred in all but the most elementary joint programs. Coproduction, for example, typically involves tooling design, fabrication process instructions, subassembly integration processes, and even final assembly integration and test know-how. All of these areas are integral to overall systems integration. Further, coproduction always requires some level of troubleshooting and the consequent correction of defects or problems, called "rework." Learning to successfully fix problems in rework often requires an understanding of the design or the construction process. Similarly, maintenance for a system can require diagnostic skills related to the original design and production skills.

For these reasons, limitations on joint development, production, and maintenance of any restricted weapons or subsystems may be a necessary component of a technology transfer control regime. Joint programs with other nations already capable of making a restricted system would offer little risk, and would presumably be freely allowed. Thus, for example, cooperative efforts to build advanced combat aircraft among the European nations would not be affected. More risk would be found in joint programs with nations allowed to purchase such systems, but not already capable of making them. At the limit, such programs could be denied entirely.

CONTROLLING DUAL-USE TECHNOLOGIES

The second control regime to be considered here has a very different focus. The intent is to control the application to weaponry of the entire, broad range of dual-use technologies. At its core, this second regime rests on the understanding that advanced conventional weaponry is coming to rely more and more on dual-use technologies. As the National Security Science and Technology Strategy says:

> Fundamentally, the spread of scientific and technical know-how is the crux of the supply side of the proliferation problem. Technological advances on which modern society depends also make it easier to design, manufacture, and use advanced weapons.[1]

At the same time, there is a need for global traffic in these technologies for commercial or civil applications. As many authors have noted, these technologies are important to economic growth, to environmental sustainability, and to the health and education of people around the world (Reinicke, 1994). Not surprisingly, the volume of trade in these technologies is large, and growing.[2] The challenge is in balancing these two factors.

Dual-use technologies—those that have both military and civilian applications—are not so straightforwardly controlled as single-use technologies, since certainty about their application is harder to achieve. Because many of the most important civilian technologies have military applications, it is critical that controls on the transfer of dual-use technologies not be so broad as to stifle the economic growth of developing nations. This would be a perverse effect since global prosperity is widely viewed as in the U.S. interest. Also, an overly constraining technology transfer regime almost certainly would substantially increase the likelihood of attempts to circumvent the controls. Therefore, the task is to devise a control regime for dual-use technologies that permits both increased trade and effective limitations.

One way of solving this apparent dilemma is to focus on controlling the *application* of dual-use technologies, rather than proscribing the technologies themselves. That is, a control regime should be based on the principle that technology transfers with commercial applications should be permitted if the seller states can be confident that dual-use technologies will be used only for nonproscribed applications. This demands a general principle of full disclosure of application in return for freer trade.

---

[1]See *National Security Science and Technology Strategy*, Executive Office of the President, Office of Science and Technology Policy, Washington, DC, 1995. Also available over the World Wide Web, URL: http://www.whitehouse.gov/White_House/EOP/OSTP/nssts/html/nssts.html

[2]National Academy of Sciences, Committee on Science, Engineering, and Public Policy, *Finding Common Ground: U.S. Export Controls in a Changed Global Environment*, National Academy Press, Washington, DC, 1991, p. 40.

The question is how to acquire that confidence. The answer must lie in the sellers' capabilities to obtain guarantees of intended application from the buyers and to assess the buyers' performance in acting in accordance with that guarantee. There are two broad approaches to assessing a buyer's performance: nonintrusive and intrusive. Among the nonintrusive methods are memoranda of understanding and agreements, national technical means of verification, limitations designed into the transferred technologies, and transparency measures. An example of the application of transparency to this problem is the Automated Technology Transfer Register suggested by Wolfgang Reinicke.[3] Among the intrusive methods are inspections and tagging.

Tagging refers to the attachment of an active system to an item to be transferred (not just a passive tag for identification during an inspection). The active system would both monitor the object tagged and communicate that information back to the United States. In practice, this means the candidate objects for tagging must be physically large systems. They can either be intended for use as is, as a machine-tool cell, or as a major component of some larger system, such as a turbine engine in a helicopter.

The tag should be capable of communicating information about the item's physical location, although some sensors may provide other kinds of information as well. The information could be communicated to a satellite or over a data link. Early versions of such devices are already in service for monitoring nuclear materials and technologies.[4]

These "smart" tags exploit the potential of several new technologies. They combine encryption, the Global Positioning System, and the emerging global wireless communication systems, such as Iridium or Orbcomm, which allows them to easily report back on the status and location of the tagged object. In principle, such tags could report the time history of position as well, to verify limitations on the deployment of some systems. For example, the United States has sold F-15s to Saudi Arabia with restrictions on their zones of deployment. Such tags could also report on the activities of a "smart" system to which they are attached. For example, a combat aircraft could report whether it had been flown at low altitude, or practiced attack profiles related to the delivery of nuclear weapons. A machine-tool cell could report whether it had made parts resembling air vehicles. Such tags could have many applications in a cooperative regime.

The position location information tagging can assess whether a dual-use technology is being integrated with other technologies, a process that would signal a military application. Modern weapon systems require the complex integration of many different technologies. Indeed, much of the qualitative superiority enjoyed by the

---

[3]See Wolfgang H., Reinicke, "Cooperative Security and the Political Economy of Nonproliferation," in *Global Engagement, Cooperation and Security in the 21st Century*, Janne E. Nolan (ed.), The Brookings Institution, Washington, DC, 1994, pp. 187ff.; and Wolfgang H. Reinicke, "From Denial to Disclosure: The Political Economy of Export Controls and Technology Transfer," in Francine R. Frankel (ed.), *Bridging the Nonproliferation Divide, The United States and India*, University Press of America, PA, 1995, pp. 269–285.

[4]Briefing to the Board by Tom Sellers, Sandia National Laboratory.

United States is the product of its prowess at systems integration. Few, if any, dual-use technologies have military potential if they are not integrated with other dual-use technologies. Usually, though not always, this process requires the physical collocation of technologies. For example, a sensor for an autonomous, precise, air-delivered weapon is usually located in close proximity to flight control technology, propulsion technology, and navigation technology. If the items embodying these technologies were tagged, it should be possible to detect when they are physically collocated, *prima facie* evidence of a violation of the buyer's guarantee. Finally, weapons system integration requires complex testing at facilities allowing full mission profiles, live warhead tests, and other unique events. The presence of a tagged component at such specialized ranges would again indicate a potential violation. At any of these points, the seller could demand an inspection or invoke sanctions.

As with all controls, all sellers of a particular technology must participate in the tagging. Buyers would gravitate to untagged items, if they were available. Tagging will probably also require buyers' cooperation. If the tag is sending data to a satellite, the buyer must permit communication when the proper satellite is overhead. Similarly, if the tag is using a data link, the buyer must connect the tag to the data link or permit someone else to. Attempts to conceal or deviate from a pattern of cooperation would be considered evidence of a potential failure of buyer performance.

There are technical obstacles and risks that must be overcome before tagging can be a reliable method for monitoring a control regime. Also, any oversight scheme should use several different methods to ensure that failure of one does not reduce deterrence of violations. Tagging may become an important oversight method for controlling technology transfers. But just as with national technical means of verification for nuclear arms control, tagging should never become the sole means of oversight.

The availability of the means to assess the buyer's adherence to guarantees forms the basis for a set of proposed decision rules for determining when a dual-use technology should be denied, sold, or sold conditionally. A dual-use technology should be denied when its military risk is *not* low and the means to reliably assess performance are *not* available. A dual-use technology should be sold when comparable substitutes are available *or* when the military risk posed by the transfer is low. A dual-use technology should be sold conditioned on a guarantee of civilian use only when reliable means exist to assess the buyer's performance of that guarantee.

A final set of technologies relevant to restrictions on advanced conventional weapons are dual-use design skills or know-how. These are the dual-use analog of the single-use design skills discussed earlier. The difference here is that the skills could be transferred in commercial agreements that do not explicitly mention restricted weapons systems. For example, maintenance agreements on civil aircraft engines can give others insights into the design of fighter engines. Once transferred, such skills are not subject to meaningful end-use controls.

In practice, the primary limitation on the transfer of these production or process technologies appears to be the interests of U.S. firms in keeping a competitive advantage over other firms. Naturally, this results in firms giving up what they see as the "least important" technologies. "Least important" is judged from the point of view of the private firm involved, but it is hard for any government to second-guess the judgment. The knowledge of the criticality of the design and production technologies is and will likely remain deepest and most protected at the firm. Beyond denying such agreements entirely, as for single-use subsystems as discussed above, the role of the government is limited. The government should work in partnership with industry to reinforce the coincidence of proprietary and military interests in restraint, and perhaps to generate new ideas.

A technically sound system of overseeing the application of dual-use technologies is useless unless violations are punished in some way. Unfortunately, some of the history of enforcing limitations on technology transfers is troubling. Under CoCom, the intention was to deny to the Communist nations many of these dual-use technologies. In one example, the United States and France agreed to sell two advanced jet engines, CFM-56s, to the People's Republic of China in 1982. Because of concerns that the Chinese might attempt to reverse engineer these engines, there were severe restrictions placed on their rights to open, disassemble, or maintain the engines. All maintenance was to be performed outside of China, for example. Additionally, the engines were to be used to re-engine a British Trident within one year, or be returned. The engines were never used to re-engine the aircraft, nor were they subject to inspection, nor were they returned. The ostensible controls on the engines had little effect on their use.

Given the difficulty in reverse engineering a modern engine, there was probably less at risk in 1982 than the CoCom regime feared. Today, the United States has several agreements with the People's Republic of China to maintain and service civilian-use jet engines.

The key point is that memoranda of agreements, or even tags, however "smart," cannot enforce a regime. Any regime must enjoy a large measure of international support for its norms, such as the Nuclear Non-Proliferation Treaty does, for its controls to be of real effect. This will be especially true of any new regime restricting conventional weapons, since existing norms restricting conventional weapons are not strong.

A PROPOSED REGIME FOR CONTROLLING TECHNOLOGIES ASSOCIATED WITH ADVANCED CONVENTIONAL WEAPONS

The character of the proposed regime for controlling the transfer of dangerous technologies flows directly from the regime proposed in Chapter Two for the control of certain advanced conventional weapons. The technologies that are logical candidates for control are those enabling the worrisome capabilities. Specifically, the weapons identified in Chapter Two as most dangerous are those with the following capabilities:

- Autonomous operation
- Precision

- Stealth

- Long range

An analytical process can disaggregate the controlled weapons into constituent subsystems and the subsystems into constituent technologies. This type of analysis is routine within the Department of Defense and the military services for technology assessments. Many were part of the general CoCom process.[5] Others were independent of CoCom, and were designed to guide U.S. defense research and development. The Army's *STAR 21 (Strategic Technologies for the Army of the Twenty-First Century)*[6] is a good example of the analytical methods used to link end-item capabilities and critical technologies. The other CoCom nations performed similar analyses to provide their national lists of controlled technologies to CoCom for assembly of the CoCom lists.[7] Evidently, the information needed to generate candidate technologies for controls has been produced regularly for other purposes, so little additional analysis would be needed to support a technology transfer control regime.

The involvement of industry will be important to the success of this classification of technologies, as it was for the CoCom process and for the internal Department of Defense analyses as well. Only with the active cooperation of industry, here and abroad, can an agreement on limitations be forged. How such industrial involvement can be managed is not clear, although both CoCom and the Chemical Weapons Convention may be useful models for emulation.

CONTROLLING STRATEGIC TECHNOLOGY

A regime like the one described above emphasizes controlling technologies in weapons under development or already in service. Not covered are technologies so early in development as to have no immediate, specific application. Yet such technologies may be used to make weapons in the longer term, and therefore might be important to control in the present. Such weapons might spur a regional arms race or destabilize a region to surprise attack. Such cases break into two categories: predictable and unpredictable.

In predictable cases a concept of operations can be defined by the technology used in a putative weapon. Examples include various antisatellite weapons, from kinetic energy impactors to ground-based lasers; ground-based antitactical ballistic missile systems; and laser dazzlers or blinders. The weapons can be well enough defined that the military in most nations can identify the key systems, subsystems, and technologies involved. This kind of analysis requires expertise that the relevant government agencies already possess, from understanding of laser propagation to damage mechanisms in sensors. If an international regime could limit any such systems, the

---

[5]Panel on the Future Design and Implementation of U.S. National Security Export Controls, pp. 336–348.

[6]See National Research Council, Board on Army Science and Technology, Commission on Engineering and Technical Systems, *STAR 21: Strategic Technologies for the Army of the Twenty-First Century,* National Academy Press, Washington, DC, 1992.

[7]Panel on the Future Design and Implementation, pp. 65, 343–344.

pattern above could be adapted to the chosen system. Because such weapons are not yet deployed, it may be easier to forge agreement on the technologies to be limited.

In contrast, unpredictable cases consist of technologies with many potential applications but with no particular application yet in mind. The so-called "strategic" technologies are an example. "Strategic" in this sense means those technologies that are having a sweeping effect on the world, such as the telecommunications and computing technologies, or the emerging biotechnologies. Such technologies could be used in many ways to create a weapon system. One popular example would be the use of computer viruses to disrupt the computer codes handling international finance. The difficulty is that there are entirely too many such potential weapons applications.

These technologies are typically being driven by the commercial sector and are fast-changing. The United States and other nations are looking to these fields for economic growth and a competitive advantage. Any limitation on them is likely to be resisted. Moreover, defining such limitations is difficult even with agreement on the need. None of these weapons applications is a straightforward extrapolation of existing weapons. Partly as a consequence, there is no well-defined concept of operations. The military agencies of most nations lack the technical understanding to analyze such ill-defined systems to the same level as they can a cruise missile, or even an antisatellite weapon. It is unclear how, under these conditions, anyone could identify any particular set of technologies to limit.

In practice, this implies that regimes to control the transfer of "unpredictable" technologies will be difficult to design and implement, at least until the military applications of the technologies become more clear.

Chapter Five

IMPLEMENTATION OF INTERNATIONAL INSTRUMENTS AND POLICY PROPOSALS

Effective control over exports of key, high-leverage weapons and components requires multinational participation. Only in those (increasingly rare) instances in which the United States is a monopolistic supplier can controls be exercised unilaterally. In other instances, unilateral restraint would be ineffectual because it would simply lead other suppliers to increase the quantity or prices of their competing weapons exports.

Consequently, in the course of the Board's deliberations, several proposals involving participation of other key countries were elicited from representatives of the Office of the Under Secretary of Defense for Acquisition, the Under Secretary of State for Arms Control and International Security Affairs, the Defense Technology and Security Administration, the Brookings Institution, management consultants from the private sector, and RAND.

Four of these proposals are briefly described and evaluated in this chapter. They have been selected to illustrate the very different perspectives of their advocates. The proposals differ widely in goals, scope, and complexity, and they would entail very different degrees of intervention in the arms market at various levels of that market. Of the four, only one—the Wassenaar Arrangement—is currently being implemented. The four are not mutually exclusive, and several possible combinations or sequences among them will be mentioned later. The proposals summarized below include: (1) an "Inner Circle" and "Concentric Circles" of participating countries; (2) The Wassenaar Arrangement/"New Forum" (a post-CoCom regime); (3) a computer-based registry system; and (4) a Market Stabilizing Mechanism.

Five principal criteria will be applied to evaluate the alternatives: the proposals' consistency with U.S. foreign and defense policies; their effectiveness in inhibiting proliferation of key, high-leverage weapons; incentive effects on suppliers and buyers; their general economic effects on U.S. defense industry (e.g., in forgone revenues); and their administrative practicability. For illustrative purposes, the four proposals will be evaluated by applying the five criteria to them.

CIRCLES OF CONTROL: INNER CIRCLE AND CONCENTRIC CIRCLES

As described by Defense Department representatives, this proposal would establish a system of free trade in (nearly) all weapons systems and related technologies among the United States and its closest allies, who would constitute, in the early stages, an "Inner Circle." Varying degrees of restraint would be imposed on trade in weapons and supporting technologies involving countries outside the Inner Circle. The proposal began as an effort to promote inter-allied cooperation and interoperability; an additional benefit of the idea is the control of the undesirable diffusion of technology. The Inner Circle concept would provide key U.S. allies with access to U.S. technology as an incentive for cooperation in the control of weapons and technology proliferation. Other countries would make up the "Concentric Circles," and the degree of restraint imposed on them would accord with several criteria, including the closeness of their alliance to the United States and the reliability of their own controls over re-exports. The issue of stringency and reliability of re-export controls applies also to the Inner Circle countries. The NATO countries differ significantly in the stringency and enforcement of their controls over arms exports and re-exports, as well as in the country destinations to which these export controls are applied. A further complication arises from the occasional disparity between the apparent stringency of formal controls and the frequency of their evasion. For example, German legislation imposes penalties of up to 15 years in prison for violations of its arms export controls, yet German exports of prohibited products have recurred with embarrassing frequency. Japan, which has also been troubled (as well as troubling others) by exports of supposedly controlled technologies, has recently sought an emollient for these troubles by announcing that its Ministry of International Trade and Industry would adopt a new system of controls "similar to control systems in place in the U.S. and Europe."

Evaluation

In regard to foreign and defense policy objectives, the Inner Circle/Concentric Circles (IC/CC) idea would promote cohesion of its members, who would experience free trade in the export of advanced weapons and technologies. Thus, the U.S. defense industry might acquire greater access to the European market, for example, while European defense producers might have more extensive access to the U.S. defense market. Nevertheless, access to national defense markets in both Europe and the United States is likely to fall considerably short of what, in the context of international trade, is referred to as "national treatment."

The IC/CC proposal would have distinctly negative effects and adverse foreign and defense policy implications *vis-à-vis* non-NATO allies outside the IC, as well as non-allied weapon suppliers such as Russia and China. Excluding them from the preferential treatment accorded IC members would arouse invidious reactions not helpful from a U.S. foreign policy standpoint.

With respect to control of arms proliferation, IC/CC might bring about enhanced control over member sources of arms exports that could otherwise destabilize regional arms balances. However, this benefit might be offset by the uncertainty connected with the effectiveness of controls over re-exports from some countries in the Inner Circle.

With respect to incentive effects, the IC/CC proposal might be expected to have a similarly "two-handed" result. On one hand, countries within the IC that would benefit from the freer trade in weapons and expanded market access might tighten their controls on exports to non-IC members to avoid jeopardizing this benefit. On the other hand, exclusion from the favored free-trade circle might provoke the excluded countries to intensify their efforts to develop and produce, and of excluded buyers to acquire, the weapons systems from which they had been excluded.

The economic effects on the U.S. defense industry would represent a negligible offset to reduced spending on research, development, and acquisition by the Department of Defense. Even this limited benefit would ensue only if, in fact, expanded access to the European market were to result. The European defense industry would presumably also acquire expanded market opportunities in the U.S. part of the IC, thereby imposing additional pressure on the U.S. defense industrial base.

With respect to administrative practicability, IC/CC would entail complex and time-consuming difficulties: for example, what weapons systems would be freely traded? Who would be in? Who would be out? How could CC members get admitted to the IC? Over what time period? These difficulties might be made more manageable by implementing the IC/CC policy in a gradual manner, beginning with, say, two or three specific weapons categories, like air- and sea-delivered missiles, and including others in light of the experience thereby gained. Similarly, membership in the IC might gradually be extended to CC members in a manner and at a pace analogous to that of moving from "Partnership-for-Peace" status to NATO membership.

THE WASSENAAR ARRANGEMENT (FORMERLY THE "NEW FORUM")

Senior representatives of the Department of State initially discussed this proposal with the Board in July 1995. The proposal has continued to evolve since that time through delicate and protracted negotiations.

The Wassenaar Arrangement on Export Controls for Conventional Arms and Dual-Use Technologies (WAECCADUT) was established in December 1995 after two years of negotiations to replace the expired CoCom regime. The 28-member Arrangement (previously referred to informally as the "New Forum") is, in fact, very different from the regime it nominally replaced; it is global, rather than focusing on targeting proscribed states, and aims to implement restraint in dealing with current problems and transparency to address future ones. Like CoCom, the Arrangement controls dual-use items, but it also deals with conventional arms sales and has a "small group" of the largest suppliers.

Regarding dual-use, members do not have a veto (as they did in CoCom), but this is seen as less important because the regime is not set up to deny transfers. Instead, the focus is on transparency, which in the case of dual-use is manifest through notification of denials. Although transparency does not preclude competitive undercutting, the expectation is that it will operate this way in practice (as did the MTCR). Specific notification deadlines are not established (just "early and timely"), but they will probably be thirty to sixty days, depending on the bureaucratic processes in member states.

A basic list of controlled technologies includes both a "sensitive" list and a "very sensitive" list. The lists are based on previous CoCom restrictions, which are continually updated and revised. Members will report every six months on transfers (denials are covered as discussed above), providing specific details in accord with the sensitivity of the item—more detail about "very sensitive" items and more general information about nonsensitive ones.

The Arrangement is not a treaty but a nonbinding agreement between members to coordinate domestic export policies. Consultations may cover such areas as general patterns of acquisition, regional tensions, and so forth. Members have agreed to adopt policies denying armaments and dual-use items to military end users in pariah states, but not necessarily to nonmilitary purchasers.[1]

For conventional arms, the focus is also on transparency. Members agree voluntarily to share information on transfers of weapons in the seven categories covered by the UN Arms Register. There will be "a little more detail" than is called for in the Register, such as descriptions of the model and type of all weapons (except for missile transfers). The United States hopes that plenary discussions will be broad, to cover areas such as destabilizing buildups, transfers of sensitive technologies and the introduction of high-tech weaponry into new regions, and regional balances and security.

Greater stock might be placed in the "small group," which is the P-5 (minus China) plus Germany and Italy—all of the major weapons exporters. This group is the legacy of the P-5 talks that followed the Persian Gulf War, and it will deal exclusively with conventional arms sales. The new aspect is that there is now a standing mechanism to address conventional arms transfers, and the potential for "multilateral restraint" is greater in this group than anywhere else. Information exchanges will be more detailed within the small group than within the entire membership, although they haven't yet agreed on notification procedures.

Evaluation

The Wassenaar Arrangement is evolving as a part of U.S. foreign and defense policy that seeks to restrict exports of destabilizing weapons through a broad consensual process among potential suppliers. While laudable in both aims and means, its status and modest progress to date raise questions about whether and how it will be able to reach binding control over proliferation of advanced systems.

Under the evolving Wassenaar Arrangement, arms proliferation (both weapons and most dual-use technologies) to the specified pariah states would be effectively denied. It is anticipated by the Arrangement's advocates that exports of some dual-use

---

[1]The United States argued unsuccessfully for extension of denials to all end users in "countries of concern;" the challenge of persuading other members of this policy remains one of the most formidable in future negotiations.

technology to these states might occur in special cases if the end user were nonmilitary and could be reliably monitored (e.g., machine tools for civil uses). Apart from the pariah states, control of arms proliferation in the rest of the world would depend on when and how the small group establishes binding criteria for allowing or proscribing weapons exports. On the other hand, if these defining criteria are delayed, or if they fail to be agreed upon, controlling proliferation would be less a reality and more a velleity.

Enforcement of the Wassenaar Arrangement's protocols largely depends on reaching consensus among members of the large group and the small group. It is arguable whether this consensus will be robust enough to offset the incentives for breakout among current arms sellers, or among potential new sellers who might be attracted to the newly restricted market.

The Wassenaar Arrangement would not have discernible economic effects on the U.S. defense industry, nor would it in any appreciable way affect current and expected reductions in U.S. defense procurement.

Finally, the administrative practicability of implementing the Arrangement's procedures and agreements inevitably presents a formidable challenge. With 28 member-countries in the full group, and six members in the small group, delays, misunderstandings, and periodic miscarriages will be hard to avoid.

COMPUTER-BASED REGISTRY SYSTEM

This proposal was presented to the Board by a Brookings Institution staff member, Wolfgang Reinicke.

The essence of the proposal is a "disclosure-based regulation" system that would reduce or eliminate the information asymmetry between government regulators and industry suppliers of advanced and advancing technology. This asymmetry represents a fundamental and arguably growing impediment to any effective control regime. The reason is that the pace of technological change enables amply motivated industry suppliers and prospective arms buyers to find ways of decomposing proscribed systems or finding substitutes for them that negate or at least dilute the regime's effectiveness.

The means for remedying this asymmetry is to require all companies involved in prospective exports of weapons or dual-use technology to register and "tag" each item throughout its product cycle—from its design to tooling to production to export—with essential information concerning its specifications, destination, recipient, and end use. All such tagged items would be checked against a "regularly updated proscribed product and destination list," and checked as well for possible piece fabrication by the same supplier or a group of suppliers.

The crux of the proposed computerized registry and tagging is to interrupt any proposed transfer that failed to meet the prescribed requirements for permissible transfers, and to permanently interdict such transfers until compliance is achieved.

Evaluation

The computer registry and warning system could be a useful adjunct and instrument for assisting in monitoring an agreed upon antiproliferation regime. As such, it would be entirely consistent with the development of U.S. foreign and defense policy in this domain.

However, the system begs the question of what the defining criteria should be for a regime designed to effectively control or proscribe transfers of destabilizing weapons and dual-use technologies. In other words, the proposed registry would be a means of assisting implementation of a control regime, rather than constituting a regime.

Once the defining criteria were clearly established, the proposed registry could be material and useful. In addressing the *incentives* of suppliers to ignore or avoid the mandatory registry, the proposal would simply *require* compliance as a matter of law. Prosecution for noncompliance would be immediately triggered by any system or component that was not entered into the computerized registry. Nevertheless, there is something of a chicken-and-egg puzzle about this process because nonregistered items would have to be identified from *outside* the system since, by assumption, their originators would have concealed them from the registry *ab initio*. And this *ex ante* concealment might itself reflect the fundamental previously noted information asymmetry that the registry was intended to redress.

Details concerning the costs and administrative practicability associated with the registry proposal were not presented in sufficient detail to permit an informed judgment about them.

MARKET STABILIZING MECHANISM

This policy instrument, briefly described to the Board by RAND staff members, builds upon research on the design and implementation of a method to stabilize the arms market so as to maintain or enhance regional military balances. The proposed Market Stabilizing Mechanism (MSM) would operate under the aegis of an MSM Council. The latter would consist of both a suppliers' group of the five or six principal supplying countries, constituting a sort of "CoCom-successor" regime, and a buyers' group consisting of the principal arms-purchasing countries. The MSM Council would focus on prohibiting or severely limiting exports of only a key subset of arms exports: namely, those weapons systems that would destabilize inter-regional or intra-regional arms balances, as defined and identified in MR-369-USDP, 1994. (See Chapter Six below.)

Effective operation of the MSM would depend critically on a process of objective analysis to determine the selected items to be controlled through the concurrence and compliance of both sellers and buyers. Compliance instruments wielded by the

MSM Council would include both "sticks" and "carrots," both penalties (for non-compliance), and compensation for forgone sales in exceptional circumstances.[2]

Evaluation

The proposed MSM would be consistent with and would advance U.S. foreign and defense policy objectives by strengthening regional military stability and controlling advanced weapons proliferation.

With respect to the control of arms proliferation, cartelizing the seller-side of the market and organizing the buying-side of the market, would work to prohibit or severely limit potentially destabilizing, high-leverage weapons sales. The targeted systems would be clearly visible and the means of restricting them transparent.

From the standpoint of incentive effects, the "free-rider" temptation for noncompliance by suppliers would be limited by the inclusiveness of the MSM and the retaliatory clout of other council members. Organizing the buyer-side of the market would avoid the "prisoner's dilemma" incentive for individual buyers to breach the stabilizing regime.

The economic effects of the proposed MSM would be reflected in only a modest dollar volume of forgone high-leverage weapons sales. Indeed, these economic effects might be cushioned if members of the buyers' cartel could be enlisted to contribute to a compensation fund to be used selectively to protect buyers from the prisoner's dilemma risk mentioned earlier.

From the standpoint of administrative practicability, the MSM option would present a major challenge. Although it would build on the previous experience of both CoCom and the MTCR, as well as the ongoing experience and process of the Wassenaar Arrangement, the two-sided (sellers and buyers) character of the MSM would entail formidable difficulties and would represent a major innovation requiring an unusual combination of ingenuity, leadership, and priority attention by the United States.

CONCLUDING OBSERVATIONS AND ASSESSMENT OF PROPOSALS

Some aspects of U.S. foreign and defense policy may warrant encouragement, rather than restriction, of arms transfers. A case in point is the Bosnian peace accords and the extent to which their durability may depend on equipping and training Bosnian Federation government forces through arms transfers from the United States and its allies.

On the other hand, if one contemplates the sustained economic dynamism of the Asia-Pacific region, with annual growth rates averaging 6 to 7 percent or more, seri-

---

[2]See *Controlling Conventional Arms Transfers: A New Approach with Application to the Persian Gulf,* MR-369-USDP, 1994, by Kenneth Watman, Marcy Agmon, and Charles Wolf, Jr. Such "exceptional circumstances" might, for example, apply to forgone sales of submarines to Iran by Russia, despite its critical foreign exchange needs.

ous concern is warranted about the possible proliferation of advanced and potentially destabilizing weapons in response to the region's increased capacity to pay handsomely for weapons imports. The onset of a worrisome arms race in the region is entirely plausible, and there already are some indications of this prospect. To prevent or at least mitigate it, international cooperation and multilateral participation by arms suppliers—and, one would hope, buyers as well—is necessary and timely.

Among the four proposals reviewed above, MSM is the most ambitious and exacting in seeking to control transfers of high-leverage, potentially destabilizing weapons. It is the only proposal that would provide a specific set of enforcement instruments—penalties and rewards—to induce compliance. It is also the only one that would explicitly include and organize potential arms buyers, as well as sellers, in exercising these instruments of control.

These advantages of MSM are associated with a notable disadvantage. Among the four proposals, MSM places the heaviest burden on U.S. initiative and leadership. For this challenge to be successfully met, the issue of arms proliferation would have to be accorded a top priority in America's foreign policy agenda—one it may be unlikely to receive.

The Wassenaar Arrangement, in contrast, is more limited in its scope and aspirations. Instead of enforcement and compliance, its watchwords are consultation and transparency. Its focus, initially, is on pariah states, rather than on the global stability of regional arms balances, which is the focus of the MSM proposal. Its scope and process are more modest than those of MSM, and consequently its implementation is likely to be more practicable.

The "Inner Circle" proposal is principally concerned with enhancing cohesion among U.S. alliance members. Control of arms proliferation is a secondary objective of the proposal, as well as a means of contributing to the primary one.

The computer-based registry is a plausible instrument that can be adapted to the contours of any of the other three proposals. It is an implementation device whose promise lies in improving the scope, content, and timeliness of the arms transfers data base.

As noted earlier, the types of international control regimes that have been described differ widely from one another, yet their wide differences do not imply mutual incompatibility. Indeed, combinations and sequences that could link the Wassenaar Arrangement, the computer-based registry, and the Market Stabilizing Mechanism are quite plausible. However, the feasibility of actually moving in such a direction would require a degree of priority attention in the policy community that is not easy to envisage in the near future.

THE ECONOMIC IMPACT OF CONVENTIONAL ARMS EXPORTS

The economic and defense industrial base effects of arms sales are often raised in discussions of arms export policy. This chapter will review the issues in three parts:

- What is the evidence on the quantitative economic and industrial impact of arms exports?

- What are the pros and cons of including economic considerations in decisions concerning arms exports?

- What are the pros and cons of other policy options concerning arms exports, such as export financing and R&D recoupment charges?

The findings of this chapter can be summarized as follows:

1. The post–cold war reduction in arms production (over 50 percent) has had major negative economic impacts on workers and localities associated with defense industries. The arms export market is small relative to this reduction, however, and is not a potential source for major alleviation of these negative impacts. Other policies must do that.

2. Although arms exports cannot alleviate the economic and industrial problems associated with the downsizing of the arms industry after the cold war, these exports can have strong positive local and regional economic impacts, as well as substantial industrial benefits for the U.S. Defense Department. Therefore, political pressures to approve arms exports to achieve these benefits are strong. However, there are also strong arguments for not permitting economic or industrial base considerations to override national security considerations in arms export decisions, especially when the arms export in question is governed by an international agreement.

3. Changes in public policy on arms exports are currently being made or considered. One recent change will permit the federal government to provide export finance guarantees for defense sales; the other would repeal the recoupment charge for R&D expenditure currently assessed on FMS sales of major defense equipment. There are two arguments for these changes. The first is that, *once it is determined that an arms sale is in the U.S. national security and foreign policy interest,* these sales should have no additional burden put on them. Since other exports are currently eligible for export finance and free of any government-imposed R&D re-

coupment charge, this argument implies that arms exports should be accorded the same treatment. The second argument is that other arms-exporting nations actively financially support their industries' sales, and, therefore, current U.S. policy does not result in a neutral playing ground for U.S. exporters. There are several arguments against such changes, however. The first is that extending export financing to arms sales would provide politically unwise encouragement of such trade at a time when weapons proliferation poses urgent security risks. (This presumably implies that the foreign policy and national security review of the sales is inadequate.) The second is that foreign arms purchasers should pay a fair share of U.S. government financed R&D expenses. Other arguments in opposition are that U.S. exporters have been successful in the market and do not need an improved playing field, and that current U.S. budget stringency makes it unwise to risk revenue losses or to incur unnecessary new outlays.

ECONOMIC AND DEFENSE INDUSTRIAL BASE EFFECTS OF ARMS EXPORTS

Arms exports have two basic economic and industrial base effects. First, they provide employment for U.S. workers and business for U.S. firms. Second, they can lower costs to the U.S. Department of Defense (DoD) for domestic procurement of arms, in two ways. First, by sharing some overhead costs with production for the DoD, or by achieving economies of scale through more efficient use of direct production resources such as labor, arms exports can lower the unit cost of specific weapons systems to the DoD. Second, arms exports may keep production lines open when U.S. government purchases have ceased for a period of time, decreasing what the DoD would have to pay to restart a cold line or to maintain a warm one. These effects will be considered in turn.

Employment Effects

The end of the cold war has resulted in a dramatic decrease in military procurement by the United States. Defense Department data show a 55 percent reduction in military procurement spending in real terms between 1987 and 1995, from $104 billion per year to $47 billion in dollars of 1995 purchasing power.[1] Associated with this almost $60 billion reduction in DoD procurement has been a large decrease in employment in industry supplying DoD—about 1.2 million jobs. In addition to this direct job loss, about 600,000 jobs indirectly generated by military procurement were lost.[2]

These job losses are not particularly large in relation to the entire U.S. economy, whose current employment is about 125 million and in which about 330,000 persons file initial claims for unemployment insurance every week. (That is every week there are about 330,000 *newly* unemployed persons who file claims for unemployment in-

---

[1] Department of Defense, Office of the Comptroller, 1995.

[2] See below for the derivation of these employment figures.

surance. Total unemployment in the United States is currently around seven and a half million persons.[3])

However, job losses associated with decreases in U.S. military procurement can be devastating for local communities, particularly those heavily dependent on defense industry. For example, the continuing weakness of Southern California's economy compared to that of the rest of the country is generally attributed to the decline of military procurement in the area, especially aerospace. These major local effects are both a serious economic problem and a serious political problem. Economically, when layoffs are highly concentrated in a few local areas, it is much more difficult for displaced workers to find new jobs.[4] Thus, unemployment and its hardships tend to be prolonged in these areas. Politically, naturally strong pressures are put on regional and federal governments to find solutions to the problem, and voters tend to hold elected officials responsible for poor economic conditions.

The question naturally follows: Do arms exports have the potential to significantly alleviate these economic problems?[5] Current U.S. arms exports generate about $10 billion per year in defense industry revenues, and generate about 200,000 direct and an additional 100,000 indirect jobs. The total world arms export market is about twice that. Therefore, arms exports could not offset the economic decline in the U.S. military products industry and employment associated with the end of the cold war, which, as indicated earlier, has resulted in the loss of 1.8 million jobs. It would thus be futile to try to use arms exports to make up for the decrease in DoD procurement. The arms export market is simply too small. To alleviate the negative economic consequences of declines in military procurement, U.S. policy cannot rely on promotion of arms exports, but will have to turn elsewhere—to job retraining and relocation, and to conversion of former military plants and workers to civilian pursuits.[6]

Table 1 shows various recent estimates of the effect of military production on employment. The studies range widely, from single system sales to overall defense spending. Based on these results, 20,000 jobs per billion dollars per year is a representative figure for direct employment—the number of persons actually working to produce the military item in question. If a worker producing a military product becomes unemployed, that worker's spending on consumer goods will decline as a re-

---

[3]All data on the overall economy are from U.S. Department of Commerce, *Survey of Current Business*, various issues, 1995.

[4]In the U.S. economy as a whole, most laid-off workers find new employment within a few months. While the unemployment rate in the United States is currently around 6 percent, only about 20 percent of those have been unemployed for six months or more, and another 15 percent between 15 and 26 weeks. However, in the Southern California region, which has been hit hard by military procurement cutbacks, unemployment is still in the 7 to 8 percent range.

[5]In this chapter, "arms exports" means "deliveries," which is the concept most closely related to employment in any given year.

[6]What are in fact appropriate policies in this area is a controversial subject in itself. The Administration established the Technology Reinvestment Program (TRP) in the Defense Department as a way to help companies and workers that relied on defense spending to convert to civilian products. The Republicans in Congress are attempting to end the program, which they interpret as wasteful pork barrel subsidies. For Fiscal Year 1996, TRP was funded at $195 million, about half the Administration proposal, and also about half the FY 1995 funding.

Table 1

Estimates of Jobs Associated with Overseas Arms Sales

Date	Author	Citation	Program	Direct Jobs/ $1 billion	Total Jobs/ $1 billion	Source of jobs/ $
4/95	National Commission for Economic Conversion and Disarmament	Gregory Bischak, *Arms Trade and Jobs*	Unspecified	Unspecified	20,000–32,000	Independent estimate
2/95	Congressional Budget Office (CBO)	"Recover the Full Cost of Military Exports," *Reducing the Deficit*, p. 86	Unspecified	20,000–25,000	Unspecified	"Advocates of arms sales"
3/30/95	Aerospace Industries Association, American League for Exports and Security Assistance, and Electronics Industries Association	"Defense Export Guarantee Facility," Defense Trade Seminar	Unspecified (loan guarantees)	20,000	35,000	Independent estimate
12/12/94	*Time*	Mark Thompson, "Going Up, Up In Arms," *Time,* Vol. 144, No. 24, pp. 46–57	1993 total U.S. overseas sales	21,334	Unspecified	"Defense experts"
10/3/94	*Nation*	Eyal Press, "Arms Sales and False Economics," *Nation*, Vol. 259, No. 10, pp. 340–344	Unspecified	Unspecified	24,295	Employment Research Associates report

Table 1—continued

Date	Author	Citation	Program	Direct Jobs/ $1 billion	Total Jobs/ $1 billion	Source of jobs/ $
7/6/94	Business Executive for National Security	"Arms Transfers and Economic Competitiveness," Draft, p. 7	Unspecified	20,652	Unspecified	Science Applications International Corporation study for American League for Exports and Security Assistance
5/94	Michael Renner	"Monitoring Arms Trade," *World Watch*, Vol. 7, No. 3, pp. 21–26	1. Guided missile OR	1. 10,242	Unspecified	"Studies in the United States"
			2. military aircraft production	2. 15,829		
4/94	*International Business*	Daniel Moskowitz, "How Far to Loosen Export Controls," *International Business*, Vol. 7, No. 4, p. 78	Eight dual-use export licensing decisions	19,436	Unspecified	Council on Competitiveness report
2/94	Joel Johnson/ AIA	"Conventional Arms Transfer Policy: An Industry Perspective," *Military Technology*, Vol. 18, No. 2, p. 30	Unspecified	14,292–16,196	Unspecified	Independent estimate
2/94	Peace Action Education Fund	"Briefing Paper: Hidden Costs of Arms Trade," p. 3	Unspecified	23,777–27,800	Unspecified	CBO
11/15/93	Joel Johnson/ AIA	*Defense News*, "Arms Exports Damage U.S. Economy"	Unspecified	14,272	23,786	Independent estimate

Table 1—continued

Date	Author	Citation	Program	Direct Jobs/ $1 billion	Total Jobs/ $1 billion	Source of jobs/ $
11/9/93	Project on Demilitari-zation and Democracy	Caleb Rossiter, Testimony before the Committee on Foreign Affairs, Subcommittees on International Operations and International Security, pp. 74–75	Unspecified	15,890	31,780	Bischak, National Commission on Economic Conversion and Disarmament
9/13/93	*Defense Week*	Andrew Weinschenk, "House, Deutch Assure Conversion Funds Won't Underwrite Weapons Sales"	Unspecified (loan guarantees)	Unspecified	27,751	Industry letter to SecDef Aspin
9/92	CBO	"Limiting Conventional Arms Exports to the Middle East," p. xv	Unspecified	23,277	Unspecified	Independent estimate
2/8/91	Science Applications International Corporation (for American League of Exports and Security Assistance)	Dr. David Louscher and Dr. William Bajusz, *The Domestic Impact of the Prospective Sale of Selected Military Equipment to Saudi Arabia*, p. 18	1. Prospective sale of defense package to Saudi Arabia (incl. tanks, missiles, fighters, etc.) 2. National average	1. 19,032 2. 19,895	1. 27,198 2. 34,729	1. Independent estimate 2. U.S. Dept. of Commerce INFORUM model
7/87	Defense Budget Project	Gordon Adams and David Gold, *Defense Spending and Employment*, p. 34	Unspecified	1. 16,782 2. 23,494	1. 2. 3. 18,387–40,903	1. CBO 2. SecDef Weinberger testimony 3. 1982 DoD Memorandum

sult of the reduction in his or her income. This will lead to additional job loss in the industries making the consumer goods, at least temporarily. These additional job losses are called the "indirect employment" effects of the defense spending. Again, based on Table 1, 10,000 jobs per billion dollars of defense spending per year, or one half the direct employment effect, is a representative figure.[7]

Economies of Scale

Many U.S. defense contractors simultaneously produce the same military item for both foreign purchase and U.S. domestic use. This leads to economies of scale, lowering costs to U.S. producers and, thus, prices to the U.S government. Cases in which military systems for both the U.S. and foreign armed forces were produced on the same line simultaneously include the F-15, F-16, and F/A-18 fighter aircraft, the M-1 tank, the AH-64 helicopter, and the C-130 transport aircraft. By absorbing some overhead, these exports further lower the cost of products sold to DoD, in accordance with Federal Acquisition Regulations (FAR) treatment of allowable cost. For example, ongoing F-16 exports by Lockheed Martin lower the current development cost of its F-22 stealth fighter in this way.

Preserving Production Lines

There are some occasions when a gap in the U.S. purchase of a weapons system would lead to a production line gap—a period of time during which the line would be idle.[8] If a line is idle, the U.S. government must either pay to keep the line "warm" during the purchase gap, or pay to restart the "cold" line. Export production and sales during a gap period can themselves keep a line alive and save the U.S. government this cost.

In the case of the M-1 and the AH-64, there were periods (of about three years duration) during which production for export was the only work on the line, after which U.S. production resumed. A recent Defense Department document estimates that the cost of some U.S. M-1 modification work was cut by one third as a result of foreign sales.[9] Whether this resulted from economies of scale from gap filling was not specified. The document also provides data about the M-1 and AH-64 production lines, showing that production for foreign military sales was the only work on the M-1 line between 1993 and 1995, bridging the end of new U.S. production and the

---

[7]The data in Table 1 were adjusted for inflation, using the GDP deflator found in the *Economic Report of the President,* January 1995. In some cases, the referenced report did not explicitly provide a figure for jobs per billion dollars, and it was derived from the data in the document. Thus, the figures in Table 1 represent, in part, interpretation of the information in the referenced reports and should not be directly attributed to them.

The overall assessments above concerning the impact of the post–cold war reduction in defense spending, and the potential of arms exports to offset it, are of course insensitive to the particular job per dollar figure chosen for the calculations, at least within the range of estimates shown in Table 1.

[8]A production line gap does not necessarily result from a Pentagon new system purchase gap because modification or overhaul work might keep the line active.

[9]*World-Wide Conventional Arms Trade (1994–2000): A Forecast and Analysis,* December 1994.

beginning of U.S. conversion work. In this case, export and domestic production shared the line when domestic production resumed. The report also indicates that foreign military sales of the AH-64 bridged the gap between the end of its sale to the U.S. Army in 1993 and the beginning of Apache Longbow procurement in 1996.

Today, there are some lines that are (or are about to be) sustained only by foreign sales, but from which there are no firm plans to purchase more output for the United States. Examples are the F-15 and F-16 fighter aircraft. Having these lines open benefits the DoD. It keeps production teams together for future projects. It also makes the option of increasing F-15 and F-16 fleets sometime in the future less expensive; the U.S. Air Force has said it would like to buy more of these fighters if its budget were increased. (The 1998 Program Objective Memorandum [POM] as of March 1996 included a submission for more F-16 purchases, for example, but whether this will survive the entire budget process is quite uncertain.)

Recap: Impact of Arms Exports on U.S. Economy

This section will summarize the ways that U.S. arms exports affect U.S. economic well-being and provide some rough quantitative estimates of the effects. The quantitative estimates are based on research results available in the existing literature and discussions with experts in the course of this study. These assessments are necessarily rough;[10] nevertheless, the exercise is illuminating in that it puts the various effects in a common framework, which would be appropriate for further, more refined analysis. In the authors' opinion, these rough order-of-magnitude estimates are not misleading, but are close to what a rigorous study would produce.

The benefits of arms exports to the U.S. economy can be addressed in a counterfactual framework: How much would it cost the United States if all arms exports were stopped? Arms exports contribute to the economy and the industrial base in three ways:

- They provide employment for workers and income for firms.

- If they are produced simultaneously with goods purchased by the U.S. Defense Department, they can lead to increased economies of scale and lower costs to the DoD.

- If they are produced during a period of hiatus of U.S. demand for the same or similar goods, they can keep production lines open and skilled workers together and employed, thus saving the DoD the cost of either maintaining or restarting the line.

If all U.S. arms exports were stopped, what would be the cost to offset the resulting economic and defense industrial base losses? A clear upper bound is $7 billion per year, the amount that foreigners actually pay the United States for arms exports. The figure cited is less than the $10 billion of total exports because about $3 billion is fi-

---

[10]In general, there has not been a great deal of serious scientific study of these issues in a quantitative fashion.

nanced through direct U.S. government grants.[11]   With this $7 billion, the United States could simply buy the goods now destined for export and store them, or give them to U.S. forces. While not a sensible policy, this conceptual artifact establishes the maximum negative industrial impact of having no arms exports. Seven billion dollars is not a small sum by any means, but it illustrates that the extreme claims by some that defense exports are vital for U.S. security and competitiveness are overblown. *At the absolute maximum,* they save us $7 billion out of a current DoD procurement budget of about $50 billion, within a defense budget of about $260 billion.

The economic benefits of arms exports in each of the three areas identified above are discussed next.

Employment for workers and income for firms. If a decrease in arms exports leads to layoffs among workers in affected firms, there will be a negative impact on the economy that has two primary components: The first is the lost compensation of the workers until they find new employment, and the second is any decrease in their lifetime earnings at their new job compared to the old job. Evidence suggests that defense workers who are laid off take longer to find new jobs than the economywide average, and that they are employed at lower wages at their new jobs—defense workers tend to be older, more skilled, more highly paid, and more regionally concentrated in recession areas than the average unemployed worker. Similar considerations apply to the profits of affected firms. Profits will fall in the immediate aftermath of a decrease in arms exports, and will not be restored until the firm's capital is redeployed in other pursuits. At the extreme, the firm's capital associated with the lost arms exports will be rendered obsolete, and the profit loss to the economy will continue until the time when the capital would have worn out anyway. The situation is analogous to that of a worker who never finds new employment, so that the associated wages are lost to the economy until the time the worker would have retired.

Taking into account the layoff time, the wage loss, the profit loss, and the time to redeploy new capital, one might expect a total loss to the economy of about $3 billion per year for about five years if all arms exports ceased. There are no precise estimates of this magnitude in the literature, because comprehensive data specific to unemployed defense workers or unutilized defense-related capital equipment are not available.   RAND research suggests that an average six-month period of unemployment ($5 billion total loss) and an average 20 percent income decrease for five years ($2 billion per year) is not unreasonable, leading to a $3 billion average annual loss.[12] This assumes that profit losses and multiplier effects are proportional to wage losses, and together average one half their value over the five years.

However, there are two important offsetting factors, each related to industrial "offsets" that are often associated with arms export packages. The first are direct off-

---

[11]The $3 billion figure is from General Accounting Office, *Military Exports: A Comparison of Government Support in the United States and Three Major Competitors,* May 1995.

[12]See Robert F. Schoeni, Michael Dardia, Kevin F. McCarthy, and Georges Vernez, *Life After Cutbacks: Tracking California's Aerospace Workers,* RAND, MR-688-OSD, 1996.

sets. As discussed in Chapter One, under these offset agreements, the arms exporter (such as the United States) agrees to procure part of the exported product in the buying country. This arrangement can range from procurement of components that are then imported to the United States and put into the product, to coproduction or even codevelopment of the product with the importer. Part of the $1.4 billion in annual U.S. arms imports is associated with direct offsets. Thus, the level of overall employment associated with arms exports is overstated to the extent that arms exports are simply re-exports of imported components. In addition, coproduction and codevelopment agreements transfer technology to importing countries, eventually giving them production capabilities, with which they can affect import substitution and compete with the United States in future export markets. These future effects are hard to estimate, but are certainly real. By helping to build up future competitors, potential future U.S. exports are lowered, offsetting somewhat the benefit associated with current exports.

Indirect offsets associated with arms sales are the procurement of items in the importing country arranged by the exporting firm as an explicit *quid pro quo* for the export sale. To the extent these are imports to the United States that would not otherwise have occurred, they lead to U.S. job loss just as much as exports lead to job gain. A 100 percent offset agreement, however, does not necessarily mean no net economic benefits to the United States: (1) Some of the offset imports may have been imported to the United States anyway. (2) Some of the offset imports may include components originally made in the United States. (3) Some imports give multiple credit to offset targets (i.e., a $1 import of certain items counts as more than $1 in offset calculations). (4) If targets are not met, escape clauses in contracts can be invoked, which while compensating the importing government to some extent do not equate to the original offset goal.

Given these considerations, there is no clear analytical estimate of true offset costs. (One could be made, but given the large number of individual contracts and their diversity, this would be a formidable task.) Since there is clearly *some* effect of offsets, assigning them a value of zero would be misleading. A notional value of $1 billion will be assigned for them, with the clear understanding that the uncertainty around this figure is high. This adjustment reduces the economic cost of losing all arms exports from $3 to $2 billion. Readers with a different assessment of offset costs can adjust the totals accordingly.

Economies of scale and keeping production lines open. There are no good estimates of defense exports' overall benefit to the DoD in terms of economies of scale and production line gap filling, but a number in the $2 billion range seems reasonable.

In summary, rough estimates yield a $4 billion annual benefit to the U.S. economy and defense industrial base from arms exports, $2 billion from employment effects, and $2 billion from cost reductions to the U.S. DoD.[13] If one believes that the $3 billion of grants for arms purchases to foreign countries would disappear in the absence of arms sales, these funds should be considered a further offset to U.S. economic benefits from arms sales, leaving a net benefit of about $1 billion. However, because these funds serve overall U.S. geopolitical and security policy, one may choose not to include them, implying a net benefit of about $4 billion.

This figure may be compared to a U.S. annual GDP of about $7000 billion, annual defense spending of $260 billion, and annual defense procurement of about $50 billion.

These relative orders of magnitude would hold for other major industrial exporting countries, such as France, Germany, and the United Kingdom. Their total arms exports are about $7 billion per year, and their combined GDP is about $5000 billion. The UK, with arms exports of about $4 billion per year and a GDP of about $1000 billion, has the highest share of arms exports in total economic activity, but that share is still relatively small.

SHOULD ECONOMIC CONSIDERATIONS BE A FACTOR IN ARMS EXPORT DECISIONS?

The White House Conventional Arms Transfer Policy Fact Sheet announcing the Presidential Decision Directive indicated that the impact of any given proposed arms sale on the U.S. defense industrial base would be one factor considered in deciding whether to allow the sale. As noted earlier in this report, the severe negative economic effects of the post–cold war military procurement decline produced great political pressures to approve arms exports that are perceived to alleviate local economic stresses in the region producing the exports. The pros and cons of such a policy will be discussed below.

Any given proposed arms export package has both foreign policy and national security implications, as well as an effect on economic and defense industrial bases. One can conceptually distinguish between these, and assess any proposed sale both in terms of its effect on foreign policy and national security and on the economy. If the foreign policy and national security impact is positive, the sale should be approved, given that the economic impact of exports will always be positive.[14] Economic factors come into consideration only when the foreign policy and national security impact of an arms transfer is potentially negative—if the foreign policy and national security impact is clearly positive, there is rarely a reason to disapprove the sale and economic considerations are irrelevant.

---

[13]We reemphasize that there are no statistically precise estimates of these magnitudes in the literature, and that these "rough estimates" could also be called "educated guesses." The order-of-magnitude is correct, however, based on the clear maximum annual loss of $7 billion noted above.

[14]Cases could be constructed that would have a negative economic impact, perhaps by straining use of a natural resource and causing shortages elsewhere in the economy, but these would be highly unusual and will not be considered further here. Of course, if one did assess this to be the case, a different kind of analysis would apply.

Thus, the process for deciding whether any given proposed arms sale is appropriate involves two steps: If the net foreign policy and national security impact is positive, approve the sale. If it is negative, one *may* want to consider economic factors.

In such circumstances, should benefits to the defense industrial base be allowed to outweigh negative national security impacts in arms transfer decisions? The argument is straightforward. Some cases that are assessed to have negative foreign policy and national security impacts may be "close calls," where negative impacts are small and uncertain. If a proposed sale has high benefits for the economy and the defense industry, one can reasonably argue that these high benefits outweigh the small and uncertain costs. This is a reasonable interpretation of the Administration's statement that it will include defense industrial considerations in the decisionmaking process.

There are two arguments against this position. The first is that any negative foreign policy and national security effects should be avoided, regardless of the cost to the defense industrial base. These effects, after all, involve political freedoms and potential military conflicts, with risks of loss of life to the U.S. armed forces and others. Whether one chooses this position or the one above—namely, that sufficiently high economic benefits can rationally offset small, uncertain national security costs, depends on underlying basic societal and political values.

There is a second, more pragmatic argument against letting economic benefits outweigh negative national security consequences in arms sale decisions. It is associated with international agreements among potential arms exporters to restrict sales in the interest of mutual and international security.

Allowing high economic or defense industrial base benefits to override even small negative security impacts would make it much more difficult to achieve international supplier coordination in arms export restraint. Once it is accepted that the positive economic/industrial implications of a proposed arms sale could legitimately offset negative regional stability implications, it is primarily a matter of judgment which of the two factors is more important. Thus, any arms transfer, no matter how negative in terms of regional security, could *in principle* be approved if its industrial benefits were perceived as high enough.

Therefore, getting international agreement on arms export restraint under this rule would face two obstacles: First, all parties must agree that the transfer is destabilizing (as is the case today). *Then,* all parties must agree that their own particular industrial benefits do not outweigh the national security costs. Since there is no natural way to make these costs and benefits commensurable, this weighing is ultimately subjective, making it difficult to demonstrate "objective" violations of any agreement.

The essence of an arms restraint agreement is that suppliers agree to forgo a certain class of transactions, regardless of individual benefit, for greater joint security. Once this class is agreed on, members of the regime cannot be allowed to opt out when they judge the individual benefit of any specific case to be especially high. Including industrial benefit considerations as a valid determinant of the acceptability of arms exports effectively increases the legitimate "opt-out" cases, seriously weakening any agreement. This is the fundamental case for not allowing economic considerations to enter arms transfer decisions when they are governed by an international agreement.

As argued elsewhere in this report, international agreements would be very helpful in restraining potentially damaging arms sales around the world. Indeed, an international agreement may well be the instrument that lets a national government resist the strong regionalized political pressures to approve an arms sale that would help alleviate local economic woes. These pressures will exist, even when it is determined by the central government that an arms sale is not in the national interest. Given the realities of national political processes, sometimes a central government may have to give in to such pressures despite its belief that the decision is wrong. International agreements can overcome the strong tendencies of local pressure politics to make decisions that are bad for the country. Including economic considerations in arms sale decisions undermines the effectiveness of international agreements, another argument against that position.

What about a policy of allowing economic considerations to play a role in decisions that are not governed by international agreements, but keeping such considerations out of those that are? There is no inherent contradiction in such a policy, but potential problems do arise. Consider a case in which a country has a monopoly on a military product not governed by an international agreement. If that country clearly allows economic considerations to influence its decisions, it will lose a certain amount of credibility in arguing in international fora that economic considerations should be ignored for other goods. Perceptions of a double standard of this type could undermine efforts to achieve or maintain international agreements in other areas. In a case where a country does not have a monopoly, complaints of unfairness by economic interests in other countries would be weakened, but still might be influential. It is therefore possible that allowing economic considerations to influence arms export decisions in areas not governed by international agreements would strengthen the hand of those who would allow them in, and thus vitiate international agreements. This is another argument against including economic considerations in arms transfer decisions.

TWO CURRENT PUBLIC POLICY ISSUES: A DEFENSE EXPORT FINANCING PROGRAM AND THE R&D RECOUPMENT CHARGE

Changes in U.S. policy toward arms exports are currently under way or in consideration. The first is the recent establishment of a defense export financing facility, and the second is possible repeal of the R&D recoupment charge now levied on exports made under the Foreign Military Sales program. This section will describe these policy change proposals, and the pros and cons of each. Both policy changes would make U.S. policy more favorable toward military exports than it currently is. Because current U.S. policy treats arms exports unfavorably relative to civilian exports, one can also characterize the two policy changes as establishing neutrality between arms and civilian exports. In this view, the changes make similar government support available for both military and civilian export sales, in theory reducing price distortions introduced by the current differential policy and "leveling the playing field" for arms exporters. In addition, the proposals are justified as responding to the policies of other arms exporting countries—U.S. competitors—which offer forms of export financing and impose no R&D recoupment charge. Again, they "level the playing field" between U.S. and foreign arms exporters.

Unlike other U.S. exports, arms exports are not eligible for Export-Import Bank financing (with some minor exceptions).[15] Pursuant to authority provided in the recently enacted FY 1996 Defense Appropriations and Authorization Acts,[16] the U.S. government will now guarantee repayment of loans made for export sales or long-term leases of U.S.-made defense equipment, services, or design and construction services to authorized countries. The total contingent liabilities of the United States for guarantees issued under the program may not exceed $15 billion in Fiscal Year 96. The Administration had opposed a Defense Export Financing Program (DEFP) citing the President's February 1995 Conventional Arms Transfer Policy, which stated that a DEFP was not needed at that time, although it might be pursued should market conditions subsequently warrant.

The legislation limits the countries for which such guarantees can be used, and many countries with low credit ratings are not eligible. Functionally, the program provides that the U.S. government will assess an "exposure fee," which is meant to meet the expected U.S. government liability associated with the program.[17] An additional administrative fee is assessed to cover Department of Defense costs directly attributable to the program. The legislation contemplates the possibility of substituting appropriations for all or part of the exposure fee; however, to date no funds have been appropriated. Despite the intent that the DEFP be self-financing, and the absence of current appropriations, pressures from advocates for greater subsidies to enact future appropriations are very likely.

Borrowers may in practice prefer the DEFP to other financing alternatives because, with the government guarantee, the lending banks may be willing to provide lower interest rates than they would in nonguaranteed transactions. Some may call this reduced interest rate a "subsidy," but it is not a cost borne by the government (as long as accumulated collected exposure fees are sufficient to cover U.S. government losses, as they are intended to be).[18]

---

[15]PL 79-173 provides exemptions from the Export-Import Bank financing prohibition. Examples are (a) some cases where the purposes of the exports are for counternarcotics, (b) for nonlethal defense articles or services, and (c) where the primary end use of the defense articles or services will be for civilian purposes.

[16]The Department of Defense Appropriations Act, 1996 (PL 104-61) was enacted (without the President's signature) on 1 December 1995, and after one presidential veto, the National Defense Authorization Act for Fiscal Year 1996 (PL 104-106) was signed into law on 10 February 1996.

[17]The Federal Credit Reform Act of 1990 defines the estimated long-term cost to the U.S. government of a loan guarantee as the difference between the net present values of government payments for defaults, delinquencies, and interest subsidies and estimated payments to the government by the borrower.

[18]There is another economic effect of the DEFP, which is equally applicable to other government loan guarantees such as the Export-Import Bank and the Overseas Private Investment Corporation: *To the extent that total borrowing for arms exports is increased,* other potential borrowers in the economy lose credit, and interest rates for all are increased. This is a simple result of the increase in demand for loan-

U.S. industry's efforts in recent years to secure a loan guarantee facility like the DEFP sought and assumed a "no cost" or "concessionary" program, at least in some instances. That is, the administrative costs of such a program, and perhaps even the fee aspects of the risk pooling necessary to cover any subsequent payment default by any single purchaser, were assumed by at least some industry advocates as being "free" to industry. As the description above of the actual DEFP implementing legislation notes, however, no appropriation has yet been made for this purpose.

In the absence of appropriations, it is reasonable to assume that the government will use a risk evaluation process similar to that used by commercial lenders and insurers, with resulting determinations for costs and fees that are essentially the same as those charged by the private lending and insurance market.[19] DEFP may well benefit U.S. exporters and potential recipient countries in either or both of two circumstances cited by advocates of such a financing mechanism. In some cases, the purchasing nation and its customer government may have otherwise been unable to secure financing of the sale from any lender, regardless of interest rate or other lending cost, because of perceived high default risk as seen by the financial community. (Of course, this case is an exception to the U.S. government charging the same costs and fees as the private market.) In such cases, a repayment guarantee bearing the full faith and credit of the United States may indeed be the factor that "makes" the sale, even if the buyer ends up paying a high service charge in order to cover—per the recent enabling legislation—all costs to the U.S. government of such backing. In other cases, potential purchasers may themselves require such a guarantee, a provision already available from the governments of other major arms exporting nations. In these instances, the guarantee merely satisfies a procedural condition of sale on the part of the purchaser, who in turn is willing and able to pay the additional costs of such a guarantee as part of the overall loan terms.

---

able funds that the increased borrowing represents, and an assessment that the supply of loanable funds is not perfectly expandable ("infinitely elastic" in economist's terms). It is similar to the "crowding out" effect of government borrowing. (Recent Administration estimates of this effect are that a 1 percent increase in real demand as a percent of GDP leads to about a 1 percent increase in real interest rates. Given these estimates, if a DEFP increased total borrowing for arms exports by $1 billion per year, long-term interest rates would rise about 7/10 of a basis point. This is a very small change in rates (i.e., from 6 percent to 6.007 percent), but would apply to all new loans and thus represent a substantial dollar amount. See *Economic Report of the President*, U.S. Government Printing Office, Washington, DC, 1995, p. 84.) If the government guarantee causes a loan to be made to an arms importer that would not otherwise have been made, other potential borrowers will not get loans. Just as there is an increase in production and employment associated with the export loan being made, there is production and employment lost as a result of other borrowers losing credit (or facing higher interest rates). In effect, the government will have made an implicit judgment that the arms importer's loan is more valuable to society than that of the potential credit recipient who does not now get credit. This outcome will replace the market outcome, which would have been the opposite.

If the arms importer would have gotten credit in the United States anyway, the crowding out effect does not occur. If the importer would have gotten the credit overseas in the absence of the DEFP, the crowding out effect in the United States is reduced to the extent that loanable funds are fungible across countries. There is strong evidence that this fungibility is not perfect, so some crowding out would still occur. (See M. Feldstein and C. Horioka, "Domestic Savings and International Capital Flows," *Economic Journal*, June 1980.)

[19]The federal government uses this same financial risk coverage calculation in the management of certain aspects of its commercial export assistance program.

For some, DEFP will represent a victory of sorts in that it provides for U.S. government guarantees of export financing of defense goods and services in a fashion similar to certain long-standing equivalent federal guarantee programs for commercial goods. For others, the legislative failure to support the program with appropriations will be disappointing, to the extent that some in industry have sought a degree of genuine subsidy to offset at least in part the concessional lending and loan forgiveness aspects of competing nations' arms export programs. It will take some time for DEFP to be established, for its availability to become an aspect of the competitive international trade arena, and for potential exporters and purchasers to use and assess the program.

An R&D recoupment charge, which accrues to the U.S. Treasury, is assessed only on government-to-government major defense equipment sales—those made through the FMS program. The rationale for the charge is the use of U.S. government funds to develop U.S.-produced weapons—costs, it is believed, that foreign purchasers of these weapons should share. In addition, if foreign customers will buy the U.S. product anyway, it is a transfer from foreign taxpayers to the U.S. Treasury.

Current and previous Administrations have proposed doing away with the recoupment charge, which would put arms exports on an equal footing with civilian exports, for which no R&D recoupment charge is made, regardless of how much the U.S. government may have paid for relevant R&D. It would also put FMS sales on an equal footing with direct commercial arms sales, for which this charge was terminated in 1992.[20] The FY 1996 Defense Authorization Act broadened the authority of the President to waive the recoupment charge, but made it contingent on finding future budgetary offsets. The Administration still supports full repeal.

PROS AND CONS OF POLICY CHANGES

This section describes two rationales for making the policy changes discussed above, and four against them.

The first argument in favor is the "policy neutrality principle," the general economic principle that public policy should be neutral to the maximum extent possible between different classes of goods and services. In particular, policy should not distort the *relative* prices of goods and services, because relative prices signal opportunity costs, and accurate incorporation of opportunity cost information into decisions will lead to efficient use of resources and maximum possible output. More precisely, public policies should distort relative prices only if there is good reason to do so. Another reason for nondiscriminatory policies is that they minimize administrative costs.

Are there any special reasons to treat arms exports differently from other exports? The major reason is that arms exports can be regionally destabilizing and detrimental to national security. For this reason, they should be regulated. However, once it

---

[20]Current exceptions to the charge are that it is not assessed on sales wholly financed by U.S. grant aid and the President may waive it on sales to NATO countries, Japan, Australia, and New Zealand.

is determined that an arms transaction has positive foreign policy and national security implications, and should thus be *allowed,* the policy neutrality argument would say there is then no reason to treat it any differently from any other export. Treating it differently at this point introduces distortions, is needlessly inefficient, and should only be done with good reason.

As noted above, arms exports are currently treated less favorably than other exports, even when it has been decided they are in the U.S. national security interest. They are not eligible for Export-Import Bank financing, and the R&D recoupment charge is imposed on FMS sales.[21]

As long as an arms export is judged to be consistent with U.S. security interests, the policy neutrality argument would say that it should be treated like any other export as far as government export financing or taxes are concerned. Historically, the Export-Import Bank and FSC provisions were added to law as a signal of disapproval of the arms trade. The policy neutrality argument would say that the appropriate place to approve or disapprove arms deals is in the formal licensing procedure. "Disapproval" through policies like the Export-Import Bank and FSC provisions just distorts the working of the economy.

Even given the policy neutrality principle, there is a plausible rationale for the R&D recoupment charge. The policy neutrality principle implies that, in general, government policy should not distort prices from what they would be in private markets. In private markets, prices in general reflect R&D costs. Since R&D for military products is financed by the government, it is reasonable to argue that the government should recover their costs in the prices it charges foreign buyers of government products.

However, it is also true that military products are generally exported much later in their product life cycle than civilian products, when "market" recoupment of R&D expenses would be much less.[22] According to the logic of the policy neutrality principle, what private markets *would* recoup for R&D is what the U.S. government *should* charge on arms exports. All things considered, there is no compelling reason to treat military products differently from other products on government-financed R&D grounds. First, current policy does not distinguish between civilian product exports based on differential government R&D support. Second, whether military or civilian products "should" carry a larger government-financed R&D burden is unclear, since military exports occur later in the product cycle, when appropriate R&D recoupment charges are likely to be low.[23]

---

[21]In addition, there is a third way in which arms exports are treated less favorably than others. Foreign Sales Corporation (FSC) tax benefits for exports are reduced by 50 percent for items on the U.S. Munitions List.

[22]Most military products are exported only well after they have been introduced to the U.S. force structure.

[23]The basis for the assertion that appropriate R&D charges for military exports may be low or zero is based on the following arguments. The policy neutrality principle is based on the premise that prices that maximize welfare are those that would occur in a private market, and that government policy should lead to prices that deviate from these only for good and specific reasons. It is typical in private markets that prices of new goods start high, and then fall. This is partially because learning by doing and other economies-of-scale type phenomena, and also partially because of competitive market pressures as other

A second argument for supporting the two policy changes is based on the fact that foreign governments subsidize their arms exports with loan guarantees and do not assess R&D recoupment charges. The result is a nonlevel playing field for U.S. exporters in their competition with foreign competitors that should be leveled through appropriate U.S. policy.

There are four arguments against establishing a Defense Export Finance Program or repealing the R&D recoupment charge: The first is based on an explicit rejection of the view that once an arms sales proposal has passed the foreign policy and national security review, it should be treated neutrally compared with civilian exports. This position asserts that arms exports, even if approved by the central national security apparatus, have the following negative aspects: They are often sold to developing countries that do not need and cannot afford them, so their purchase diverts scarce resources from economic development. In addition, these exports can fuel regional arms races and instability. This asserts that it is appropriate to discourage arms sales, even after a foreign policy and national security review has found them acceptable, and it implies that the foreign policy and national security review is inadequate in screening out exports that are unwise from the U.S. point of view. Therefore, policy that is less favorable to arms exports than to civilian products is appropriate because it helps to correct this inadequacy.

A second argument applies to the R&D recoupment charge only and is based on a simple perception that it is just and equitable for foreign customers to bear part of the U.S. government-financed R&D, regardless of whether it is the most efficient economic outcome.

The third argument for opposing these policy changes is the mirror image of the "level playing field" argument in favor of them. It is based on the current successful U.S. performance in world export markets, of which the United States has about a 50 percent share. This success is taken as evidence that the playing field must be sufficiently level; otherwise, U.S. exporters would not be so successful. A more sophisticated version of this argument has been made in a DoD forecast of world conven-

---

products compete for the buyers' purchases. This implies that R&D recoupment tends to occur early in the product life cycle. Since most arms are exported late in the product life cycle, the appropriate R&D recoupment is likely to be low.

In fact, in private markets, some goods will not recoup their R&D costs at all, while others will recoup them many times over. This is almost equivalent to saying that some new products are failures and some are great successes. When deciding to embark on an R&D project leading to a new product, the firm will try to project the future time path of price and sales of the product that will maximize profit, and will undertake the R&D project if such projections are favorable enough. After the product has been developed, of course, the firm's price/volume realization is dictated by overall market conditions, including buyer acceptance of the product and the presence of competing products. Since neither of these can be predicted with certainty before the project is undertaken, whether the firm recoups its R&D in fact depends on these unknowns.

Thus, the appropriate R&D recoupment charge for U.S. arms exports may be positive, zero, or negative, depending on the system. In fact, the appropriate charge on successful systems will likely be high, while that on relatively unsuccessful systems will be zero. This is the opposite of the current system, which attempts to allocate charges across total sales, thus charging more on poor sellers.

Given these conceptual difficulties in choosing the appropriate charge, the general market phenomenon of falling prices over the product cycle, and the fact that the U.S. government does not assess such charges on other kinds of exports (health care products developed with government funds, for example), the policy neutrality principle leads to a position of no R&D recoupment charge.

tional arms trade.[24] In it, the future world market for arms exports was analyzed, and the likely influence of policy measures such as a Defense Export Financing Program was assessed. The results of the study show that only a very small part of the market (about 6 percent) was sensitive to these kinds of policies. The vast majority of market share allocation was found to be determined by political alliance, technical characteristics of weapons, after-market service of weapons, desire for interoperability or continuity of supplier, or desire for diversity of supply. For this large majority of the market (about 94 percent), policy changes such as the DEFP were found to have no impact on market share.

In a different study, the Government Accounting Office (GAO) attempted to assess whether U.S. exporters suffered a competitive disadvantage as a result of foreign government policies.[25] It concluded that there was no way to determine whether U.S. or foreign exporters were more favorably treated by their governments, because of U.S. exports financed through the Foreign Military Financing (FMF) program.[26]

A fourth argument against these changes is that in the current period of U.S. budget stringency, no policies that reduce revenue or increase outlays should be adopted. This argument suggests that the long-run importance of improving the budget balance supersedes, at least for now, any marginal benefits that may be gained by more neutral policies or level playing fields. A counter to this argument is that these policies might pay for themselves by increasing exports enough that other tax revenue increases would offset the negative budget impacts. There is no persuasive quantitative evidence on this score. In addition, the current practice of assessing the R&D recoupment charge only when arms exports are made via FMS (and not when made through direct commercial sales) will likely result in the loss to the U.S. government of the intended revenue, as buyers switch purchases to direct commercial sales to avoid the R&D charge.

THE ISSUE OF OFFSETS

Two arguments have been made that the U.S. government should not allow, or should significantly restrict, the use of offset provisions as a part of arms sales. The first argument concerns "direct" offset—shared production or assembly of the weapon system or some of its components with the buyer. These offsets, it is argued, represent unhealthy technology transfer, a *de facto* giving up of control by the United States to a potential new producer. A counterargument is that this issue should be addressed in the foreign policy and national security review of any specific proposed arms package, but not by means of an indiscriminate blanket policy. The technology transfer aspects of major direct offset provisions in the past, such as the F-16 European Production Group, the Japanese F-15 Coproduction agreement, and the

---

[24]*World-Wide Conventional Arms Trade (1994–2000): A Forecast and Analysis*, December 1994.

[25]GAO, *Military Exports: A Comparison of Government Support in the United States and Three Major Competitors*, May 1995.

[26]In FY 96, FMF will provide grants of about $3 billion for U.S. defense goods and services, and support loans of about $500 million.

Republic of Korea K-1 tank development and production contract, have been reviewed this way. Because such export/coproduction packages have been and can in the future be appropriately handled during foreign policy and national security review, there is no need for additional provisions.

The second argument concerns both direct and indirect offsets, and is based on the resulting transfer of jobs from the United States to the buyer country.[27] The counterargument projects that some arms exports may be completely lost if offsets are restricted, leading to lower economic benefits and jobs than an arms export package with offsets would. It is noted that many U.S. exports of high-technology items (from power-generation equipment to industrial machinery to transportation vehicles) are associated with a broad and varied set of direct and indirect offset arrangements, and these exports have brought major net economic and job creation benefits to the United States. More broadly, this kind of micromanagement of business dealings by the U.S. government is seen as counterproductive, susceptible to special-interest pressures, and needlessly restricting commercial arrangements that are mutually beneficial to exporter and importer. By focusing on one aspect of complex business contracts (offsets), it impedes the working of the normal commercial market that tends to maximize economic benefits.

SUMMARY

This chapter has reviewed the effects of conventional arms exports on the economic and industrial base and described the costs and benefits of several policy options associated with those exports. The world arms export market is small relative to the decline that has occurred in the U.S. defense industrial base. Therefore, arms exports cannot alleviate the economic problems associated with that decline. However, these economic difficulties do lead to pressures to approve export sales. An international agreement to limit arms will be most effective if economic or industrial concerns do not override national security considerations.

---

[27]The earlier discussion of economic benefits from arms exports described these effects, and noted that all offset provisions do not necessarily result in lost U.S. jobs.

Chapter Seven

U.S. GOVERNMENT ARMS EXPORT-CONTROL PROCESS

This chapter describes and evaluates the current process for controlling exports of weapons and dual-use technologies. Suggestions for improving the process in light of the changing international security environment and the expansion of technological capabilities around the world are also discussed.

The United States has a complex set of laws and procedures to control exports of weapons and associated dual-use technologies. These laws and regulations were developed in the post–World War II international environment in which the United States was the Western leader in technology and military power and the Soviet Union and its allies were an agreed-upon common enemy. The primary objective of the weapons and dual-use export controls was, and is, to protect the national security of the United States by preventing enemy acquisition of threatening capabilities. In addition, these controls are tools of foreign policy through which countries supporting U.S. policies are rewarded with access to U.S. weapons and technologies, and countries acting against U.S. objectives are punished by withholding such items.

A review of the laws, legislative history, regulations, other reports, and interviews with current practitioners shows that the issues raised in this report, and in this chapter, are not new topics of debate. History reflects continuing tension over issues such as the appropriate balance between industry desires to export and foreign policy or national security desires to control; whether the United States can, and should, lead by example in controlling particularly sensitive items; and how to manage the implementation of export controls within the government and internationally. As the balance between these competing demands has shifted, the laws and regulations have been modified to support the current trend, but always within the split framework set up in the post–World War II world where control of weapons is managed separately from control of technologies.

THE CURRENT PROCESS

Weapons exports are administered and controlled by the State Department, whereas exports of dual-use items are administered and controlled by the Commerce Department. The Treasury Department's Office of Foreign Assets Control administers embargo-type controls, most of which impose prohibitions on financial and trade transactions with target countries. Some of these regulations interact with, or defer to, Commerce Department regulations; generally, however, export prohibitions are part of a larger set of economic measures. For both weapons and dual-use items extensive procedures are in place to ensure that other interested agencies, primarily the Defense Department, the Arms Control and Disarmament Agency, the Energy Department, the Treasury Department, and the intelligence community, have a voice in determining what is to be controlled and in reviewing particular license applications. These agencies all have agendas and points of view, and their input is critical to successful decisions and overall policy implementation.

Weapons Controls

Arms exports are statutorily regulated by the Arms Export Control Act (AECA), whose antecedents date to the Battle Act of 1954.[1] The AECA authorizes the President to control the export and import of defense articles and services, an authority he has traditionally delegated to the Secretary of State. The Department of State controls all licenses for weapons exports through the International Transfer in Arms Regulation (ITAR), which contains a list of proscribed export destinations, a list of regulated weapons (the Munitions List), procedures for applying for export licenses, and penalties for failure to comply with the regulations.

The Munitions List is compiled by the State Department with the concurrence of the Department of Defense. It is updated on an *ad hoc* basis as needed to accommodate changes in weapons systems technology or data or changes in international regimes in which the U.S. participates. Munitions List items are articles, services, and related technical data designated as defense articles and defense services (pursuant to Sections 38 and 47(7) of the Arms Export Control Act). By law, all weapons are subject to export control; however, deciding whether a component is a defense article or dual-use item can be subjective. Determining whether an item is to be regulated by the State Department or Commerce Department can have significant consequences for the government's ability to control its export.

A critical difference in the implementation of weapons controls and technology controls is the criteria by which controls are imposed. Weapons or munitions export control "implementation guidance" is handled by various offices in the State Department's Bureau of Political Military Affairs, depending on whether the export item is controlled through an international regime or simply according to United States interests. U.S. conventional weapons transfers are now controlled by U.S. policy only, and both overall policy guidance and review of contentious cases are undertaken by a single office.

The oversight offices work with licensing officials to ensure thorough and appropriate review of cases, including referrals to other agencies as necessary. However, given the range of criteria and issues involved, decisions on major weapons are largely made on a case-by-case basis. Among the criteria considered are regional stability, the military and other needs of the procuring country, and concerns over

---

[1]Mitchel B. Wallerstein, with William W. Snyder, Jr., "The Evolution of U.S. Export Control Policy: 1949–1989," in National Academy of Sciences, *Finding Common Ground: U.S. Export Controls in a Changed Global Environment*, National Academy Press, Washington, DC, 1991, pp. 311–312.

support for terrorists and drug trafficking. The regulations allow the government considerable flexibility to deny or approve licenses based on any one of a large number of foreign policy and national security concerns. While considerations of foreign availability of substitute weapons plays a role in these decisions, it is not a decisive criterion, as is the case with most items controlled by the Commerce Department.

Dual-Use Technology Controls

Dual-use technology exports are statutorily regulated by the Export Administration Act, whose antecedents date to the 1940s. This law's initial purpose was to ensure that sufficient quantities of critical technologies remained at home to support U.S. consumption needs during World War II.[2] The law and associated regulations have since been expanded to support efforts to keep certain enabling technologies out of the hands of hostile states. The Missile Technology Control Regime (MTCR), nuclear nonproliferation, chemical, and biological regimes are all supported through this law, as was the CoCom regime.[3] The law is implemented through regulations that identify the commodities to be controlled (through the Commodity Control List [CCL]), the countries for which certain items are controlled, and the justification for the control (national security or foreign policy grounds). Although the Export Administration Act (EAA) has expired, the law and associated regulations continue to be enforced under the International Emergency Economic Powers Act (IEEPA).

The Commodity Control List regulating dual-use technologies consists of items on the Military Critical Technologies List (MCTL) and the Nuclear Referral List (NRL). The MCTL is updated annually by the Defense Department in a process that includes industry representation as well as widespread interagency review. However, there is no routine process for updating the NRL and changes to it are dependent upon updates made to the international regime. There are provisions for businesses to recommend that an item be removed from the overarching CCL because the same or comparable items are available from foreign sources. Adding items to the list requires the support of the Defense Department or, in the case of nuclear technologies, the Department of Energy. Unlike the Munitions List, the CCL is intended to be as limited as possible while still supportive of U.S. national security and foreign policy objectives.

The Commerce Department manages the export license reviews of items on the CCL. It has significantly less flexibility to deny license applications than does the Department of State because control of nonmilitary items is the exception rather than the rule. The controls exercised by the Commerce Department were established primarily to (1) support established multilateral agreements, or (2) punish countries supporting terrorists, drug trafficking, or otherwise engaged in activities deemed counter to U.S. interests. Exports that would be in contravention of multilateral

---

[2]National Academy of Sciences, *Finding Common Ground: U.S. Export Controls in a Changed Global Environment*, National Academy Press, Washington, DC, 1991, pp. 61–62.

[3]By agreement among former CoCom members, the Commerce Department continues to enforce CoCom regulations despite the disestablishment of the formal regime.

agreements or U.S. policies are prohibited. Outside these explicit restrictions, export licenses can be denied only if the sale would be detrimental to U.S. interests and there is no comparable item available from foreign sources. This "no foreign availability" criterion is commonly cited as an impediment to the imposition of controls and a frequent reason given for relaxation of existing controls. It has become increasingly difficult to meet the no foreign availability standard as technological capabilities have proliferated and the United States is no longer the sole producer of many technologies identified as "critical." Although the widespread availability of items labeled "critical" may in fact mean the technology should no longer be defined as "critical" (for example, lower-end computers and associated technologies), the mere existence of one other supplier should not carry the same inference. Yet the existence of one other supplier (particularly one suspected or known to be willing to sell) may be sufficient to overturn a U.S. control. Because dual-use criteria for denial are much more narrow than those applied by the State Department, exporters prefer to have items listed on the CCL rather than as defense articles on the Munitions List.

Interagency Consultations

Both the weapons and dual-use export control processes have built-in mechanisms for consulting with other interested agencies. In addition to providing the bulk of the input for the lists of controlled items—the Munitions List and the MCTL—the Defense Department provides criteria for case referral to both the State Department and the Commerce Department. The proportion of cases referred has fluctuated over time but is currently about 25 percent for the State Department's munitions cases and about 10–15 percent for the Commerce Department's dual-use cases. The Defense Department has also provided specific criteria for cases it does not need to see, further bounding the problem of case referrals. The Energy and Treasury Departments, with narrower areas of interest, have also provided referral guidelines to State and Commerce. ACDA has its own internal arrangements with the State Department for review of munitions cases and works with the Commerce Department as well. DoD and ACDA review is required for all munitions cases that require congressional approval (those exceeding a threshold of $14 million for major defense equipment, and $50 million for any defense article or service). Weapons export cases arranged through the Defense Security Assistance Agency (DSAA) must be coordinated with the State Department before approval.

Formal interagency groups are routinely convened to discuss cases related to the MTCR, chemical and biological regimes, and the Nuclear Nonproliferation Treaty. These interagency groups do not review each license application, but gather to discuss the few contentious cases identified as needing interagency discussion (coordination can be obtained without convening an interagency meeting). No equivalent group exists, however, to review conventional weapons exports, although interagency coordination and discussions are held on contentious conventional weapons and technology exports. The interagency groups, whether formal or informal, provide input and guidance to the lead agency—Commerce for technology and State for weapons—but the licensing decision is left to the lead agency. Agencies uncomfortable with the lead agency decision may "appeal," which then elevates the decisionmaking and coordination to the next highest level of government. Such appeals depend on the lead agency's prompt notification of others as to the decision reached. The majority of appeals for both dual-use items and weapons are resolved at the Assistant Secretary level or below.

Enforcement

Enforcement of the laws and regulations pertaining to the export of arms and dual-use technologies is split among a number of agencies. The Commerce and State Departments run separate programs to verify that sales are going to declared buyers, and that those buyers are using items appropriately. These efforts are further supported by Customs and other law enforcement personnel. The laws and regulations provide for sanctions against exporters and importers who break the law. These sanctions, against U.S. and foreign businesses or other governments, differ across the licensing organizations and regimes. In a recent attempt to strengthen sanctions, a new standard has been imposed against sellers who "know or have reason to know" their products might be diverted. Many in industry are concerned about the implementation of this law and the interpretation that will be given to "have reason to know."

EVALUATION OF THE CURRENT PROCESS

As with many governmental processes, the export-control laws and regulations have both intended and unintended consequences. Any lack of clarity in the policy or procedures for decisionmaking result in bureaucratic wrangling and tactical maneuvering. The fact that the Export Review Board operates at the Cabinet Secretary level contributes to policy confusion because so few cases make it to this level that cabinet decisions do not inform or reinforce policy objectives laid out elsewhere. A more effective mechanism, which the National Security Council has used extensively elsewhere, would be to convene a senior working group at the assistant secretary (or even under secretary) level, as the primary decision mechanism in disputed matters. This group's seniority over those administering the review process, and their ability to meet more regularly, could improve the process significantly. In the current system, information control gives bureaucratic control; systems for information sharing are seen as equalizers and somewhat threatening to those who exercise authority.

The regulations and processes described above have played an important role in protecting U.S. security and have provided a meaningful foreign policy tool. However, neither the regulatory framework nor the processes for implementing it have kept pace with fundamental changes in the international security environment or with technological innovation. Failure to adjust to these fundamental changes threatens the continued success of U.S. export-control policies.

The world has changed significantly since the immediate post–World War II period, which provided the foundation for the laws and regulations in use today. The decision in the late 1940s and 1950s to separate the regulation of military weapons from technologies could be justified because military technology led civil technologies, so it was relatively easy to distinguish between civil and military uses of particular items. Further, the United States had the technological lead among its allies, so that it could virtually singlehandedly control the proliferation of technologies through purely national regulations. The issue of foreign availability was either non-existent or very limited. Finally, a clear threat to the United States could be identified in the Soviet Union and associated bloc countries, a threat also felt by our allies. It was this common threat that provided the basis for multinational export controls, such as CoCom, as other nations became able to compete with the United States in the production and export of sophisticated weapons and technology.

With the dissolution of the Soviet Union, this export-control process is now operating in a fundamentally different environment. The dissolution of a monolithic enemy, combined with loss of unilateral U.S. control of many of the weapons and technologies once considered critical to protect, has contributed to the fragmentation of the review process. Without the common threat, it has become more difficult for agencies with different roles and missions to agree on what constitutes a threat to U.S. security. This is borne out by difficulties in arriving at interagency decisions that are both internally consistent and consistent with U.S. and international policies.

The blurring of lines between defense and civil technology, and the shift in innovation leadership to the civilian or commercial sector, have led to a weakness in the government's ability to assess the potential threats technologies pose. The Department of Defense and other government agencies are not staffed to make these assessments, and the purposeful separation of the regulation of technology from weapons makes this task even more difficult. Despite the best efforts of government officials to implement export-control laws and regulations effectively and efficiently, the separation of weapons and technology seems ill-suited to the needs of current and future administrators.

The significant differences in the stringency of review criteria for weapons and dual-use technologies lead to jurisdictional debates. Jurisdictional tensions generally arise from the need to define items either as defense articles, and therefore subject to State Department review, or as items on the MCTL subject to Commerce Department review. Many government officials have noted an increase in the number of jurisdictional issues raised in recent years as export controls have been adjusted to account for changes in the international security environment. Foreign availability combined with the dissolution of the Soviet Union has encouraged decontrol of many items previously on the MCTL. While decontrol may simply imply a reduction in the number of recipients that are prohibited from receiving a particular type of technology, and not the complete absence of regulation, coordination of decontrol decisions has been a problem in the export licensing community. An example recently highlighted by the GAO and in the media is the stealth coatings that were controlled on the CCL by Commerce. As a result of Commerce Department approval of exports subsequently opposed by the Defense and State Departments, stealth coatings have now been transferred to the Munitions List, for control by the State Department. As noted earlier, the State Department has greater latitude to deny export applications for items it controls than does the Commerce Department. Such jurisdictional issues are not only time-consuming and difficult for industry, but highlight the fact that our two-track control system has significant gaps.

In theory, the issue of gaps should be covered by the referral process through which the lead agencies, as recipients of the license applications, refer cases to other interested organizations such as Defense, State, Energy, or the intelligence community. This process works well for 90–95 percent of the cases received, but there are numerous reports of cases that should have been, but were not, referred.[4]

The convening of separate interagency groups, while efficient from the perspective of discussing particular regimes, will be ineffective for future increasing needs for crosscutting analyses of trends and capabilities. These groups will need to focus on linkages between civilian technologies and weapons, and are likely to find that items previously associated with only one type of weapon may now apply across the board. Close coordination will be required to ensure that these separate groups do not make decisions counter to the interests of other regimes.

To take an example, items covered under the MTCR may be listed either on the Munitions List or on the Commodity Control List. Depending on which regulation controls the export, a particular set of activities will be set in play in response to an application. For items on the Munitions List, the State Department will manage the review process including any necessary interagency coordination. Items on the CCL will be managed by the Commerce Department, although any interagency meeting necessary will be convened by the State Department. If the various staff-level interagency groups cannot reach a decision, or if the lead agency reaches a decision another finds unacceptable, the decision may be elevated and appealed. While some of the players at the staff level are the same for technology and weapons, many are not, making consistent decisionmaking and policy implementation difficult.

Although the regulatory frameworks and lists are managed separately, the Department of State convenes and chairs all the formal interagency working groups. When working groups are unable to resolve their disagreements, the issues are raised to a higher level, to a committee chaired by representatives of either the Secretary of State or the Secretary of Commerce. Thus, there is no independent consolidator of information or arbitrator in this process until an issue reaches the President. The lack of an independent actor earlier in the process, in a time of increased complexity, makes it difficult to arrive at consistent decisions.

The policy and structural problems outlined above are compounded by administrative inefficiencies. Lack of a common database for all types of export licenses leads to inefficiencies in the use of staff time and impedes the establishment of historical case files to support license application reviews. License applications requiring coordination among a number of offices or organizations must generally be photocopied and mailed to the other interested parties. Time lost to mail delivery is time away

---

[4]U.S. GAO, *Nuclear Nonproliferation, Export Licensing Procedures for Dual-Use Items Need to Be Strengthened*, GAO/NSIAD-94-119, April 1994; U.S. GAO, *Export Controls, Some Controls Over Missile-Related Technology Exports to China Are Weak*, GAO/NSIAD-95-82, April 1995; U.S. GAO, *Export Controls, Concerns Over Stealth-Related Exports*, GAO/NSIAD-95-140, May 1995.

from substantive review. The move to strict time limits on dual-use reviews and pressure to reduce the review times of munitions applications make it even more imperative that information be available instantly to all participants in the review process. This includes not only license application information but intelligence and enforcement information and data on previous sales to the end user, country, and region.

Maintaining an electronic database available to the entire licensing community would not only allow more time to focus on the case at hand, but would provide a means of tracking decisions over time. It has been noted by some that on a small scale, license applications that may have been denied initially are frequently approved upon the second or third submittal simply because different license application processors use slightly different screening criteria. With access to a historical database, such reversals would presumably occur only as a result of a change in policy or the world situation, not simply as a result of differences in the interpretation of regulations.

With the increasing globalization of the arms industry and increased commercialization of weapons technologies the analysis of data relating to sales also becomes increasingly complex. The intelligence community, primarily DIA (in support of the Department of Defense) and CIA (in support of the rest of the licensing community) are still in the process of shifting their concern with exports from the Soviet empire to the world at large. Lack of information about allied and non-aligned nations' equipment and capabilities continues to hamper intelligence evaluations of the impact of particular sales on particular global regions. As with the rest of the government, technical expertise has been difficult to recruit and retain, making it difficult to support efforts to understand the links between technologies and weapons production.

In today's uncertain international environment, the intelligence community's support is critical. The questions of what end-user countries should we be concerned with now, and what products will we want to control, or wish we had controlled, ten years from now need to be addressed in an organized fashion.

The enforcement structure associated with export controls mirrors the separate regulatory processes with separate organizations responsible for dual-use and weapons exports. Coordination of overseas activities seems particularly weak, with inspections sometimes made by personnel with little or no expertise or training in dual-use technologies or weapons.[5] Enforcement authorities could, in fact, provide considerable useful information to the intelligence and regulatory communities on the extent to which technology items seem to be connected to weapons programs, but this would require considerably more technical expertise and greater coordination among the various enforcement agencies than is currently the case.

---

[5]See, for example, GAO/NSIAD-94-119, Chapter 5, "Methods Used to Deter and Detect Diversions Have Limitations"; and GAO/NSIAD-95-82, p. 3.

CONCLUSIONS

While the objective of controlling weapons and dual-use items that directly threaten the United States remains clear, our objectives are no longer as clear for weapons and countries that pose no direct threat to U.S. territory. When the United States had the technological lead, U.S. objectives could be pursued largely through unilateral actions. U.S. objectives were tied to U.S. foreign policy concerns and views about the "right" amount of militarization for particular regions or countries. However, as the number of countries manufacturing weapons and technologies comparable to those produced by the United States has grown, the U.S. ability to control the flow of weapons into other regions has diminished.

The processes in place to support current policy and policies anticipated for the future lack certain attributes critical to success. In particular, agency roles for advocacy, review, and decisionmaking are often inseparable, contributing to confusion over priorities and making it difficult to achieve consistent decisions. The lack of a strong and independent adjudicator to force decisions that are both internally consistent and consistent with national and international policy will continue to be a problem as the complexity of cases brought to the interagency process grows. The separation of weapons from technology controls has also contributed to an artificial divide that threatens our ability to successfully identify technologies for control.

Although the Administration has a Conventional Arms Transfer policy, it lacks the procedural and regulatory tools necessary for fully effective implementation. Guidelines for restricting arms exports are largely implemented on a case-by-case basis, and regulations restricting sales of dual-use technologies associated with conventional weapons are limited and not well linked to conventional weapons proliferation concerns.

Across the government, access to information necessary for informed decisionmaking is inadequate, tending to reflect institutional boundaries and antiquated data systems. Feedback mechanisms, primarily in the enforcement and intelligence communities, are dominated by specific agency concerns and play a smaller role than is necessary in informing the review process and supporting decisions on future directions.

The considerable uncertainty in the international security environment combined with increased diffusion of dual-use technologies throughout the world has created an environment in which it is critical that the regulatory framework integrate technology and weapons controls. At the same time, the regulatory framework must be flexible enough to accommodate changes in policies and in weapons and technology controls. An integrated legal framework and list of weapons and associated technologies, and an independently managed license review process would provide better support for implementation of arms proliferation policies.

IMPLEMENTING CHANGES IN THE EXPORT CONTROL PROCESS

The export licensing process, particularly in regard to conventional weapons and associated technologies, can be improved in many areas. Some changes would require restructuring of government agencies and staffs or rewriting of laws, whereas others may be more easily implemented with beneficial results.

A commitment to developing a common database will not only improve processing consistency but is critical to the success of any other steps taken to make the governmentwide export licensing system more efficient. The critical capabilities of such a system should be determined by an interagency group, but would at a minimum include transmission of all license application materials electronically to all potential participants, a common database of cases that could be queried in a number of ways, and a trends analysis as cases are entered into the system and a historical database is built. The common electronic database must have good multilevel security and control to manage "read and write" capabilities. Many of the organizations involved in the process already maintain electronic databases and the new system should take advantage of these by creating links and adding connectivity rather than creating an entirely new system. An example of a governmentwide common database is RaDiUS, which contains information on all federal R&D projects. The RaDiUS database is fed by individual agency databases that can be accessed by authorized personnel through the Internet, using Netscape. The database engine is ORACLE with a user-friendly query tool layered on top.

While creating a new database system will incur significant costs, possibly on the order of $10 million, industry experience shows that initial investments in this area have a rapid payoff. This should translate into faster, more consistent, government export licensing decisions, a historical record for tracking trends, and a system for feeding reports required by Congress, the United Nations, and nonproliferation regimes such as the new one agreed to at Wassenaar. In the current information management environment, large portions of such a system should be available commercially with, perhaps, some modifications to protect classified and proprietary information—a capability already integral to many business management systems. The ability to link such information is well under way with the establishment of the Internet, INTELINK, and SIPRNet, among others.

Another important step is the integration of technology and weapons controls into one legal and regulatory framework. This would help address concerns about the artificial separateness of technology and weapons by focusing attention on their points of convergence. This step would ease jurisdictional disputes over whether items should be classified as defense articles or placed on the CCL, as presumably there would be one list of weapons and associated technologies with prohibitions or restraints on their export to particular regions or nations. Technologies not deemed to be critical to the production or use of weapons might be regulated separately.

While it is useful to have a large number of governmental players and interests represented in the export-control decisionmaking process, the process as currently managed has difficulty making consistent decisions on the small subset of issues generating interagency interest. This situation could be improved by more aggressive intervention on the part of the NSC staff to use cases to establish policy precedents that could then guide agency staff decisionmakers.

Previous reports and commissions have examined the issue of "one stop shopping" with respect to export licenses, and many have recommended that at least the administrative functions be consolidated in one agency. Particularly if a common database is to be established and maintained, it would be useful to establish one agency as the central administrator and coordinator of all weapons and related-technology export licenses.

The establishment of a central administrator must be clearly distinguished from establishment of one agency to manage and implement U.S. export controls. In the latter case, the single agency implementer should be an independent arbitrator, able to integrate information, arbitrate decisions, and enforce policy guidance. Whether such an agency would absorb the export-control staffs of all other agencies or operate as a clearing house and integrator of their inputs should depend on the extent to which the multiple agency views are deemed critical to successful policy implementation.

At present, the Arms Control and Disarmament Agency (ACDA) is the only agency of the U.S. government with a clear arms control perspective. Because it has this sole focus it is less likely to be captured by competing interests in the business, military, or regional/foreign policy communities. As is the case with all the agencies involved in the export-control process, ACDA lacks expertise in all the specialties needed to make consistently good licensing decisions. However, it does have experience working with all the other organizations involved and in working in consultation with others. A major impediment to ACDA's effectiveness as the lead agency in this area is its lack of cabinet-level leadership, which will hamper its ability to enforce decisions.

Intelligence resources contributing to this effort must be linked to the ongoing reviews and debates so that their input can be used both by policymakers and implementers. Experience tells us the windows for acting to limit the proliferation of a weapons system or technology are small and we must take action as soon as a problem area is identified if we are to have a chance at success.

MEETING PARTICIPANTS, BRIEFERS, AND OTHER CONTRIBUTORS

February 22, 1995

Participants and Attendees

William Clements	National Security Council
COL Robert Fitton	Defense Security Assistance Agency
Robert Litwak	National Security Council
Joe Marty	Department of State (PM/SRP)
H. Diehl McKalip	Defense Security Assistance Agency
Ralph Novak	Office of the Secretary of Defense (Policy Support)
Dan Poneman	National Security Council
Deanna Powers	Defense Security Assistance Agency
John Richards	Department of Commerce (Bureau of Export Administration)
Joe Smaldone	Arms Control and Disarmament Agency
Lin Wells	Office of the Secretary of Defense (Policy Support)
Len Zuza	Office of Management and Budget

March 15, 1995

Participants and Attendees

Gordon Adams	Office of Management and Budget
Sumner Benson	Defense Technology Security Administration
Walter Earle	Defense Technology Security Administration
Robert Feldhune	Defense Intelligence Agency
COL Robert Fitton	Defense Security Assistance Agency
Ken Flamm	Office of the Secretary of Defense (Acquisition and Technology)
Dan Grynaviski	Defense Intelligence Agency
Martha Harris	Department of State (Export Control Matters)
Gary Koblitz	Defense Intelligence Agency
Caryn Leslie	Central Intelligence Agency
Robert Litwak	National Security Council
Gayland Lyles	Central Intelligence Agency
H. Diehl McKalip	Defense Security Assistance Agency
Joe Marty	Department of State (PM/SRP)
Eric Newsom	Department of State (PM)

Ralph Novak   Office of the Secretary of Defense (Policy Support)
Pete Petrihos   Department of State (PM/SRP)
Dan Poneman   National Security Council
Deanna Powers   Defense Security Assistance Agency
Victoria Prescott   Defense Intelligence Agency
John Pulju   Central Intelligence Agency
John Richards   Department of Commerce (Bureau of Export
                                   Administration)
Larry Scheinman   Arms Control and Disarmament Agency
Greg Schlickenmaier   Central Intelligence Agency
Joe Smaldone   Arms Control and Disarmament Agency
Pete Verga   Office of the Secretary of Defense (Policy Support)
Lin Wells   Office of the Secretary of Defense (Policy Support)
Len Zuza   Office of Management and Budget

Briefings

Dan Poneman and representatives of other agencies, *Background on the Conventional Arms Transfer PDD and Agency Positions*

John Pulju, Victoria Prescott, *Intelligence Issues: Technology Transfer, Multinational Intelligence Sharing, Non-Proliferation Enforcement Issues*

Ken Flamm, *Overview of Arms Market Forecast and Production Capacity Issue; Inner Circle Concept*

Martha Harris, Pete Petrihos, *Post-CoCom Efforts: Relationship Between the Conventional Arms Transfer Policy and the Regional Conventional Arms Transfer Policy for Central Europe*

April 18, 1995

Participants and Attendees

Floyd Banks   Assistant Deputy Director for International
                                   Negotiations (OJCS/J-5)
Sumner Benson   Defense Technology Security Administration
Col. Steve Boyce   Joint Chiefs of Staff (OJCS/J-5)
Belinda Canton   Central Intelligence Agency
Tony Chavez   Office of Management and Budget
Ken Crelling   Defense Intelligence Agency
Michael Dixon   Department of State (DTC)
Walter Earle   Defense Technology Security Administration
Lt.Col. Mike Ehrlich   Joint Chiefs of Staff (OJCS/J-5)
Lee Feinstein   Department of State (Export Control Matters)
Ken Flamm   Office of the Secretary of Defense (Acquisition and
                                   Technology)
Dan Grynaviski   Defense Intelligence Agency
Martha Harris   Department of State (Export Control Matters)
Jan Lodal   Principal Under Secretary of Defense (Policy)

H. Diehl McKalip	Defense Security Assistance Agency
Joe Marty	Department of State (PM/SRP)
Deanna Powers	Defense Security Assistance Agency
Victoria Prescott	Defense Intelligence Agency
John Pulju	Central Intelligence Agency
LTG Thomas Rhame	Defense Security Assistance Agency
Giovanni Snidle	Arms Control and Disarmament Agency
James Swanson	Defense Technology Security Administration
Peter Sullivan	Defense Technology Security Administration
Lt.Col. John Woodward	Arms Control and Disarmament Agency

RAND
Marcy Agmon
Greg Treverton
Kathi Webb

Briefings

Lt.Col. John Woodward, *Arms Control Concerns; Regional Focused Supplier Restraints; Regionally Focused Demand/Supply Arrangements; Diplomatic Initiatives; Process Issues*

Ken Flamm, *Follow-up on the Global Arms Market Forecast*

May 9, 1995

Participants and Attendees

Sumner Benson	Defense Technology Security Administration
Tyrus Cobb	Business Executives for National Security
Aaron Cross	IBM
David Evans	Business Executives for National Security
COL Robert Fitton	Defense Security Assistance Agency
Bruce Jackson	Lockheed-Martin
Joel Johnson	Aerospace Industries Association
Ralph Novak	Office of the Secretary of Defense (Policy Support)
Deanna Powers	Defense Security Assistance Agency
John Richards	Department of Commerce (Bureau of Export Administration
Maj. Bill Snyder	Office of the Secretary of the Air Force (AQ/XM)
Bill Schneider	Defense Trade Advisory Group (DTAG)

RAND
Marcy Agmon
James Bonomo
Michael Kennedy
Greg Treverton
Ken Watman
Kathi Webb

Briefings

Ken Watman, *Limiting the Perils of Arms Trade at Limited Cost*

Bill Schneider, *Export Credit Financing*

John Richards, *New Approaches for Cooperation; Industrial Base Issues*

Tyrus Cobb, Business Executives for National Security, *Presentation*

May 16, 1995

Participants and Attendees

Tom Barksdale	MITRE
Joe Smaldone	Arms Control and Disarmament Agency
Joe Marty	Department of State (PM/SRP)
Peter Sullivan	Defense Technology Security Administration
John Richards	Department of Commerce (Bureau of Export Administration)
Len Zuza	Office of Management and Budget

RAND
Marcy Agmon
James Bonomo
Michael Kennedy
Ken Watman
Kathi Webb
Charles Wolf

Briefings

Tom Barksdale, *Trade and the Health of the U.S. Defense Industrial Base; Foreign Technological Competitiveness; Implications of Foreign Defense Industrial Policies on U.S. Security; Technology Transfer Risk Management*

June 12/13, 1995

Participants and Attendees

Greg Bischak	National Commission on Economic Conversion & Disarmament
Tom Cardamone	Council for a Livable World Education Fund
Frank Cevasco	IPAC, Inc.
William J. Durch	The Henry L. Stimson Center
Suzanna Dyer	BASIC
Ken Flamm	Office of the Secretary of Defense (Acquisition and Technology)
Natalie Goldring	BASIC
Steve Goose	Arms Project/Human Rights Watch

Dennis Gormley   Pacific Sierra Research
Geoffrey Kemp   Carnegie Endowment for International Peace
Lora Lumpe   Federation of American Scientists
Andrew Pierre   Carnegie Endowment for International Peace
Tom Sellers   Sandia National Laboratories
David Tarbell   Defense Technology Security Administration

RAND
Marcy Agmon
James Bonomo
Michael Kennedy
Ken Watman
Kathi Webb
Charles Wolf

Briefings

Dennis Gormley, *French Apache Cruise Missiles*

Tom Sellers, *Monitoring Mechanisms*

Geoffrey Kemp, *Arms Control and the Middle East*

Frank Cevasco, *Arms Control and Industry*

Lora Lumpe, *Overview of Proliferation Issues*

July 13, 1995

Participants and Attendees
Gen. John R. Landry (Ret.)   National Intelligence Council
Lynn Davis   Department of State
Warren Olson   Defense Security Assistance Agency
Wolfgang Reinicke   The Brookings Institution

RAND
Marcy Agmon
James Bonomo
Michael Kennedy
Ken Watman
Kathi Webb
Charles Wolf

Briefings

Lynn Davis, *Update on the New Forum*

Wolfgang Reinicke, *The Political Economy of Export Controls and Technology Transfer*

Other Contributors or Sources of Information and Assistance

Government Staff

Sumner Benson	Defense Technology Security Administration
Russ Burns	Defense Intelligence Agency
William Denk	Department of Commerce
Walter Earle	Defense Technology Security Administration
John Ehrman	Central Intelligence Agency
Lee Feinstein	Department of State
Stephen Geis	Department of State
Richard F. Grimmett	Congressional Research Service
Hilary Hess	Department of Commerce
Robert Litwak	National Security Council
Robert Maggi	Department of State
Terry McAfee	Defense Intelligence Agency
George Menas	Defense Technology Security Administration
John Richards	Department of Commerce
Joe Smaldone	Arms Control and Disarmament Agency
Jim Swanson	Defense Technology Security Administration
Len Zuza	Office of Management and Budget

Government Support

Col. Robert Fitton	Defense Security Assistance Agency
Deanna Powers	Defense Security Assistance Agency
Lt. Colonel Joe McAndrew	Defense Security Assistance Agency
Ralph Novak	Office of the Secretary of Defense (Policy Support)
Edward Rader	Office of the Secretary of Defense (Policy Support)
Pete Verga	Office of the Secretary of Defense (Policy Support)

RAND

Marcy Agmon
James Bonomo
Michael Kennedy
Maren Leed
Jonathan Pollack
Greg Treverton
Ken Watman
Kathi Webb
Charles Wolf

Others

Martin Kennedy	British Embassy
Simon Webb	British Embassy

DOCUMENTS

This appendix includes four documents:

- Legislation requesting the President to establish the Advisory Board on Arms Proliferation Policy

- Executive Order 12946: President's Advisory Board on Arms Proliferation Policy

- Charter of the President's Advisory Board on Arms Proliferation Policy

- Executive Order 12981: Administration of Export Controls

TITLE XVI—ARMS CONTROL MATTERS

Subtitle A—Programs in Support of the Prevention and Control of Proliferation of Weapons of Mass Destruction

SEC. 1601. STUDY OF GLOBAL PROLIFERATION OF STRATEGIC AND ADVANCED CONVENTIONAL MILITARY WEAPONS AND RELATED EQUIPMENT AND TECHNOLOGY. *President.*

(a) STUDY.—The President shall conduct a study of (1) the factors that contribute to the proliferation of strategic and advanced conventional military weapons and related equipment and technologies, and (2) the policy options that are available to the United States to inhibit such proliferation.

(b) CONDUCT OF STUDY.—In carrying out the study the President shall do the following:

(1) Identify those factors contributing to global weapons proliferation which can be most effectively regulated.

(2) Identify and assess policy approaches available to the United States to discourage the transfer of strategic and advanced conventional military weapons and related equipment and technology.

(3) Assess the effectiveness of current multilateral efforts to control the transfer of such military weapons and equipment and such technology.

(4) Identify and examine methods by which the United States could reinforce these multilateral efforts to discourage the transfer of such weapons and equipment and such technology, including placing conditions on assistance provided by the United States to other nations.

(5) Identify the circumstances under which United States national security interests might best be served by a transfer of conventional military weapons and related equipment and technology, and specifically assess whether such circumstances exist when such a transfer is made to an allied country which, with the United States, has mutual national security interests to be served by such a transfer.

(6) Assess the effect on the United States economy and the national technology and industrial base (as defined by section 2491(1) of title 10, United States Code) which might result from potential changes in United States policy controlling the transfer of such military weapons and related equipment and technology.

Establishment. (c) ADVISORY BOARD.—(1) Within 15 days after the date of the enactment of this Act, the President shall establish an Advisory Board on Arms Proliferation Policy. The advisory board shall be composed of 5 members. The President shall appoint the members from among persons in private life who are noted for their stature and expertise in matters covered by the study required under subsection (a) and shall ensure, in making the appointments, that the advisory board is composed of members from diverse backgrounds. The President shall designate one of the members as chairman of the advisory board.

(2) The President is encouraged—

(A) to obtain the advice of the advisory board regarding the matters studied pursuant to subsection (a) and to consider that advice in carrying out the study; and

(B) to ensure that the advisory board is informed in a timely manner and on a continuing basis of the results of policy reviews carried out under the study by persons outside the board.

(3) The members of the advisory board shall receive no pay for serving on the advisory board. However, the members shall be allowed travel expenses and per diem in accordance with the regulations referred to in paragraph (6).

(4) Upon request of the chairman of the advisory board, the Secretary of Defense or the head of any other Federal department or agency may detail, without reimbursement for costs, any of the personnel of the department or agency to the advisory board to assist the board in carrying out its duties.

(5) The Secretary of Defense shall designate a federally funded research and development center with expertise in the matters covered by the study required under subsection (a) to provide the advisory board with such support services as the advisory board may need to carry out its duties.

(6) Except as otherwise provided in this section, the provisions of the Federal Advisory Committee Act (5 U.S.C. App.), and the regulations prescribed by the Administrator of General Services pursuant to that Act, shall apply to the advisory board. Subsections (e) and (f) of section 10 of such Act do not apply to the advisory board.

Termination date.

(7) The advisory board shall terminate 30 days after the date on which the President submits the final report of the advisory board to Congress pursuant to subsection (d)(2)(B).

(d) REPORTS.—(1) The Advisory Board on Arms Proliferation Policy shall submit to the President, not later than May 15, 1994, a report containing its findings, conclusions, and recommendations on the matters covered by the study carried out pursuant to subsection (a).

(2) The President shall submit to Congress, not later than June 1, 1994—

(A) a report on the study carried out pursuant to subsection (a), including the President's findings and conclusions regarding the matters considered in the study; and

(B) the report of the Advisory Board on Arms Proliferation Policy received under paragraph (1), together with the comments, if any, of the President on that report.

4829

Federal Register

Vol. 60, No. 15

Tuesday, January 24, 1995

Presidential Documents

Title 3—

The President

Executive Order 12946 of January 20, 1995

President's Advisory Board on Arms Proliferation Policy

By the authority vested in me as President by the Constitution and the laws of the United States of America, including section 1601 of the National Defense Authorization Act, Fiscal Year 1994 (Public Law 103–160), and the Federal Advisory Committee Act, as amended (5 U.S.C. App. 2) ("Act"), except that subsections (e) and (f) of section 10 of such Act do not apply, and section 301 of title 3, United States Code, it is hereby ordered as follows:

Section 1. *Establishment.* There is established within the Department of Defense the "President's Advisory Board on Arms Proliferation Policy" ("Board"). The Board shall consist of five members who shall be appointed by the President from among persons in private life who are noted for their stature and expertise regarding the proliferation of strategic and advanced conventional weapons and are from diverse backgrounds. The President shall designate one of the members as Chairperson of the Board.

Sec. 2. *Functions.* The Board shall advise the President on implementation of United States conventional arms transfer policy, other issues related to arms proliferation policy, and on other matters deemed appropriate by the President. The Board shall report to the President through the Assistant to the President for National Security Affairs.

Sec. 3. *Administration.* (a) The heads of executive agencies shall, to the extent permitted by law, provide to the Board such information as it may require for the purpose of carrying out its functions.

(b) Members of the Board shall serve without compensation, but shall be allowed travel expenses, including per diem in lieu of subsistence, as authorized by law, including 5 U.S.C. 5701–5707 and section 7(d) of the Act, for persons serving intermittently in government service.

(c) The Department of Defense or the head of any other Federal department or agency may detail to the Board, upon request of the Chairperson of the Board, any of the personnel of the department or agency to assist the Board in carrying out its duties.

(d) The Secretary of Defense shall designate a federally funded research and development center with expertise in the matters covered by the Board to provide the Board with such support services as the Board may need to carry out its duties.

(e) The Department of Defense shall provide the Board with administrative services, facilities, staff, and other support services necessary for the performance of its functions.

Sec. 4. *General.* (a) The Board shall terminate 30 days after the date on which the President submits the final report of the Board to the Congress.

(b) For reasons of national security or for such other reasons as specified in section 552(b) of title 5, United States Code, the Board shall not provide public notice or access to meetings at which national security information will be discussed. Authority to make such determinations shall reside with the Secretary of Defense or his designee who must be an official required to be appointed by and with the advice and consent of the Senate.

(c) Information made available to the Board shall be given all necessary security protection in accordance with applicable laws and regulations.

(d) Each member of the Board and each member of the Board's staff shall execute an agreement not to reveal any classified information obtained by virtue of his or her service with the Board except as authorized by applicable law and regulations.

William J. Clinton

THE WHITE HOUSE,
January 20, 1995.

[FR Doc. 95-1925
Filed 1-20-95; 5:01pm]
Billing code 3195-01-P

**CHARTER OF
THE PRESIDENT'S ADVISORY BOARD ON
ARMS PROLIFERATION POLICY**

A. OFFICIAL DESIGNATION: The President's Advisory Board on Arms Proliferation Policy.

B. OBJECTIVES AND SCOPE: Pursuant to Title XVI, Section 1601 of the National Defense Authorization Act for Fiscal Year 1994, the President's Advisory Board on Arms Proliferation Policy (hereinafter, the Board) shall advise the President on the implementation of the United States conventional arms transfer policy, other issues related to arms proliferation policy, and on other matters deemed pertinent to the subject and requested by the President.. The Board will operate in accordance with the provisions of Public Law 92-463, the Federal Advisory Committee Act (5 U.S.C. App.), except that subsections (e) and (f) of Section 10 of such Act shall not apply and except where the Board is being utilized by the Central Intelligence Agency. Executive Order 12946, Jan 20, 1995, governs the Board's functions.

C. PERIOD OF TIME REQUIRED: The Board shall terminate 30 days after the date on which the President submits the Board's final report to Congress. The Board shall provide its final report to the President no later than May 15, 1995 unless sooner extended by the President.

D. OFFICIAL TO WHOM THE COMMITTEE REPORTS: The Board shall report to the President of the United States through the Assistant to the President for National Security Affairs.

E. THE AGENCY RESPONSIBLE FOR PROVIDING NECESSARY SUPPORT: The Department of Defense shall provide the Board with administrative services, facilities, staff, and other support services necessary for the performance of its functions.

F. MEMBERSHIP: The President shall appoint five (5) members to the Board from among private life with the stature and expertise related to matters outlined in the objectives and duties of the Board. The President shall designate one of the members as Chairperson of the Board.

G. ESTIMATED ANNUAL OPERATING COSTS AND STAFF SUPPORT YEARS: It is estimated that the total annual costs of operations for travel, per diem, consultant fees, staff support, and other incidental costs, will not exceed $600,000. Full time equivalent staff support years are anticipated to be one (1) years of effort.

H. NUMBER OF MEETINGS: The Board will meet monthly, unless called more frequently by the Chairperson. For reasons of national security or for such other reasons as specified in Section 552(b) of title 5, United States Code, the Board shall not provide public notice or access to meetings at which national security information will be discussed. Authority to make such determinations shall reside with the Secretary of Defense or his designee who must be an official required to be appointed by and with the advice and consent of the Senate.

I. TERMINATION DATE: The Board shall terminate 30 days after the date on which the President submits the Board's final report to Congress. This charter must be renewed two years from the date filed below.

J. DATE CHARTER FILED: 27 JAN 1995

THE WHITE HOUSE

Office of the Press Secretary

For Immediate Release   December 6, 1995

EXECUTIVE ORDER
#12981
- - - - - - -

ADMINISTRATION OF EXPORT CONTROLS

By the authority vested in me as President by the
Constitution and the laws of the United States of America,
including but not limited to the International Emergency Economic
Powers Act (50 U.S.C. 1701 et. seq.) ("the Act"), and in order to
take additional steps with respect to the national emergency
described and declared in Executive Order No. 12924 of August 19,
1994, and continued on August 15, 1995, I, WILLIAM J. CLINTON,
President of the United States of America, find that it is
necessary for the procedures set forth below to apply to export
license applications submitted under the Act and the Export
Administration Regulations (15 C.F.R. Part 730 et. seq.) ("the
Regulations") or under any renewal of, or successor to, the Export
Administration Act of 1979, as amended (50 U.S.C. App. 2401
et. seq.) ("the Export Administration Act"), and the Regulations.
Accordingly, it is hereby ordered as follows:

Section 1. License Review. To the extent permitted by
law and consistent with Executive Order No. 12924 of August 19,
1994, the power, authority, and discretion conferred upon the
Secretary of Commerce ("the Secretary") under the Export
Administration Act to require, review, and make final
determinations with regard to export licenses, documentation, and
other forms of information submitted to the Department of Commerce
pursuant to the Act and the Regulations or under any renewal of,
or successor to, the Export Administration Act and the
Regulations, with the power of successive redelegation, shall
continue. The Departments of State, Defense, and Energy, and the
Arms Control and Disarmament Agency each shall have the authority
to review any export license application submitted to the
Department of Commerce pursuant to the Act and the Regulations or
under any renewal of, or successor to, the

Export Administration Act and the Regulations. The Secretary may refer license applications to other United States Government departments or agencies for review as appropriate. In the event that a department or agency determines that certain types of applications need not be referred to it, such department or agency shall notify the Department of Commerce as to the specific types of such applications that it does not wish to review. All departments or agencies shall promptly respond, on a case-by-case basis, to requests from other departments or agencies for historical information relating to past license applications.

Sec. 2. Determinations. (a) All license applications submitted under the Act and the Regulations or any renewal of, or successor to, the Export Administration Act and the Regulations, shall be resolved or referred to the President no later than 90 calendar days after registration of the completed license application.

(b) The following actions related to processing a license application submitted under the Act and the Regulations or any renewal of, or successor to, the Export Administration Act and the Regulations shall not be counted in calculating the time periods prescribed in this order:

(1) Agreement of the Applicant. Delays upon which the Secretary and the applicant mutually agree.

(2) Prelicense Checks. Prelicense checks through government channels that may be required to establish the identity and reliability of the recipient of items controlled under the Act and the Regulations or any renewal of, or successor to, the Export Administration Act and the Regulations, provided that:

(A) the need for such prelicense check is established by the Secretary, or by another department or agency if the request for prelicense check is made by such department or agency;

(B) the Secretary requests the prelicense check within 5 days of the determination that it is necessary; and

(C) the Secretary completes the analysis of the result of the prelicense check within 5 days.

(3) Requests for Government-To-Government Assurances.

Requests for government-to-government assurances of suitable end-use of items approved for export under the Act and the Regulations or any renewal of, or successor to, the Export Administration Act and the Regulations, when failure to obtain such assurances would result in rejection of the application, provided that:

      (A) the request for such assurances is sent to the Secretary of State within 5 days of the determination that the assurances are required;

      (B) the Secretary of State initiates the request of the relevant government within 10 days thereafter; and

      (C) the license is issued within 5 days of the Secretary's receipt of the requested assurances.
Whenever such prelicense checks and assurances are not requested within the time periods set forth above, they must be accomplished within the time periods established by this section.

      (4) Multilateral Reviews. Multilateral review of a license application as provided for under the Act and the Regulations or any renewal of, or successor to, the Export Administration Act and the Regulations, as long as multilateral review is required by the relevant multilateral regime.

      (5) Consultations. Consultation with other governments, if such consultation is provided for by a relevant multilateral regime or bilateral arrangement as a precondition for approving a license.

      Sec. 3. Initial Processing. Within 9 days of registration of any license application, the Secretary shall, as appropriate:

      (a) request additional information from the applicant. The time required for the applicant to supply the additional information shall not be counted in calculating the time periods prescribed in this section.

      (b) refer the application and pertinent information to agencies or departments as stipulated in section 1 of this order, and forward to the agencies any relevant information submitted by the applicant that could not be reduced to electronic form.

(c) assure that the stated classification on the application is correct; return the application if a license is not required; and, if referral to other departments or agencies is not required, grant the application or notify the applicant of the Secretary's intention to deny the application.

Sec. 4. Department or Agency Review. (a) Each reviewing department or agency shall specify to the Secretary, within 10 days of receipt of a referral as specified in subsection 3(b), any information not in the application that would be required to make a determination, and the Secretary shall promptly request such information from the applicant. If, after receipt of the information so specified or other new information, a reviewing department or agency concludes that additional information would be required to make a determination, it shall promptly specify that additional information to the Secretary, and the Secretary shall promptly request such information from the applicant. The time that may elapse between the date the information is requested by the reviewing department or agency and the date the information is received by the reviewing department or agency shall not be counted in calculating the time periods prescribed in this order. Such information specified by reviewing departments or agencies is in addition to any information that may be requested by the Department of Commerce on its own initiative during the first 9 days after registration of an application.

(b) Within 30 days of receipt of a referral and all required information, a department or agency shall provide the Secretary with a recommendation either to approve or deny the license application. As appropriate, such recommendation may be with the benefit of consultation and discussions in interagency groups established to provide expertise and coordinate interagency consultation. A recommendation that the Secretary deny a license shall include a statement of the reasons for such recommendation that are consistent with the provisions of the Act and the Regulations or any renewal of, or successor to, the Export Administration Act and the Regulations and shall cite both the statutory and the regulatory bases for the recommendation to deny. A department or agency that fails to provide a recommendation within 30 days with a statement of reasons and the statutory and regulatory bases shall be deemed to have no objection to the decision of the Secretary.

Sec. 5. Interagency Dispute Resolution. (a) Committees. (1)(A) Export Administration Review Board. The Export

Administration Review Board ("the Board"), which was established by Executive Order No. 11533 of June 4, 1970, and continued in Executive Order No. 12002 of July 7, 1977, is hereby continued. The Board shall have as its members, the Secretary, who shall be Chair of the Board, the Secretary of State, the Secretary of Defense, the Secretary of Energy, and the Director of the Arms Control and Disarmament Agency. The Chairman of the Joint Chiefs of Staff and the Director of Central Intelligence shall be nonvoting members of the Board. No alternate Board members shall be designated, but the acting head or deputy head of any member department or agency may serve in lieu of the head of the concerned department or agency. The Board may invite the heads of other United States Government departments or agencies, other than the departments or agencies represented by the Board members, to participate in the activities of the Board when matters of interest to such departments or agencies are under consideration.

(B) The Secretary may, from time to time, refer to the Board such particular export license matters, involving questions of national security or other major policy issues, as the Secretary shall select. The Secretary shall also refer to the Board any other such export license matter, upon the request of any other member of the Board or the head of any other United States Government department or agency having any interest in such matter. The Board shall consider the matters so referred to it, giving due consideration to the foreign policy of the United States, the national security, the domestic economy, and concerns about the proliferation of armaments, weapons of mass destruction, missile delivery systems, and advanced conventional weapons and shall make recommendations thereon to the Secretary.

(2) Advisory Committee on Export Policy. An Advisory Committee on Export Policy ("ACEP") is established and shall have as its members the Assistant Secretary of Commerce for Export Administration, who shall be Chair of the ACEP, and Assistant Secretary-level representatives of the Departments of State, Defense, and Energy, and the Arms Control and Disarmament Agency. Appropriate representatives of the Joint Chiefs of Staff and of the Nonproliferation Center of the Central Intelligence Agency shall be nonvoting members of the ACEP. Representatives of the departments or agencies shall be the appropriate Assistant Secretary or equivalent (or appropriate acting Assistant Secretary or equivalent in lieu of the Assistant Secretary or equivalent) of the concerned department or agency, or appropriate Deputy Assistant Secretary or equivalent (or the appropriate acting

Deputy Assistant Secretary or equivalent in lieu of the Deputy Assistant Secretary or equivalent) of the concerned department or agency. Regardless of the department or agency representative's rank, such representative shall speak and vote at the ACEP on behalf of the appropriate Assistant Secretary or equivalent of such department or agency. The ACEP may invite Assistant Secretary-level representatives of other United States Government departments or agencies, other than the departments and agencies represented by the ACEP members, to participate in the activities of the ACEP when matters of interest to such departments or agencies are under consideration.

(3)(A) Operating Committee. An Operating Committee ("OC") of the ACEP is established. The Secretary shall appoint its Chair, who shall also serve as Executive Secretary of the ACEP. Its other members shall be representatives of appropriate agencies in the Departments of Commerce, State, Defense, and Energy, and the Arms Control and Disarmament Agency. The appropriate representatives of the Joint Chiefs of Staff and the Nonproliferation Center of the Central Intelligence Agency shall be nonvoting members of the OC. The OC may invite representatives of other United States Government departments or agencies, other than the departments and agencies represented by the OC members, to participate in the activities of the OC when matters of interest to such departments or agencies are under consideration.

(B) The OC shall review all license applications on which the reviewing departments and agencies are not in agreement. The Chair of the OC shall consider the recommendations of the reviewing departments and agencies and inform them of his or her decision on any such matters within 14 days after the deadline for receiving department and agency recommendations. As described below, any reviewing department or agency may appeal the decision of the Chair of the OC to the Chair of the ACEP. In the absence of a timely appeal, the Chair's decision will be final.

(b) Resolution Procedures. (1) If any department or agency disagrees with a licensing determination of the Department of Commerce made through the OC, it may appeal the matter to the ACEP for resolution. A department or agency must appeal a matter within 5 days of such a decision. Appeals must be in writing from an official appointed by the President by and with the advice and consent of the Senate, or an officer properly acting in such capacity, and must cite both the statutory and the regulatory bases for the appeal. The ACEP shall review all departments' and agencies' information and recommendations, and the Chair of the ACEP shall inform the reviewing departments and agencies of the majority vote decision of the ACEP within 11 days from the date of receiving notice of the appeal. Within 5 days of the majority vote decision, any dissenting department or agency may appeal the decision by submitting a letter from the head of the department or agency to the Secretary in his or her capacity as the Chair of the Board. Such letter shall cite both the statutory and the regulatory bases for the appeal. Within the same period of time, the Secretary may call a meeting on his or her own initiative to consider a license application. In the absence of a timely appeal, the majority vote decision of the ACEP shall be final.

(2) The Board shall review all departments' and agencies' information and recommendations, and such other export control matters as may be appropriate. The Secretary shall inform the reviewing departments and agencies of the majority vote of the Board within 11 days from the date of receiving notice of appeal. Within 5 days of the decision, any department or agency dissenting from the majority vote decision of the Board may appeal the decision by submitting a letter from the head of the dissenting department or agency to the President. In the absence of a timely appeal, the majority vote decision of the Board shall be final.

Sec. 6. The license review process in this order shall take effect beginning with those license applications registered by the Secretary 60 days after the date of this order and shall continue in effect to the extent not inconsistent with any renewal of the Export Administration Act, or with any successor to that Act.

Sec. 7. Judicial Review. This order is intended only to improve the internal management of the executive branch and is not intended to, and does not, create any rights to administrative or judicial review, or any other right or benefit or trust responsibility, substantive or procedural, enforceable by a party against the United States, its agencies or instrumentalities, its officers or employees, or any other person.

WILLIAM J. CLINTON

THE WHITE HOUSE,
   December 5, 1995.

# # #

Acharya, Amitav, "Why the Rush in Arms Upgrading in Southeast Asia?" *Asian Defence Journal,* April 1994, pp. 27–30.

Adams, Gordon, and David Gold, *Defense Spending and the Economy: Does the Defense Dollar Make A Difference?* Defense Budget Project, Washington, DC, July 1987.

Anoushiravan Ehteshami, "Iran Boosts Domestic Arms Industry," *International Defense Review,* April 1994, pp. 72–73.

Anthony, Ian (ed.), *Arms Export Regulations,* Oxford University Press, Oxford, 1991.

Arms Control Reporter, Institute for Defense and Disarmament Studies, Cambridge, Massachusetts, 1992 and 1995.

Arms Exports Cost Jobs, National Commission for Economic Conversion and Disarmament, Washington, DC, 26 January 1994.

"Arms Exports Damage U.S. Economy," *Defense News,* 15 November 1993.

"Arms Sales: Boom," *Economist,* Vol. 332, No. 7876, 13 August 1994, pp. 24–28.

Arms Sales Monitor, Federation of American Scientists, Washington, DC, 1991–1995.

"Arms Transfers and Economic Competitiveness," Draft, Business Executives for National Security, Washington, DC, 6 July 1994.

Axelrod, Seth J., *U.S. Legislation, Regulations and Executive Orders Pertaining to Nonproliferation Treaties and Regimes,* RAND, PM-478-OSD, Santa Monica, California, October 1995.

Banks, Howard, "Aerospace and Defense," *Forbes,* Vol. 15, No. 1, 4 January 1993, pp. 95–97.

BASIC, *Chronicling an Absence of Restraint: The 1995 UN Arms Register,* British-American Security Information Council Occasional Paper #13, Washington, DC, November 3, 1995.

Beaver, Paul, "Gulf Markets: China's Rich Harvest," *Jane's Defence Weekly,* 13 February 1993, p. 48.

Bischak, Gregory, *Arms Trade and Jobs*, National Commission for Economic Conversion and Disarmament, Washington, DC, April 1995.

Bischak, Gregory, "Do U.S. Arms Transfers Enhance Economic and Military Security?" National Commission for Economic Conversion and Disarmament, Washington, DC, 1993.

Bitzinger, Richard, "The Globalization of the Arms Industry: The Next Proliferation Challenge," *International Security*, Vol. 19, No. 2, Fall 1994, pp. 170–198.

Blank, Stephen, "Russia Arms Exports and Asia," *Asian Defence Journal*, March 1994, pp. 72–79.

Borrus, Amy, Stewart Toy, and Eric Schine, "Meet Bill Clinton, Arms Merchant," *Business Week*, 28 June 1993, p. 32.

Braybrook, Roy, "South Africa Back in Business at Farnborough," *Asia-Pacific Defence Reporter*, October–November 1994, pp. 34–35.

British-American Security Information Council, *A European Code of Conduct on the Arms Trade*, Washington, DC, May 1995.

Brower, Kenneth, "North Korean Proliferation—The Threat to the New World Order," *Jane's Intelligence Review*, August 1994, pp. 376–380.

Bruce, James, "A New Arms Race in the Gulf," *Jane's Intelligence Review*, October 1995, pp. 37–39.

Buissiere, Robert, "A Europe of Security and Defense," *NATO Review*, No. 5, Vol. 43, September 1995, pp. 31–35.

Cappaccio, Tony, "Arms Makers Fret Over Next Saudi Sale," *Defense Week*, Vol. 11, No. 51, 12 December 1990.

Chalmers, Malcolm, Owen Greene, Edward J. Laurance, and Herbert Wolf (eds.), *Developing the UN Register of Conventional Arms*, University of Bradford, United Kingdom, 1994.

Chalmers, Malcolm, and Owen Greene, *The UN Register of Conventional Arms: Examining the Third Report*, University of Bradford, United Kingdom, November 1995.

Cobb, Tyrus W., "Arms Transfers and Economic Competitiveness," Business Executives for National Security, draft paper, July 6, 1994.

Cole, Jeff, and Sarah Lubman, "Going Great Guns in Post–Cold War Era," *Wall St. Journal*, 28 January 1993, p. A1.

Communiqué Issued Following the Meeting of the Five on Arms Transfers and Non-Proliferation, Department of State, July 9, 1991.

Communiqué Issued Following the Meeting of the Five: Guidelines for Conventional Arms Transfers, Department of State, October 18, 1991.

Confidence-Building in the Middle East: Regional Developments, The Henry L. Stimson Center, Washington, DC, 5 October 1995.

Congressional Budget Office, *Limiting Conventional Arms Exports to the Middle East*, Congressional Budget Office, Washington, DC, September 1992.

Congressional Presentation for Promoting Peace, prepared by the Department of State and the Department of Defense, FY 1995.

Congressional Presentation, *Foreign Operations, FY 1996*, Department of State, Washington, DC, 1995.

Congressional Research Service, *Changing Perspectives on U.S. Arms Transfer Policy*, Appendix II, Washington, DC, September 25, 1981,.

Covault, Craig, "New French Missiles Expand Attack Options," *Aviation Week & Space Technology*, January 9, 1995, pp. 44–45.

Craddock, Ashley, "U.S. Arms," *Mother Jones*, Vol. 19, No. 5, September 1995, pp. 41–48.

Deagon, Brian, "Why Tech Export Curbs May Be a Futile Exercise," *Investor's Business Daily*, 23 October 1995, p. A8.

Deltac Limited and Saferworld, *Proliferation and Export Controls: An Analysis of Sensitive Technologies and Countries of Concern*, Doveton Press, Great Britain, 1995.

"Denel Today and Tomorrow," *Military Technology*, February 1995, pp. 50-59.

Dhiravegin, Likhit, "The Multilateralisation of Pacific-Asia: Rethinking the ARF," *Asian Defence Journal*, November 1994, pp. 42–47.

Director of Naval Intelligence, *Posture Statement*, 1994.

Export Administration Act of 1969, United States Code, *Congressional and Administrative News*, 91st Congress, First Session, 1969, Vol. 1, *Laws, Legislative History*, West Publishing Company, St. Paul, Minnesota, pp. 937–944.

Export Administration Act of 1969, United States Code, *Congressional and Administrative News*, 91st Congress, First Session, 1969, Vol. 2, *Legislative History, Proclamations, Executive Orders, Reorganization Plans, Tables and Index*, West Publishing Company, St. Paul, Minnesota, pp. 2705–2722.

Export Administration Act of 1979, United States Code, *Congressional and Administrative News*, 96th Congress, First Session, 1979, Vol. 1, *Legislative History*, West Publishing Company, St. Paul, Minnesota, pp. 93 STAT. 503–93 STAT. 536.

Export Administration Act of 1979, United States Code, *Congressional and Administrative News*, 96th Congress, First Session, 1979, Vol. 2, *Legislative History*, West Publishing Company, St. Paul, Minnesota, pp. 1147–1197.

Export Administration Act of 1994, Final Draft: Administration Proposal, February 2, 1994.

Export Administration Regulations, Parts 730–772, Proposed Rule, United States Department of Commerce, Bureau of Export Administration, April 11, 1995.

Export Controls, Concerns Over Stealth-Related Exports, Report to the Chairman, Subcommittee on Acquisition and Technology, Committee on Armed Services, U.S. Senate, United States General Accounting Office, GAO/NSAID-95-140, May 1995.

Export Controls, Some Controls Over Missile-Related Technology Exports to China Are Weak, Report to the Chairman, Committee on International Relations, House of Representatives, United States General Accounting Office, GAO/NSAID-95-82, April 1995.

Federal Document Clearing House, Inc., Congressional Testimony by Lynn E. Davis, Under Secretary of State, "Appropriations Foreign Operations Arms Transfer Policy," May 23, 1995.

Federal Document Clearing House, Inc., Congressional Testimony by Mitchel B. Wallerstein, Deputy Assistant Secretary of Defense, "Foreign Operations Arms Transfer Policy," May 23, 1995.

Federal Information Systems Corporation, Hearing of Senate Governmental Affairs Committee and the Permanent Subcommittee on Investigations, "Chemical and Biological Weapons," February 9, 1989.

Federal Information Systems Corporation, Hearing of Senate Governmental Affairs Committee and the Permanent Subcommittee on Investigations, "Chemical and Biological Weapons," February 10, 1989.

Federal Information Systems Corporation, Hearing of Senate Governmental Affairs Committee and the Permanent Subcommittee on Investigations, "Nuclear Proliferation," May 2, 1989.

Federal Information Systems Corporation, Hearing of the Senate Governmental Affairs Committee, "Chemical Biological Materials," May 18, 1989.

Federal Information Systems Corporation, Remarks of John D. Holum, U.S. Arms Control and Disarmament Agency, July 1995.

Feinstein, Lee, "Bush Unveils Long-Awaited Middle Eastern Arms Control Plan," *Arms Control Today*, June 1991, pp. 27–28.

Feldstein, M., and C. Horioka, "Domestic Savings and International Capital Flows," *Economic Journal*, June 1980.

Fisher, Scotty, "Country Briefing: Israel," *Jane's Defence Weekly*, 18 February 1995, pp. 29–38.

Flamm, Don, "U.S. Conventional Arms Transfers: Rhetoric and Reality," *Asian Defence Journal*, May 1994, pp. 33–39.

Foss, Christopher F. (ed.), *Jane's Armour and Artillery 1994–95*, Janes' Information Group, Alexandria, Virginia, 1994.

Fulghum, David A., "Army Pushes Missiles for UAV Use," *Aviation Week & Space Technology*, August 28, 1995, p. 23.

Fulghum, David A., "International Market Eyes Endurance UAVs," *Aviation Week & Space Technology*, July 10, 1995, pp. 40–42.

Gaddy, Clifford G., and Melanie L. Allen, *Russian Arms Sales Abroad: Policy, Practice, and Prospects*, The Brookings Institution, Washington, DC, September 1993.

Gaffney, Henry H., Jr., *Worldwide Defense Expenditures (excluding the United States)*, Center for Naval Analyses, Alexandria, Virginia, June 1995.

Glashow, John, and Theresa Hitchens, "Thailand to Get AMRAAMs in F/A-18 Fighter Package," *Defense News*, 8–14 January 1996.

Global Arms Trade, "Commerce in Advanced Military Technology and Weapons," Congress of the United States, Office of Technology Assessment, June 1991.

Goldring, Natalie, "Arms Control or Arms Out of Control: Trends in Arms Sales After the Cold War," in Elizabeth J. Kirk, W. Thomas Wander, and Brian D. Smith (eds.), *Trends and Implications for Arms Control, Proliferation and International Security in the Changing Global Environment*, American Association for the Advancement of Science, Washington, DC, 1993.

Goldring, Natalie J., "Toward Restraint: Controlling the International Arms Trade," *Harvard International Review*, Vol. XVII, No. 1, Winter 1994/95.

Gormley, Dennis M., *French Land-Attack Cruise Missiles: Objectives, Programs, and Prospects*, Pacific-Sierra Research Corporation, Washington, DC, May 1995.

Gormley, Dennis M., and K. Scott McMahon, "Land-Attack Cruise Missile Proliferation: Prospects and Policy Implications," prepared for *Fighting Proliferation: New Concerns for the '90s*, Air University Press (forthcoming), draft dated August 1995.

Gormley, Dennis M., and K. Scott McMahon, *Controlling the Spread of Land-Attack Cruise Missiles*, AISC Paper Number 7, American Institute for Strategic Cooperation, Marina del Rey, California, January 1995.

Government Accounting Office, *Military Exports: A Comparison of Government Support in the United States and Three Major Competitors*, Washington, DC, May 1995.

Government Printing Office, *Economic Report of the President*, February 1995.

Grimmett, Richard, *Conventional Arms Transfers to Developing Nations, 1987–1994*, Congressional Research Service, Washington, DC, August 4, 1995.

Harrison, Glennon J., *Export Controls: Background and Issues,* CRS Report for Congress 94-30E, Congressional Research Service, Library of Congress, Washington, DC, 12 January 1994.

Harshberger, E. R., *Long Range Conventional Missiles: Issues for Near-Term Development,* RAND, N-3328-RGSD, Santa Monica, California, 1991.

Hartung, William D., *Conventional Arms Proliferation: Rethinking U.S. Policy,* Business Executives for National Security, December 1993.

Hartung, William D., "Hidden Costs of Arms Sales: briefing paper," Peace Action Education Fund, Washington, DC, February 1994.

Hartung, William D., "Reforming the Arms Transfer Decisionmaking Process: Coming in from the Cold War," testimony to Hearings on Conventional Arms Transfer Policy, Washington, DC, May 23, 1995.

Harvey, John, et al., *A Common-Sense Approach to High-Technology Export Controls,* Center for International Security and Arms Control, Stanford, California, March 1995.

Helmoed, Romer Heitmann, "South Africa's Arsenal," *Military Technology,* November 1994, pp. 10–32.

Hitchens, Theresa, "Thais Use AMRAAM as U.S. Fighter Buy Lever," *Defense News,* September 4–10, 1995.

Hove, Captain Richard Andres, and Captain Eric John von Tersch, *CoCom and the Future of Conventional Arms Exports in the Former Communist Bloc,* Defense Technical Information Center, Fort Belvoir, Virginia, December 1993.

"Inhumane Weapons Convention," *Arms Control Reporter,* Institute for Defense and Disarmament Studies, Cambridge, Massachusetts, October 1995, pp. 860-3.1–860-3.7.

Institute for Foreign Policy Analysis, Inc., *Old Challenges in a New Era: Addressing America's Cold War Legacy,* Cambridge, Massachusetts, January 1995.

International Security Assistance and Arms Export Control Act of 1976, United States Code, *Congressional and Administrative News,* 94th Congress, Second Session, 1976, Vol. 1, West Publishing Company, St. Paul, Minnesota, pp. 90 STAT. 729–90 STAT. 769.

International Security Assistance and Arms Export Control Act of 1976, United States Code, *Congressional and Administrative News,* 94th Congress, Second Session, 1976, Vol. 3, *Legislative History,* West Publishing Company, St. Paul, Minnesota, pp. 1378–1454.

International Traffic in Arms Regulations (ITAR), 22 CFR 120-130, OCR International, Inc., Rockville, Maryland, July 22, 1993.

Johnson, Joel, "Conventional Arms Transfer Policy: An Industry Perspective," *Military Technology*, Vol. 18, No. 2, February 1994, pp. 30–33.

Johnson, Joel, "In Search of a Sensible Arms Transfer Policy," *Military Technology*, Vol. 15, No. 10, October 1991, pp. 12–14.

Johnson, Joel, Testimony Before the Committee on Foreign Affairs, Subcommittees on International Security and International Relations, 103rd Congress, First Session, 9 November 1993, U.S. Government Printing Office, Washington, DC, 1994.

Karp, Aaron, "The Demise of the Middle East Arms Race," *Washington Quarterly*, Vol. 18, No. 4, Autumn 1995, pp. 29–51.

Kemp, Geoffrey, *The Control of The Middle East Arms Race*, Carnegie Endowment for International Peace, 1991.

Kemp, Geoffrey, *The Elements for Middle East Arms Control*, Carnegie Endowment for International Peace, Washington, DC, May–June 1995.

Khripunov, Igor, "Russia's Arms Trade in the Post–Cold War Period," *Washington Quarterly*, Vol. 17, No. 4, Autumn 1994, pp. 79–94.

Kuzion, Taras, "Ukraine's Military Industrial Plan," *Jane's Intelligence Review*, August 1994, pp. 352–355.

Leahy, Patrick, "The CCW Review Conference: An Opportunity for U.S. Leadership," *Arms Control Today*, September 1995, pp. 20–24.

Lewin, David, "A Victim of the End of the Cold War," *Mechanical Engineering*, Vol. 116, No. 7, July 1994, p. 36.

Lewis, J.A.C., "Gulf Markets: Middle Eastern Promise," *Jane's Defence Weekly*, 13 February 1993, pp. 43–44.

Lewis, Peter, "Privacy for Computers? Clinton Sets the Stage for a Debate on Data Encryption," *New York Times*, 11 September 1995, p. D7.

Lodgaard, Sverre, "Global Security and Disarmament: Regional Approaches," *Bulletin of Peace Proposals*, Vol. 22, No. 4, Fall 1991, pp. 377–386.

Lorell, Mark A., *Troubled Partnership: A History of U.S.-Japan Collaboration on the FS-X Fighter*, RAND, MR-612/2-AF, Santa Monica, California, 1995.

Lorell, Mark A., *Troubled Partnership: An Assessment of U.S.-Japan Collaboration on the FS-X Fighter*, RAND, MR-612/1-AF, Santa Monica, California, 1995.

Lorell, Mark, and Julia Lowell, *Pros and Cons of International Weapons Procurement Collaboration*, RAND, MR-565-OSD, Santa Monica, California, 1995.

Louscher, David, William Bajusz, J. Kaplan, and S. Rippeth, *The Domestic Impact of the Prospective Sale of Selected Military Equipment to Saudi Arabia*, Science

Applications International Corporation (prepared for the American League for Exports and Security Assistance), Arlington, Virginia, 8 February 1991.

Lumpe, Lora, "Sweet Deals, Stolen Jobs," *The Bulletin of the Atomic Scientists*, September/October 1994, pp. 30–35.

McNamara, Thomas E., Assistant Secretary of State for Political-Military Affairs, *Statement before the Subcommittee on International Finance and Monetary Policy of the Senate Banking, Housing, and Urban Affairs Committee*, Washington, DC, September 21, 1995.

Mann, Paul, "Washington Outlook," *Aviation Week and Space Technology*, July 10, 1995, p. 21.

Markusen, Ann, and Joel Yudken, *Dismantling the Cold War Economy*, Basic Books, New York, 1992.

Martov, Andrei, "Russia's Asian Sales Onslaught," *International Defense Review*, May 1994, pp. 49–54.

Marvel, K. Barry, "International Offsets: An International Trade Development Tool," *Contract Management*, October 1995.

Military Balance, 1994–95, 1995–96, International Institute for Strategic Studies, London.

MITRE, *Defense Trade Influences on U.S. National/Economic Security*, for Presidential Advisory Board on Arms Proliferation Policy, Washington, DC, May 16, 1995.

Moodie, Michael, "Constraining Conventional Arms Transfers," *Annals of the American Academy of Political and Social Science*, 535, September 1994, pp. 131–145.

Moskowitz, Daniel, "How Far To Loosen Export Controls," *International Business*, Vol. 7, No. 4, April 1994, p. 78.

National Academy of Sciences, Committee on Science, Engineering, and Public Policy, *Finding Common Ground: U.S. Export Controls in a Changed Global Environment*, National Academy Press, Washington, DC, 1991.

National Research Council, Board on Army Science and Technology, Commission on Engineering and Technical Systems, *STAR 21: Strategic Technologies for the Army of the Twenty-First Century*, National Academy Press, Washington, DC, 1992.

National Security Planning Associates and Institute for Foreign Policy Analysis, *Defense Conversion and Arms Transfers: The Legacy of the Soviet-Era Arms Industry*, Washington, DC, and Cambridge, Massachusetts, June 1993.

National Security Planning Associates, *UN Transparency in Armaments: A Current Assessment & Future Prospects*, prepared for the Defense Nuclear Agency, January 1995.

National Security Science and Technology Strategy, Executive Office of the President, Office of Science and Technology Policy, Washington, DC, 1995. Also available over the World Wide Web, URL: http://www.whitehouse.gov/White_House/ EOP/OSTP/nssts/html/nssts.html

1991 Annual Report, McDonnell Douglas, St. Louis, Missouri, 19 February 1992.

Nolan, Janne E., *Trappings of Power: Ballistic Missiles in the Third World*, The Brookings Institution, Washington, DC, 1991.

Office of the Deputy Secretary of Defense, *Report on Nonproliferation and Counterproliferation Activities and Program*, Washington, DC, May 1994.

Offices of Inspector General, and the U.S. Departments of Commerce, Defense, Energy, and State, *The Federal Government's Export Licensing Processes for Munitions and Dual-Use Commodities*, Special Interagency Review, Final Report, September 1993.

O'Prey, Kevin P., *The Arms Export Challenge: Cooperative Approaches to Export Management and Defense Conversion*, The Brookings Institution, Washington, DC, 1995.

Pace, Scott, G. P. Frost, I. Lachow, D. R. Frelinger, D. Fossum, D. Wassem, and M. M. Pinto, *Assessing National Policies for the Global Positioning System*, RAND, MR-614-OSTP, 1995.

Pages, Erik R., and Tyrus W. Cobb, *Industrial Policy Ascendant: The Rise of Economic Security and Its Impact on American Defense Priorities*, Business Executives for National Security, Washington, DC, September 1994.

Panel on the Future Design and Implementation of U.S. National Security Export Controls, pp. 336–348.

Pierre, Andrew J., "Conventional Arms Proliferation Today: Changed Dimensions, New Responses," in Elizabeth J. Kirk, W. Thomas Wander, and Brian D. Smith (eds.), *Trends and Implications for Arms Control, Proliferation and International Security in the Changing Global Environment*, American Association for the Advancement of Science, Washington, DC , 1993.

Powell, Stewart M., "A Forecast of the Arms Trade," *Air Force Magazine*, September 1995, pp. 76–80.

Press, Eyal, "Arms Sales and False Economics," *Nation*, Vol. 259, No. 10, pp. 340–344.

Protsenko, Aleksandr, "How It Is Done: Weapons Abroad," *Obshchaya Gazeta*, 6–12 July 1995.

"Recover the Full Cost of Military Exports," *Reducing the Deficit: Spending and Revenue Options*, Congressional Budget Office, Washington, DC, February 1995, pp. 86–87.

Reed, Carol, "Russia Sharpens Its Export Skills," *Jane's Defence Weekly,* 9 July 1994, pp. 28–29.

Reinicke, Wolfgang H., "Cooperative Security and the Political Economy of Nonproliferation," in Janne E. Nolan (ed.), *Global Engagement, Cooperation and Security in the 21st Century,* The Brookings Institution, Washington, DC, 1994, pp. 175–234.

Reinicke, Wolfgang H., "From Denial to Disclosure: The Political Economy of Export Controls and Technology Transfer," in Francine R. Frankel (ed.), *Bridging the Nonproliferation Divide, The United States and India,* University Press of America, Lanham, Maryland, 1995, pp. 269–285.

Renner, Michael, "Monitoring Arms Trade," *World Watch,* Vol. 7, No. 3, May 1994, pp. 21–26.

Revelle, Daniel J., and Lora Lumpe, "Third World Submarines," *Scientific American,* August 1994, pp. 16–21.

Richards, Peter, "Disarmament and Employment," *Defense Economics,* Vol. 2, 1991, pp. 295–311.

Schneider, William Jr., "A Role for Defense Export Credit Financing of U.S. Exports in U.S. Conventional Arms Transfer Policy," presented to President's Advisory Board on Arms Proliferation Policy by the Chairman, Defense Trade Advisory Group, Bureau of Political Military Affairs, U.S. Department of State, Washington, DC, May 9, 1995.

Schoeni, Robert F., Michael Dardia, Kevin F. McCarthy, and Georges Vernez, *Life After Cutbacks: Tracking California's Aerospace Workers,* RAND, MR-688-OSD, 1996.

Sharpe, Captain Richard (ed.), *Jane's Fighting Ships 1995–96,* Jane's Information Group, Alexandria, Virginia, 1995.

"Singapore Defence Industries: Moving Ahead in a Tough Market," *Asian Defence Journal,* December 1994, pp. 62–68.

Steinberg, Gerald, "Middle East Arms Control and Regional Security," *Survival,* Spring 1994, pp. 126–141.

The Henry L. Stimson Center, "Confidence-Building in the Southern Cone: Regional Developments," Washington, DC, 11 December 1995.

The White House, *Conventional Arms Transfer Policy Fact Sheet,* February 1995.

Thompson, Mark, "Going Up, Up in Arms," *Time,* Vol. 144, No. 24, 12 December 1994, pp. 46–57.

Turner, Richard T., *Sustaining the Nation's Aerospace Technology—The Currency of Collaboration,* 1995 Handley Page Lecture, The Royal Aeronautical Society, 27 April 1995.

U.S. Arms Control and Disarmament Agency, *Report to Congress 1994: Threat Control Through Arms Control*, U.S. GPO, Washington, DC, pp. 40–47.

U.S. Arms Control and Disarmament Agency, *World Military Expenditures and Arms Transfers*, U.S. GPO, Washington, DC, various issues.

U.S. Arms Exports and Defense Industry Transition: Backgrounder, Defense Budget Project, Washington, DC, 3 May 1993.

U.S. Congress, Office of Technology Assessment, *Global Arms Trade*, OTA-ISC-460, U.S. GPO, Washington, DC, June 1991.

U.S. Departments of Commerce, Defense, Energy, and State, *The Federal Government's Export Licensing Processes for Munitions and Dual-Use Commodities, Final Report*, September 1993.

U.S. Department of Commerce, *Survey of Current Business*, various issues, 1995.

U.S. Department of Commerce, Bureau of Export Administration, *The New Export Administration*, Washington, DC, October 1994.

U.S. Department of Defense, Office of the Under Secretary of Defense (Acquisition and Technology), *World-Wide Conventional Arms Trade (1994–2000): A Forecast and Analysis*, Department of Defense, Washington, DC, December 1994.

U.S. Department of Defense, Inspector General, *Defense Industrial Base Policies and Procedures: Inspection Report*, 95-INS-08, June 1995.

U.S. Department of Defense, Office of the Under Secretary of Defense (Comptroller), *National Defense Budget Estimates—FY 1996*, March 1995.

U.S. Department of Defense, Security Assistance Agency, *Foreign Military Sales, Foreign Military Construction Sales and Military Assistance Facts*, September 1994.

U.S. Executive Office of the President, Office of Science and Technology Policy, *National Security Science and Technology Strategy*, Washington, DC, 1995.

U.S. Joint Chiefs of Staff, *National Military Strategy of the United States of America*, Washington, DC, 1995.

United States General Accounting Office, *Export Controls, Concerns Over Stealth-Related Exports*, GAO/NSIAD-95-140, May 1995.

United States General Accounting Office, *Export Controls, Some Controls Over Missile-Related Technology Exports To China Are Weak*, GAO/NSAID-95-82, April 1995.

United States General Accounting Office, *Military Exports: A Comparison of Government Support in the United States and Three Major Competitors*, GAO/NSIAD-95-86, May 1995.

United States General Accounting Office, *Military Exports: Recovery of Nonrecurring Research and Development Costs*, GAO/NSIAD-95-147, May 1995.

United States General Accounting Office, *Nuclear Nonproliferation, Export Licensing Procedures for Dual-Use Items Need to Be Strengthened*, GSAO/NSIAD-94-119, April 1994.

United States, The White House, Office of the Press Secretary, *Conventional Arms Transfer Policy Fact Sheet*, January 1995.

United States Code, Title 22, various chapters.

Utgoff, Victor A., et al., *Changing Face of Conventional Arms Control*, Defense Technical Information Center, January 1994.

Wallerstein, Mitchel B., with William W. Snyder, Jr., "Appendix G: The Evolution of U.S. Export Control Policy: 1949–1989," in National Academy of Sciences, *Finding Common Ground: U.S. Export Controls in a Changed Global Environment*, National Academy Press, Washington, DC, 1991.

Watman, Kenneth, Marcy Agmon, and Charles Wolf, Jr., *Controlling Conventional Arms Transfers: A New Approach with Application to the Persian Gulf*, RAND, MR-369-USDP, Santa Monica, California, 1994.

White House Fact Sheet, *Middle East Arms Control Initiative*, 29 May 1991.

Wolf, Charles Jr., K. C. Yeh, Anil Bamezai, Donald Henry, and Michael Kennedy, *Long-Term Economic and Military Trends, 1994–2015: The United States and Asia*, RAND, MR-627-OSD, Santa Monica, California, 1994.

Wood, Suzanne, Martin F. Wiskoff, and Callie J. Chandler, *Illegal Technology Transfer: Patterns of U.S. Export Control Violations 1981–1993*, Vol. II, Defense Technical Information Center, Fort Belvoir, Virginia, October 1994.

Wright, LTC W. Richard, *U.S. Conventional Arms Transfer Policy*, Defense Technical Information Center, March 1993.

Report of the
Presidential Advisory Board on Arms Proliferation Policy

Dr. Janne E. Nolan, Chair

Edward Randolph Jayne II

Ronald F. Lehman

David E. McGiffert

Paul C. Warnke

This report was created by the President's Advisory Board on Arms Proliferation. The RAND monograph, *Arms Proliferation Policy: Support to the Presidential Advisory Board* (MR-771), a companion study, is available from RAND, 1700 Main St., Santa Monica, CA 90407.

Report of the

Presidential
Advisory Board on
Arms Proliferation
Policy

Dr. Janne E. Nolan, Chair

Edward Randolph Jayne II

Ronald F. Lehman

David E. McGiffert

Paul C. Warnke

Title XVI, Section 1601 of the National Defense Authorization Act for Fiscal Year 1994 mandated the creation of the President's Advisory Board on Arms Proliferation Policy to conduct a study of (1) the factors that contribute to the proliferation of strategic and advanced conventional military weapons and related equipment and technologies, and (2) the policy options that are available to the United States to inhibit such proliferation. The five-member Board was established by Executive Order 12946 on January 20, 1995,[1] and tasked to advise the President on implementation of United States conventional arms transfer policy, other issues related to arms proliferation policy, and other matters deemed appropriate by the President. Areas specified for study in the Board's Terms of Reference include trends in the international arms market, instruments of restraint, export financing facilities, and the relationship between arms exports and the defense industrial base.[2]

In its initial conception of the Board, Congress envisioned it as a participant in the development of the Clinton Administration's conventional arms transfer policy, which was finalized in February 1995 in a Presidential Decision Directive (PDD). In fact, the timing of the Board's appointment was such that this PDD had been released before the Board began its deliberations. The Board has accordingly undertaken both to examine the policy itself and to make recommendations on how to proceed with the next steps. Further, the Board offers recommendations for the government's administrative and policy processes.

The Board understands that conventional weapons transfer to friendly regimes can contribute to national security. And it understands that, particularly because militarily-useful technologies are increasingly commercial in origin, the vigor of our export economy can be limited by export controls. For both these reasons, it is incumbent on those concerned with controlling the transfer of conventional weapons and technologies not to overreact. On the other hand, unregulated proliferation of conventional arms and technologies—particularly in their more advanced forms and to

---

[1]Executive Order 12946 is appended to this document.

[2]See Marcy Agmon, James Bonomo, Michael Kennedy, Maren Leed, Kenneth Watman, Katharine Webb, and Charles Wolf, Jr., *Arms Proliferation Policy: Support to the Presidential Advisory Board*, Appendix B, MR-771-OSD, 1996, for texts of these documents.

pariah states—can drastically undermine regional stability and hence U.S. national security. It can promote arms races. By enhancing the capability of potential adversaries, it can increase the risk to U.S. military personnel in the event of war. Finally, conventional weapons can serve as delivery systems for weapons of mass destruction.

The Board has a healthy respect for the difficulties associated with establishing effective controls on conventional weapons. Our focus is on increasing security through control and risk reduction in the transfer of conventional weapons and technologies. The Board does not advocate a single approach or regime, but instead emphasizes the criticality of U.S. leadership, of genuine long-term policy commitment, and of an Executive Branch policy process that can accurately and efficiently execute current and future conventional arms control policies.

Further, given the long and complex legislative history of conventional arms control and the structure and functioning of the various organizations in the Executive Branch that are responsible for policy and administration in this area, the Board is convinced of the need for closer legislative-executive cooperation. The inherently transnational character of the arms market and the absence of consensus among governments regarding common policy objectives also make it clear that efforts to elicit other countries' support for new initiatives should be given the highest priority. Executive Branch initiative, with the backing of Congress, is essential to this task.

In fashioning its recommendations, the Board did not examine and does not propose changes in the substantive U.S. legislative standards that govern the export of weapons and related technologies. Furthermore, the Board has not attempted to go into detail regarding the structure of regimes for the control of technology and conventional arms, leaving that task to the National Security Council (NSC) policy process. There are several promising concepts presented here. Likewise, we have outlined a series of process improvements without trying to dictate technical solutions or assignments of lead responsibilities among the affected agencies. Again, we look to the NSC process to execute needed improvements.

In executing its mandate, the Board met frequently throughout 1995 and into 1996. Board members were ably assisted by two key groups. Within the government, the Defense Security Assistance Agency provided outstanding staff support, administrative skills, and coordination of the many meetings and presentations. We were supported in our detailed analytic efforts, and in our research for data and alternative policy and process approaches, by RAND. The RAND team worked closely with the Board to produce the companion study, MR-771-OSD, an effort that addresses many of the specific issues brought to us in the course of our deliberations. The Board commends the RAND analysis and findings to those interested in this topic.

The Board neither endorses nor rejects the detailed aspects of the RAND study. In key areas of both policy and process, however, the RAND approach is consistent with the Board's thinking, and we hope that the Administration and the Congress will pursue initiatives that reflect the spirit and thrust of these ideas, if not their detailed characteristics.

The Board appreciates the many presentations, discussions, and written materials provided to us by governmental and private organizations and interested individuals. Our recommendations reflect a genuine effort on our part to consider the range of issues and policy alternatives that were raised in these discussions.[2]

---

[2]See RAND's companion report, MR-771-OSD, for an outline of Board meetings, meeting participants and attendees, presentations to the Board, and other contributors.

CONTENTS

Chapter One

THE CONVENTIONAL WEAPONS CHALLENGE

Since the end of the cold war the constant dollar value of conventional weapons exported by the six major suppliers has dropped by more than half, mostly because of a sharp decline in exports from the former Soviet Union.[1] Accompanying this overall decline in exports, domestic arms procurement in supplier countries also has dropped precipitously, leaving excess weapons production capacity worldwide. As a result, economic pressures to export advanced weapons and technologies have increased, exacerbated by a growing interest in high-end weapons and technology stimulated in part by the Gulf War. At the same time, the Coordinating Committee on Multilateral Exports (CoCom) was disbanded. Although this left in place national laws controlling transfers, it meant that the only remaining formal international controls were limited to those on weapons of mass destruction and related missile technologies. The recently concluded Wassenaar Arrangement holds promise for restraining both conventional arms and weapons-related technology exports, but it is too early to judge its potential impact.

The control of conventional arms and technology exports has always been subordinate in priority to other forms of military trade regulation. The nuclear nonproliferation regime owes its genesis to the monopoly on nuclear capabilities maintained for many years by the five declared nuclear powers and is held together by a widespread consensus about the unique dangers of nuclear weapons. In the case of chemical and biological weapons, eliciting multinational support for a restraint regime is possible in large measure because of the less than compelling military utility of these weapons among the advanced powers and the opprobrium raised by the grave risks they pose to noncombatants.

The proliferation of conventional arms and technologies, by contrast, shares few of these attributes. The monopoly among a few suppliers for all but the most advanced armaments is already shattered, the dangers of proliferation are disputed by many, and the perceptions of utility tend to overwhelm any moral opprobrium. Conventional weapons transfers also have been seen as a benign alternative to nuclear proliferation and remain the most common instrument of dissuasion in efforts

---

[1]The value of former Soviet weaponry is based on the equivalent constant dollar value of comparable Western equipment. For further reading on how these calculations are made, see "Estimating and Interpreting Defence Economic Data," in *The Military Balance, 1994–1995*, International Institute for Strategic Studies, Brassey's, London, 1994, pp. 278–285. Also see the Board's discussion in Chapter Three of the need to consider estimates based on methods other than dollar-value comparisons.

to stop new states from acquiring nuclear weapons. The principal formal international conventional arms transfer restraint arrangement, the Missile Technology Control Regime (MTCR), restricts the sale of ballistic and cruise missiles, largely because of their association with nuclear, chemical, or biological weapons delivery.

The problem is made more difficult by the absence of internationally accepted criteria for determining what kinds of arms and technology exports are undesirable. It is impossible as a practical matter to classify most weapons and technologies as either offensive or defensive. A tank, for example, could be either, depending on the proclivities of the user. And while it may be possible at any given time to identify potential aggressors, today's peace-loving state may be tomorrow's pariah or *vice versa*.

The experience of the U.S.-led coalition war against Iraq indicates the dangers of a *laissez-faire* approach to the international trade in conventional arms and technologies. Western militaries confronted an Iraqi arsenal made up largely of weapons and technologies provided by the industrialized countries, prompting recognition that the political will to control the military technology trade was far too weak. Since then, however, the predominant focus of policy innovations has remained on nuclear, chemical, biological, and missile technologies. The real challenge yet to be addressed in the United States and other advanced countries is how to preserve superior conventional military capabilities and a healthy industrial base without a chronic dependency on exports of the kind that can accelerate diffusion of weapons and technology beyond what is prudent.

Bureaucratic inertia compounds the difficulty of meeting this challenge. The illumination of a new problem, or the assignment of urgent priority to an existing issue, is often greeted with less than enthusiasm by policymakers and bureaucrats. Aside from the crush of daily business in the Departments involved, today's budget constraints are unparalleled in recent decades. Nonetheless, the Board is strongly convinced that control of conventional arms and technology transfers must become a significantly more important and integral element of United States foreign and defense policy if the overall goals of nonproliferation are to succeed.

Among the many reasons for this conviction, five stand out. First, "conventional" weapons—i.e., those with destructive mechanisms that are not nuclear, chemical, or biological—have in some cases attained degrees of military effectiveness thought of in the past as associated only with nuclear weapons. Further, certain advanced systems can be used to deliver weapons of mass destruction.

Second, as the world's economies develop technologically, the current and potential future sources of advanced conventional weapons steadily expand beyond the handful of nations previously designing and building such systems. This changing and increasingly diffuse character of the international technology market further complicates the effective application of international controls.

The effects of this diffusion are diverse and profound. Supplier instruments, like the missile technology cartel, work only in proportion to the clout of the members and their relative monopoly on the products they are trying to control. Over thirty-five countries are able to export conventional weapons[2] (admittedly of widely varying levels of capability) and some suppliers have indicated they would not support a restraint regime until they have a more equal share of the arms market. In areas of weaponry where domestic procurement needs have fallen sharply, such as fighter aircraft and naval vessels, the consensus in favor of controls is even weaker.

The third reason stems from the sum of the economic stresses and discontinuities brought on by the fall of the former USSR and the Communist governments in key east European states, the decline in U.S. defense procurement budgets, and the downsizing of military force structures throughout the world. These events have caused both governments and their defense industrial base to become significantly more aggressive in trying to sell products abroad that they had previously bought for or sold to their own armed forces.

Fourth, trends in the technology market presage declining control by governments over the disposition of defense-related innovations. Critical technologies vital to defense, from supercomputers to biotechnologies to fiber optics, are increasingly commercial in origin. As developing countries establish their own weapon industries, they too become more capable of tapping into new sources of commercial and dual-use goods without reference to constraints imposed by larger powers. In the future, an ever-shrinking percentage of technology will be subject to direct government controls, testing the viability of supplier cartels or trade restrictions for all but a select number of the most advanced technologies.

Fifth, certain transfers may have a substantial adverse effect on American national security policy and on the security of U.S. personnel deployed overseas, especially if an American military presence is maintained in key regions such as Asia and the Persian Gulf. Heavily armed countries that are (or become) politically unstable could pose a direct threat to the security of deployed U.S. personnel or America's allies. In many contingencies, the proliferation of advanced weaponry could constrain U.S. policy options by making the human and material risks and costs associated with forward deployment prohibitively high.

In the face of the economic forces detailed above, alliances and individual nations that heretofore have been counted upon to take conservative and restrictive approaches to sales of state-of-the-art conventional weaponry today show much less, if any, inclination to do so. The demise of CoCom, with its structured and reasonably disciplined approach to the control of conventional arms and related technologies, left a major gap in the international coordination of national export control policies. An opportunity for filling this gap may lie in the new Wassenaar Arrangement on Export Controls for Conventional Arms and Dual-Use Goods and Technologies, discussed in the next chapter, but thus far agreements reached have fallen well short of U.S. goals.

---

[2]*World Military Expenditures and Arms Transfers, 1993–94*, U.S. Arms Control and Disarmament Agency, Washington, D.C., 1994.

Finally, we note that the challenge to restrain such proliferation includes the demand side of the equation. Desired levels of security cannot be achieved by supplier action alone. The dangers inherent in proliferation will not be eliminated in many parts of the world until changes occur in two key areas. First, the political nature of certain regimes in power must change. Second, responsible nations must improve security arrangements in their respective regions. A more comprehensive collective economic, political, military, and diplomatic strategy will be necessary to create the conditions for such change.

Chapter Two

NEGOTIATION OF AN INTERNATIONAL CONTROL REGIME

The Board believes that the first priority for the U.S. government is to continue, with a greater dedication of resources, to push for international consensus and control mechanisms to limit selected conventional weapons and technologies. The fundamental principles of national, international, and regional security, and arms control must be the basis for that consensus. U.S. leadership is essential; nothing will happen without it.

WHERE TO START

The Board believes that sustainable, multilateral progress on an issue as controversial as arms and technology exports will best be served by beginning with modest objectives that can be expanded over time. This suggests that any initiative should start with incremental or technical measures that are relatively noncontroversial in countries' domestic politics, and which might therefore gain early support. The idea is to minimize the political burden that initiatives would bear at the outset in order to develop the fundamental infrastructure—both domestic and international—that would permit the institutionalization of arms restraint. Given the novel nature of this kind of diplomacy, there is much to be learned even from technical discussions. Such dialogue can create the procedures and institutions which could in turn lead to success in more ambitious undertakings.

Discussions of technical issues—from global bans on potentially destabilizing weapons or technologies to tighter restrictions on clients' disposition of dual-use technologies received from the larger powers—need not be seen as either a substitute for, or a sacrifice of, the larger objective of developing more general codes of conduct. Making progress in areas that involve a minimum of controversy could lead to the development of agreed criteria for more far-reaching application.

The Wassenaar Arrangement appears to incorporate such an approach. Concluded in December 1995, the Arrangement is still a work in progress, and the outcome of future negotiations will determine its effectiveness. In its initial form, the Arrangement covers sales of both conventional arms and militarily-useful technologies, but relies on the policies of individual nations for enforcement. Transparency measures are expected to allow for cooperative efforts, as members share information on sales of military goods. Important U.S. objectives such as prior notification of transfers and more comprehensive data sharing, however, have not been accepted in the initial agreements.[1]   It is nevertheless the Board's view that the Arrangement represents a practical and potentially promising forum in which to address the dangers of proliferation of conventional weapons and related technologies.

CONTROL OF WEAPONS

Control of end items could focus on advanced conventional weapons and on especially repugnant weapons of lesser military utility. In many ways, the most threatening advanced conventional weapons are those that possess certain characteristics, including autonomous (fire-and-forget) operation, high accuracy, long range, and/or the ability to defeat countermeasures. Examples include submarines, stealth aircraft, advanced missiles, and directed energy weapons. The combination of high military effectiveness, low substitutability and low opportunity cost could serve as guidelines for selecting candidates for this approach.[2]

Another approach would be to emphasize restraint in the sale of weapons that raise international concerns because of the risks they pose to noncombatants or because of their perceived repugnance even when used on the battlefield. A candidate list of such weapons, known by some as "weapons of ill-repute," would include certain incendiary and fragmentation weapons, weapons easily diverted to terrorist use such as advanced man-portable air defense systems, and weapons currently under U.S. and international review, such as blinding lasers and antipersonnel mines.[3] Discussions of global bans on the export of weapons in which no government has a significant military stake and that pose particular risks to noncombatants could be a reasonable starting point for beginning a multinational dialogue on technology transfer restraint.

The significance of controls on weapons of ill-repute would initially be far more political than military. Achieving agreement even on broad principles or codes of conduct for the sales of such weapons, however, could serve as a foundation for more ambitious undertakings. Such efforts could build on existing instruments such as the 1980 Convention on Conventional Weapons (CCW, also known as the Inhumane Weapons Convention), which prohibits weapons that produce fragments not detectable by x-rays, incendiary weapons, and some land mines.[4]

---

[1]The hoped-for progress on these issues was not realized at the Vienna meeting of the Wassenaar participants on April 3–4, 1996. Talks will resume after the Russian elections in July.

[2]Weapons have low substitutability when alternatives are prohibitively costly or nonexistent; low opportunity cost refers to minimizing the economic losses for potential sellers. For further details on this proposal, see the companion report, MR-771-OSD, Chapter Three.

[3]Historically, the definition of "weapons of ill repute" included the concept of low military utility. As more significant technology has been packaged into smaller and smaller devices and weapons, however, some rather high-utility weapons have become targets of the same proliferation/control concerns as were land mines, incendiary bombs, and the like. For example, man-portable anti-aircraft missiles and blinding lasers, which by any measure have significant military utility in various scenarios, have come to be viewed as part of the subset of items for which the threat to noncombatants and the risk of diversion to terrorist use can be severe, thus the "weapons of ill repute" label.

[4]The United States has not ratified Protocol 3 of the CCW, which restricts the use of incendiary weapons.

CONTROL OF TECHNOLOGIES

Key technologies are those with potentially significant military applications, including certain "dual-use" technologies, along with a smaller set of "military-only" items such as fuse or warhead technologies. This broad category of items, in the form of hardware in some cases but "knowledge" in others, may move in international trade in what is on the surface a nonmilitary and therefore nonproblematic way. Given today's weapon systems engineering and the growing roles of sensing, data processing, and communication technologies in the effectiveness of advanced weapons and military operations, uncontrolled proliferation of relevant technology is highly undesirable.[5]

Supplier restrictions still have a critical role to play in identifying and targeting the technologies that are almost exclusively pertinent to weapons development—that are not "dual-use." Many vital inputs for missile development, such as advanced guidance needed for missile accuracy, remain in the hands of just a few suppliers, and such commerce can be segregated from routine trade. In addition, export control policies are needed that are effective in a technology market in which there are many channels of supply, where many advanced technologies that can contribute to weapons development have wholly legitimate nonmilitary applications, and where economic imperatives make a competitive trading system inevitable.

In short, the growing weakness of supply-side restraints flowing from the commercialization of military technologies argues for a control system that begins to shift the focus away from controls only on exports to controls on the actual end use of technologies. Likewise, for items that are commercial in origin but have dual or multiple uses—from biotechnologies to space systems—nonproliferation efforts increasingly will have to shift away from an exclusive focus on supply controls toward monitoring the application of technologies. Although current agreements include end-use assurances, they have not been reliably enforced. The Board believes that a credible system of end-use assurances is essential and can be achieved.

Such end-use arrangements will require profoundly greater levels of transparency in the international trading system and a more effective system of enforcement. Like-minded states independently and together must enhance their monitoring, verification, and compliance policies and capabilities. Moreover, judging from the cases of Iraq and North Korea, multinational cooperation to isolate and penalize violators must go well beyond today's levels.

TRANSPARENCY

Transparency both within the decisionmaking process of individual nations and among trading nations will play an ever more critical role as more and more nations develop advanced industries. Although recognition of this fact will not alone meet the challenge, it does provide a principle around which efforts can be focused. The

---

[5]See MR-771-OSD, Chapter Three, for a discussion of various proposals for the control of the transfer of military technologies.

Board believes that important deficiencies in transparency exist within the Executive Branch of the United States, as discussed in Chapter Five, and that these should be relatively easy to address. The problem of significant improvement in international transparency is more daunting.

The Board heard many proposals for greater transparency, most of them technical. Their viability will require a greater degree of cooperation and common purpose among trading nations than now exists. An obstacle to progress in this regard is that a transparency requirement for reporting and monitoring the disposition of sensitive technology would seem to impose added regulatory burdens for industry and for recipients, as could the administration of sufficient sanctions to deter misuse. It is true that a new system would have to be devised and be seen as reliable. However, if this could reduce intrusions on legitimate trade, now at the core of grievances about existing regimes, while still protecting credible nonproliferation objectives, reduced regulations could result and be welcomed by participants.

Western enterprises that manufacture and trade dual-use products have long adhered to cumbersome requirements for prior approval under restrictions imposed by national legislation, CoCom, or more selective regimes such as the MTCR. Many of these arrangements were directed against the former Soviet Union and its Warsaw Treaty allies and have lost much of their original political rationale. But there is still a strong inclination to continue them against countries of concern such as Iraq.

Countries choosing not to join a transparency regime could be denied access to its benefits, or given access on significantly more restrictive terms, at costs that become more directly calculable by governments and individuals. By seeking to advance the principle of free trade for all compliant states, and providing a clear incentive to suppliers and recipients to abide by monitoring arrangements in return for greater market access, the regime could remove many of the political impediments currently hampering control initiatives, including the perception of discriminatory application among potential recipients.

TRANSPARENCY, INTERNATIONAL NEGOTIATIONS, AND INDUSTRIAL COOPERATION

Whether a new control regime should begin as a comprehensive multinational effort, engaging both suppliers and recipients at the outset, or should start with the major advanced countries will depend on prevailing political conditions and the scope of restraint proposals envisioned. A multinational regime could be pursued on several tracks, however, consisting of supplier negotiations and separate recipient negotiations, with regional restraint regimes being considered over time. This could supplement national, bilateral, and informal efforts.

At the international level, a multinational secretariat with the mandate to monitor proliferation in an integrated manner could help redress the problems posed by the fragmentation of existing arrangements and bolster their effectiveness. Such a mechanism could help formalize and streamline control guidelines, establish procedures for routine consultations among participants, and anticipate new technological and political challenges. While it could build on the operational experiences of such institutions as CoCom and the UN Special Commission, the new organization would have to avoid being seen as a supplier cartel. A supplier arrangement that attempts to minimize or avoid consultation with recipient countries would likely be regarded as high-handed and self-defeating. Accordingly, the Board urges that the evolving Wassenaar process strive to ensure such broad and inclusive consultation.

To make such a regime work, particularly as regards technology controls, cooperation with industry is essential. In the United States, for example, restraint policies have been imposed by the government after only limited consultation with industry. One result has been industry antagonism and efforts to undercut unpopular policies through Congress or the media. But industry has a potentially vital role to play in a future restraint regime. As the main source of expertise on technology and usually the party most involved in actual transactions, industry may be the best means by which governments can track compliance with restrictions on exported products. Industry could help identify relevant building blocks and "fingerprints" for particular proscribed technologies and devise safeguards and other end-use restrictions to prevent the diversion of civilian or dual-use equipment to military application.

We think industry may well prove supportive of at least selective export controls for advanced dual-use products that raise international security concerns. Facing continued conflicts over the permissibility of exports of supercomputers and associated software, for example, IBM set about in 1990 to help devise credible end-use assurances that would prevent diversion of civilian computers to military uses while permitting freer trade with legitimate clients.

Chapter Three

INTERNATIONAL INSTITUTIONAL DEVELOPMENT

With modest exceptions, international concern about conventional proliferation has not been translated into effective policy implementation. Following a series of negotiations beginning in 1991, for example, a majority of members of the General Assembly approved a proposal in December of that year to establish an international registry of arms exports and imports, under the auspices of the UN Secretary-General. The Permanent Five (P-5) members of the Security Council (the United States, Russia, China, Britain, and France) also began discussions of procedures and negotiated guidelines for prior notification of arms contracts, an important initiative whose implementation failed earlier in the decade but was revisited during negotiations of the Wassenaar Arrangement. The "Small Group" of Arrangement members, which includes four of the Permanent Five (not China) along with Italy and Germany, continues to discuss notification procedures.

At a minimum, the arms registry, if it succeeds, will represent an important move toward greater transparency in the international defense trade system and a resumption of P-5 cooperation may prove critical in troubled regions. The Board wishes to emphasize that important international efforts such as these will not advance without better data on arms and technology sales. The Board believes that current estimates of the international arms market made in dollars or other currencies, however useful, cannot substitute for comprehensive data on disaggregated quantities and specific types of transfers. Indeed, they can mislead assessments of international security consequences and estimates of economic implications. Also, a much more detailed approach to quantity and quality must be developed, in any case, if the transparency regimes anticipated in this report are to have the desired effects.

Within international lending institutions such as the International Bank for Reconstruction and Development, the International Money Fund, and the more recently established European Bank for Reconstruction and Development, there is growing interest in linking international financial assistance to various norms of military behavior, including defense expenditures and, more ambitiously, compliance with treaties. This represents a marked shift in attitude among institutions that for decades promulgated the formal fiction that a country's defense sector should not be included in evaluations of its economic performance, political stability, and other variables that go into decisions about credit or aid eligibility.

Bilateral aid agencies, such as the U.S. Agency for International Development and Japan's Ministry of Foreign Affairs, have made it explicit that they will consider military behavior in granting aid. Further examples of this linkage may be found in various Western arrangements to provide financial and material assistance to former Soviet bloc countries.

Direct financial inducements are being used increasingly for advancing efforts to constrain the diffusion of former Soviet weapon designers and engineers from lending their expertise to defense industries in developing nations. The recent increase in the membership of the MTCR may also be a basis for discussions of additional conventional weapons technologies, including more comprehensive understanding about advanced cruise missiles. The regime has grown from an initial membership of seven in 1987 to twenty-eight members to date, of which Russia, South Africa, and Brazil are the most recent. In addition, while not official members, China, Israel, and Ukraine have agreed to abide by MTCR guidelines.

The possibility of aid to countries to establish export control programs needs examination. There is precedent: With the assistance of Western specialists, the Russian government has announced plans to set up a special body, composed of senior officials from departments in the foreign policy, industry, economics, finance, and security ministries, for exercising political control over arms exports. It may be that the Wassenaar Arrangement could provide a forum for exploring such initiatives.

In evaluating candidate regimes, the Board heard from a number of officials in the responsible agencies—Departments of Defense, State, and Commerce, Arms Control and Disarmament Agency (ACDA), etc.—regarding conceptual approaches to new restraints. The ideas put forth included several aimed at creating incentives or mitigating economic losses for prospective signatories of such regimes. In all likelihood, these ideas will continue to be analyzed and debated in the ongoing U.S. government policy process.

The Board has looked closely at these ideas, and believes that two of them warrant brief description and comment here. One proposed incentive would involve a system of free defense trade in nearly all existing advanced weapons and related technologies within a signatory group as a "carrot" for regime members agreeing to rigorous transfer restraints on agreed items to third parties. The Board doubts the feasibility of this concept. Access to U.S. technology and weapons should continue to require a broad determination by the United States as to shared policy and values with the recipient, often including specific security treaty participation or other agreements.

Providing such access to a constraint regime signatory simply in return for agreement not to sell certain items to third parties could have a perverse effect on nations not already possessing significant defense technology or production capacity. In such cases, proliferation might in fact be increased through "incentive" transfers to those who heretofore had no such access. In our view, proliferation involving one or more recipient countries does not represent a useful incentive for restraint regimes, the very purpose of which is to reduce or halt that same proliferation elsewhere.

The second incentive the Board finds inappropriate is one based on the technological superiority of the United States and certain key allies. Some officials postulated using membership in joint weapons development or production programs, and others suggested offering access to specific dual-use or defense technologies as well, as carrots to certain nations to induce their acceptance of restraint regime rules. The Board sees a potential proliferation problem in this approach as well.

In addition, we believe that there are problems of practicality with these concepts. Past efforts at major multinational weapons development or production programs have for the most part failed to deliver their touted economic benefits for either the United States or its partners. As a result, industry and its shareholders—as well as a number of governments—show little interest today in such arrangements, except on extremely favorable economic terms. As for using technology transfer as a regime incentive, there is a further question. Since industry in the United States, Europe, and Japan holds proprietary claim to most such technologies—especially those developed commercially—it is not feasible for the United States or other governments to offer simply to "give" this knowledge to a prospective regime member. The legal obstacles in determining proprietary rights and establishing compensatory value for such transfer, plus the obvious federal budget impact of any required compensation, are probably insuperable.

Our purpose in this discussion is not to discourage broad, creative thinking in pursuing new restraint concepts. Nor do we want to understate the potential value of incentives for inducing participation by nations with obvious economic reasons to seek markets for their arms industries. The Board also recognizes that the desire for full participation in other high-technology markets has provided nonproliferation incentives for many nations. However, we believe that the primary motivation for national and multinational restraint is and should be the resulting genuine increase in national security derived from nonproliferation of advanced weaponry.

Another area for examination is the rationalization and integration of existing nonproliferation regimes. The United States alone currently participates in at least six distinct control arrangements to restrict nuclear, chemical, and biological weapons, missiles, select conventional weapons, and dual-use technologies. They each have had varied histories and political fortunes, and contain different mechanisms for surveillance, control, enforcement, and administration.

Even as they operate as separate entities, in practice the regimes face similar legal, regulatory, and administrative challenges. Over time, the phenomenon of weapons proliferation has in and of itself become synergistic as more countries seek to acquire proscribed weapons, weapons production technology, and material as part of concerted national strategies. Violations experienced within the various regimes often involve the same arms traders and conduits of clandestine transfer, and thus pose common intelligence and enforcement challenges as well. International intelligence sharing, shared procedures for monitoring and inspections of trade flows, joint preparation of lists of controlled items and end-users, and a concerted effort to marshal political support for enforcement would obviously benefit from streamlining existing national and multinational enforcement mechanisms.[1]

These measures might be implemented by the Wassenaar Arrangement, which would receive data collected through national licensing procedures. Data sharing and transparency measures to promote the desired restraint would have to be accompanied by an international consensus that concealment of information should be subject to penalties, just as there must be punitive measures for violations of internationally accepted norms.

The principle of open disclosure and cooperative enforcement is already imbedded in the Chemical Weapons Convention, which has been signed by 160 nations to date. Similar undertakings include, *inter alia,* the U.S. effort to recast the premises and guidelines of the Export Administration Act, continued development of the Wassenaar Arrangement, and support for more intrusive challenge inspections pursuant to the Nuclear Non-Proliferation Treaty.

Again, the history of past efforts to limit armaments teaches us that restraints depending solely on supplier cartels are insufficient and are further weakened when they appear discriminatory. As with the effort to control drug trafficking or other illicit forms of trade, control agreements must ultimately focus on the demand side. It is in regional contexts that conventional balances deserve the most attention, but where consultative mechanisms are the least developed. For restraint initiatives to be considered seriously outside of the advanced countries, they will require devising new mechanisms for regional security consultations that can bring new states into a broader security partnership.

Regardless of how much progress in arms restraint agreements is or is not achieved, the development of common understandings to guide crisis management and crisis resolution among nations will become increasingly important as regional power alignments become more diffuse and clients more militarily capable. Bilateral and multilateral regional security talks, as have been pursued in the Middle East and South Asia in recent years, are in and of themselves a vital undertaking that in turn could serve as the foundation for agreements on arms shipments tailored to specific areas. Such initiatives are unlikely to succeed, however, if the major suppliers are engaged in intense competition for arms markets motivated by their respective domestic interests.

---

[1] Perhaps the most important example of the benefits of an integrated approach to nonproliferation is the case of Iraq. By combining nuclear, chemical, biological, and missile technologies under Resolution 687—the blueprint for the disarmament of Iraq—the UN Security Council explicitly recognized the need for an integrated approach to the detection and destruction of the Iraqi arsenal. Combined verification efforts, in turn, have proven vital to the effectiveness of 687. Many of these lessons could apply to other control regimes.

Chapter Four

DOMESTIC ECONOMIC AND INDUSTRIAL BASE ISSUES

The Board's review included examination of issues regarding the defense industrial base and associated employment. The Board heard from both government and industry representatives on these subjects, and from interested scholars and citizens, and looked closely at the economic impact of controlling conventional arms transfers.

In response to the profound decline in Department of Defense procurement over the past five years, U.S. industry has downsized, shut down, and otherwise restructured many production facilities and weapons assembly lines. Some firms have exited the business in particular weapons categories, but there remain one or more producers active in each key product area. Further, while the global trade in conventional arms has dropped significantly from the historic highs of the mid-eighties, the U.S. totals have remained relatively constant. In today's shrinking international arms market, the United States has thus significantly increased its market share, from an average of 21 percent in the 1980s[1] to a 1994 level of 52 percent of the total world volume.[2]

Nevertheless, as specific sales are reviewed and key regional transfer policies debated (the Middle East and South Asia are perhaps the most significant examples), U.S. industry has put forward declining DoD procurement budgets and the value of "warm" production lines as arguments for approval. Indeed, a number of "mainline" weapon system production lines today are operating solely to meet foreign sales requirements, with no budgeted DoD procurement of those systems for U.S. use. Examples include the F-15 fighter, the M1 main battle tank, and the Harpoon antiship missile.

THE ROLE OF ECONOMIC CRITERIA

As discussed more extensively later in this chapter, the Board finds that U.S. arms transfer policy can and should be developed and executed separately from issues of maintenance of the defense industrial base, which we believe are better handled by specific DoD industrial base policy. We do not believe that arms sales that would be rejected on the basis of foreign policy and national security considerations should be

---

[1]Average U.S. share of world arms exports, 1983–1989; from U.S. Arms Control and Disarmament Agency, *World Military Expenditures and Arms Transfers, 1993–1994*, February 1995, p. 15.

[2]U.S. share of all arms deliveries worldwide in 1994. See Richard F. Grimmett, *Conventional Arms Transfers to Developing Nations, 1987–1994*, Congressional Research Service, August 4, 1995, p. CRS-82.

approved simply to preserve jobs or keep a production line open. The Board believes it is essential that the U.S. government take steps to make this policy clear at home and abroad.

A policy approving arms transfers solely for industrial base reasons would undercut and perhaps even preclude the very sorts of new and effective international restraint regimes we urge here. If any participating country is allowed to use its independent judgment regarding its own internal economic circumstances as a rationale to transfer a weapon or technology, the whole purpose and nature of a restraint regime would be subverted. Accordingly, the Board believes that it is not only appropriate but mandatory that the United States and other nations agree to handle legitimate domestic economic and defense industrial base issues through other policies and actions, rather than allow them to circumvent restraint agreements for particular weapons and technologies.[3]

The erosion of restraint driven by this sort of economic competition could have severe consequences. The United States and its allies have been fortunate in that their soldiers, sailors, and airmen have seldom had to face in combat advanced conventional weapons of their own manufacture. The few examples, however, are troubling. The Board is concerned that domestic political pressures already strong in major supplier countries could increase significantly the number of risky sales in the name of jobs or the economy. A disturbing image is forming: ever more transfers driven by shrinking defense industries placing increasingly more capable weapons in troubled regions. The exporting states in turn feel compelled to develop and produce even more advanced weapons to counter this proliferation. This increasingly vicious circle is indeed worthy of prevention or early treatment.

FINANCING OF ARMS SALES

The Board also reviewed instances where, under current law, U.S. arms sales are at an economic disadvantage both in competition with equivalent foreign products and as compared with other U.S. exports. As a matter of principle, the Board believes that free trade without the price distorting mechanism of government subsidies is a desirable goal. Excessive government involvement frequently inhibits free trade and reinforces unhealthy special-interest relationships between governments and industries within their jurisdiction, particularly with government owned or subsidized companies. In the case of arms sales, this can lead to strong domestic pressures to make sales of weapons or technologies that may be unwise from an international security perspective. Certain sales to Iraq are a case in point.

U.S. policy toward government financing of its own exports should support the goal of reducing or eliminating subsidies on a global basis.[4] Compromise legislation passed and signed into law in February 1996 creates a defense financing facility de-

---

[3]See discussion in MR-771-OSD, Summary.

[4]This argument is not meant to preclude various forms of U.S. government aid to other nations, such as training assistance, development loans, and outright grants of equipment.

signed to provide government loan guarantees. The selling company or its foreign customer must pay an "exposure fee" to cover potential U.S. government liability. Such an approach can help American companies meet the requirement for government-backed loans that some foreign governments demand. The Board fears that pressure to use the new defense financing facility to provide genuine subsidies will grow unless the goal of reducing and eliminating subsidies among competing suppliers is advanced. The Board believes that the Administration and the Congress should work together to develop and implement a strategy to gain multinational restraint on all manner of price distortion and unfair trade practices.

THE R&D RECOUPMENT CHARGE

Current law provides that when certain weapons developed for U.S. use are sold abroad by the U.S. government, a charge is to be added to the price and remitted to the Department of Defense. This requirement, intended to recover part of the U.S. government's original investment, is called an R&D recoupment charge. The case-by-case application of this charge has historically been both uneven and controversial. Various administrations have obtained numerous exceptions from Congress, allowing the charge to be reduced or waived for foreign policy reasons. General exceptions currently exist in law for individual nations, including NATO allies.

Industry has argued that the charge discriminates against defense contractors, since such recoupment rules have no such parallel in other areas where the U.S. government has made major R&D investments in developing and purchasing capital equipment—for example, power generation, telecommunications, computer systems, and nuclear reactor technology. Further, American firms cite the R&D recoupment charge as a clear and sometimes significant price discriminator against them as they compete for sales in third countries against foreign producers. These foreign competitors have no equivalent added costs, and may even benefit from overt or covert subsidies from their respective governments. Based upon its review of this issue, the Board supports the Administration's stated intent to seek repeal of the current R&D recoupment charge.

OFFSET PROVISIONS

The Board also heard differing opinions on a long-standing issue regarding arms transfers—the negotiation of offset provisions in sales contracts that involve agreements to buy one or more aspects of the weapon program in question in the purchasing country's own economy, very much like the current approach by foreign automobile producers selling in the United States. Such direct offset agreements can also involve conducting final assembly, integration, and test tasks in the purchasing countries, similar again to the automotive market's trend to shift foreign product final assembly onshore to the United States.

Nations purchasing arms are sometimes unable to provide cost competitive or technologically suitable weapons components, and in such cases often use indirect offset as a way to defray part of the costs of their purchase and the negative trade balance impact of such major imports. U.S. and other exporting weapons producers have in these instances agreed to purchase or broker a wide variety of nondefense items from the purchasing country, or to make equity investments in commercial enterprises there.[5]

The Board notes that certain opponents of current arms control policy, along with organized labor, argue that the U.S. government should prohibit, or at least significantly restrict, offset agreements as a part of arms sales. Primary reasons voiced in support of this position are that offsets can involve destabilizing proliferation (as in providing design or manufacturing expertise) and that, similarly, they create economic loss both through near-term diversion of jobs overseas and through the long-term risk of strengthening foreign competitors in the marketplace. On the first point, the Board agrees that all transfers of arms and related technology warrant careful government review, especially when the transaction creates a new military or industrial capability abroad. However, if offset provisions pass such an examination, the economic aspects of each sale should be left to the producer and purchaser.[6]

In considering the second issue, that of job loss, which applies both to direct and indirect offsets, the Board finds no persuasive argument for U.S. policy constraints other than the same basic arms/technology transfer criteria noted above.[7] The long and successful history of U.S. commercial trade in high-technology items (from power-generation equipment to industrial machinery to transportation vehicles) is full of direct and indirect offset arrangements, and the net benefit to the U.S. economy has been substantial. The overall economic and employment impact of foreign trade—of which offsets are a small subset—is highly positive. In summary, the Board believes that once a proposed transaction meets U.S. policy on arms control and transfer restraint, that same transaction's specific business terms between seller and buyer should not be artificially altered for economic reasons by the governments involved.

---

[5]Indirect offset examples from past sales show great diversity and creativity on the part of the buyers and sellers. The list includes consumer goods of all types, commitments to a certain volume of tourist trade (involving airline tickets, hotel and tour group reservations, and visits to certain designated regions), bartering of various foodstuffs into the U.S. or other economies, and joint venture equity investments in everything from powerplants to hotels to commercial and industrial real estate and construction.

[6]A long series of major arms exports with significant offset, from the original F-16 European Production Group in the late 1970s to the Japanese F-15 co-production arrangement, through the Korean K-1 tank development, to the more recent Japanese F-2 (formerly FS-X) fighter development, have all involved this type of major government review and item-by-item approval for the direct offset involved.

[7]If the alternative to granting offset demands could be simply retaining complete workshare (all jobs) here, then U.S. industry would (and in some cases actually can) do so. In cases where a U.S. firm faces no credible competition and where the buyer has a strong security rationale for the weapon in question, American firms have been able to negotiate without significant offset concessions. In most instances today, however, U.S. and other producers use offset as well as other economic concessions to secure business in a competitive environment. In that market, winning while conceding a portion of workshare through offset results in the creation or extension of American jobs. It is important to remember that if the alternative is that the U.S. firm loses the sales contract, the U.S. economy ends up losing every one of the jobs involved.

THE DEFENSE INDUSTRIAL BASE

The final economic issue reviewed by the Board involves arguments by some in the U.S. defense industry who contend that robust foreign arms sales are critical for sustaining an adequate defense industrial base.[8] The Board rejects any notion that stepping back from well-conceived arms restraint policies is the way to ensure the health of our defense industrial base. The radical restructuring and adjustment to much smaller markets in the world's defense industries will, as the RAND and other studies document, continue into the foreseeable future. The export market is much too small to offset the overall decline in defense procurement. Hence, the existence of export sales opportunities for U.S. firms, while obviously valuable in preserving jobs and production lines in many cases, will not be sufficient to allow the affected companies to forgo the downsizing required for their survival.

As President Clinton has stated, U.S. defense firms and their labor forces should not be the scapegoats of sweeping sectoral change. The Administration has created a defense industrial conversion program to help American companies adjust to the decline in procurement. Contractors who do not succeed in diversifying out of defense production will still face difficult problems of excess capacity and job losses, but arms exports that would not otherwise be approved are not the proper remedy. Likewise, means other than questionable arms sales are available to maintain or reconstitute essential elements of the defense industrial base.

In short, the Board believes that, in general, the best solution to overcapacity in defense industries, in the United States and worldwide, is to reduce supply rather than increase demand. For that reason, the Board has concerns about any cooperative approach or cartel that would constitute a floor for rather than a constraint on arms sales. Some companies now in the world arms market are not competitive and are financial drains on their respective nations' economies. With due regard to the complexities involved, the Board believes that an approach that discourages subsidizing or otherwise maintaining uneconomical defense industries makes the most sense. Unwise arms sales remain unwise no matter how many jobs are involved; moreover, those jobs are protected only in the short term.

---

[8]On this subject, the Board commends the reader to the RAND analysis, MR-771-OSD, Chapter Five.

IMPROVING THE GOVERNMENT'S PROCESSES FOR EXPORT CONTROL POLICY AND ADMINISTRATION

As we stated in the Introduction, good policy and good process go hand in hand. The present U.S. system of export controls is, however, so dispersed that the line between policy formulation and its implementation is murky and day-to-day administration is less efficient than it should be. More specific attention at the senior policymaking level is needed. A December 6, 1995 Presidential Executive Order[1] on export controls restructures the review process for dual-use licenses, but it is too early to judge its impact.

The outcome of deliberations over technology and arms sales often is influenced by the relative clout of the agencies involved, the perceived importance of the recipient in domestic political terms, and even the expertise or endurance of individual participants involved in evaluating cases. Bureaucratic warfare, rather than analysis, tends to be the *modus operandi* in what is often a protracted process of plea bargaining and political compromise that may not reflect long-term national objectives.

In its examination of arms proliferation policy, the Board recognizes that U.S. goals are neither solely nor even primarily in the arms control arena. The composite national security strategy, foreign policy, and domestic agenda of the government reflects an attempt to optimize among incommensurate and not always complementary objectives. Thus, the interagency process created to make decisions should represent effectively the diverse views of the various departments and agencies created to address different objectives of the United States. Certainly, for example, the State Department must weigh diplomatic considerations, the Defense Department must consider its own programs and overseas security relationships, and the Commerce Department must look to trade. All of the major departments also have an interest in preventing the proliferation of weapons and technologies of concern, but in each case that perspective is subject to countervailing pressures at all levels of decision-making.

Separate export review mechanisms grew up first for weapons and later for dual-use technologies. Consequently, there are unnecessary differences and duplication between these two processes.[2] Further, the process by which the various responsible

---

[1] Executive Order 12981 may be found in MR-771-OSD.

[2] Under the Arms Export Control Act, the State Department administers controls on the export of weapons and related technology and services, based on the U.S. Munitions List, with input from the Defense,

21

agencies review individual export requests, and are able to communicate their positions to the designated coordinating department or agency, is cumbersome and outdated. Unlike similar government policy processes within a single agency, the export licensing mechanism has seen little modernization or upgrade, largely because of the challenge of getting broad interagency agreement on information system hardware, software, and operating procedures.

There is nothing inevitable about this situation. The solution rests with a sustained effort by senior policymakers, particularly the President and the National Security Council. Because export controls are justified on national security and foreign policy grounds and because of the many agencies involved, the National Security Council must take the lead in fundamental policy formulation. The Board does not here try to lay out exactly what policy mechanisms the NSC should use—obviously, different agencies will have different points of view and a means to give them a voice in policymaking and to resolve major disputes is required. But the NSC's role should be more than that of a mediator. It should take the lead in formulating policy and issuing policy guidance. This will require deeper institutionalization of the export control policymaking process—a process that today is episodic and tends to produce guidance at such a high level of generality as to be much less useful than it should be.

The day-to-day administration of export controls can also be greatly improved. The most prominent players in export control decisions are now the State Department, the Commerce Department, and the Treasury Department (which implements various country-specific embargoes under the International Emergency Economic Powers Act). Although the Defense Department does not make final licensing decisions, its views and those of the Arms Control and Disarmament Agency heavily influence those decisions. The Board found reason to be concerned that due regard may not be given to nonproliferation issues, absent a clear voice representing that perspective at all levels, including the Oval Office. The Board believes that this responsibility has rested primarily with the United States Arms Control and Disarmament Agency since 1961. Until such time as the threat from proliferation is greatly diminished, the Board believes that such an independent agency is essential and a further strengthening of its nonproliferation mandate is warranted.

As already indicated, these agencies have different and often conflicting missions. As a result, too much time is spent in settling disputes and not enough in operating the export control system; senior policymakers often lack a balanced view of important policy issues; regulations overlap and sometimes conflict; enforcement jurisdictions overlap; and information flow within and among agencies is inadequate, inefficient, or both.

Energy, and Treasury Departments, the Arms Control and Disarmament Agency, and the Intelligence Community. Under the Export Administration Act (EAA) and its antecedents, exports of dual-use items are administered and controlled by the Commerce Department, with input from the same agencies. Over time, the EAA and associated regulations have been expanded from their initial focus on ensuring adequate domestic supplies of critical technologies during World War II to support for efforts to keep certain enabling technologies out of the hands of hostile states. The MTCR, nuclear nonproliferation, and chemical and biological weapons control regimes are all supported through this law, as was the CoCom regime. Although the EAA expired in 1994, the law and associated regulations continue to be enforced through Executive Order 12924, issued pursuant to the International Emergency Economic Powers Act.

Proponents of consolidation of some or all elements of the arms and dual-use technology export application, review, and approval process into a single organization cite two primary benefits of such change. To the extent that multiple offices, staffs, registration and analysis procedures, forms, data systems, and review processes could be rationalized and consolidated, there could be significant budgetary savings. In addition, the many American businesses—both large and small—seeking permission to export would benefit from the cost, time, and consistency advantages of so-called "one-stop shopping." American business has a legitimate concern that its international competitors gain an advantage from the relatively inconsistent and slow-moving U.S. regulation of technology exports.

Such consolidation could, as a first step, include the administrative aspects of case applications and information service for applicants. It could also be expanded to provide individual approval/denial decisions in clear-cut cases where the responsible policy agencies were comfortable delegating such authority without requiring formal interagency review. At the extreme, it is conceivable that a set of statutory revisions could transfer and consolidate legal authority for essentially all cases in a single department, agency, or office.

While the Board takes no position as to where and in what form such consolidation would best be accomplished, it agrees that the Executive Branch should pursue such an approach. Even if only the first two steps noted above were executed—processing of applications and approval authority for certain routine or noncontroversial cases—the efficiencies would be significant. In addition, the government's ability to then share and distribute transfer information both internally and externally would also be enhanced. Such increased efficiency and transparency would further many U.S. interests and goals, both in nonproliferation policy and elsewhere. While consolidation all the way to the third step described here has potential benefits, it also raises other questions regarding both feasibility (securing the complex legislative agreement and change required) and desirability (overall policymaking consolidation by its nature can reduce the interplay of the different responsibilities and perspectives at Defense, State, Commerce, Energy, ACDA, and other interested departments and agencies). The Board accordingly believes the Administration's focus should be on the first two areas, where the benefits clearly outweigh the costs and risks.

Whether or not consolidation takes place, an investment in modern data base management is badly needed; it will save money and make for more consistent and intelligent application of policy in the long-run. The development of such a regime has been frustrated by failure to get interagency agreement on information system hardware, software, and operating procedures, and by lack of adequate funding.

In summary the Board recommends the following principles to guide this much-needed innovation and improvement in the interagency process.

1. Given the many interests involved, the NSC process must be used, and used effectively. A senior official from the NSC staff, as opposed to any of the affected agencies, should lead this extensive effort, with the clear goal of promptly improving

the decisionmaking effectiveness and efficiency for all arms and dual-use technology export issues.

2. Insofar as possible without new legislation, the President should, by executive order, merge the administrative and routine decisionmaking arms and technology transfer control processes, and should ensure maximum efficiency and interagency coordination, as well as the integration of their information more fully into the policy process.

3. Through the NSC process, a package of legislative and regulatory changes to integrate the current transfer regulations into a single, coherent framework should be developed and proposed to the Congress.

4. The Administration should identify and empower a responsible agency or organization, working closely through the NSC interagency process, to develop an integrated management information system for use by all agencies involved in the export control process. This new system should be optimized for efficient electronic exchange of information on license applications; reporting requirements for the United Nations, other international organizations, and the U.S. government; and for direct interconnect with the intelligence and enforcement communities as they both input and draw information from the license application and review process. The Administration should propose and the Congress agree to a one-time appropriation to fund procurement and installation of the system.

5. The Administration should continue and redouble its current efforts to increase the intelligence community's focus and capabilities to understand and monitor key conventional weapons capabilities, overt and covert export to third parties of such weapons or technologies, and the potential near- and longer-term impact for U.S. and allied joint commanders and forces.

Chapter Six

SUMMARY

Advisory Boards such as ours invariably grapple with broad mandates, changing circumstances, and widely diverse interests concerned with the substance of Board charters. As we have noted, our approach has been to review and offer recommendations on both policy and process. We have endeavored to review the Administration's current policies regarding conventional arms control, and have commented only where we concluded it appropriate. We are under no illusions as to our limitations in addressing but a few of the myriad interests and issues of great concern to the various parties concerned with arms proliferation policy.

At the core of our recommendations is our belief in the value, indeed the necessity, of strong U.S. leadership in the quest for more effective arms control in the nation's interest. This leadership must come from the top, involving the President, his Cabinet, and the Congress. As we have stated, within the Executive Branch that initiative requires in the first instance, more policy-oriented interagency coordination and execution of policy, which in turn requires a strong focal point of administration leadership. We believe that leadership can and must come from the National Security Council's long-standing interagency process. That NSC-led process, in addition to selecting and implementing the kind of advanced conventional arms restraint regime postulated here, must also address the thorny question of governmental process the Board has highlighted. There is no doubt that *how* we make policy and *how* we make individual arms or technology transfer decisions is absolutely critical to achieving U.S. arms control goals.

We believe that it is of great importance to reemphasize a point about focus. The Board's recommendations for both policy and process are built on a long-term commitment to improvement and progress, rather than on any discrete preferred regime or proposed organizational realignment. The world struggles today with the implications of advanced conventional weapons. It will in the future be confronted with yet another generation of weapons, whose destructive power, size, cost, and availability can raise many more problems even than their predecessors today. These challenges will require a new culture among nations, one that accepts increased responsibility for control and restraint, despite short-term economic and political factors pulling in other directions. While the image of a "journey" has become almost trite in today's culture, it is just such a concept that perhaps best describes the strategy for success in achieving necessary restraint on conventional arms and strategic technologies, and the resulting increase in international security.

The Administration has in recent months, in parallel with the Board's deliberations, taken steps such as the Wassenaar Arrangement, which could be the key to more enduring and comprehensive successes in restraint and control. Leaders in the Administration and in the Congress should be heartened to know that there is no shortage of individuals, in and out of government, whose energy and commitment can contribute to the ongoing effort. We are proud to have been a part of that dialogue, and are committed to continuing our participation. We summarize here the major recommendations put forward in our report:

- Effective restraint requires international cooperation. U.S. leadership is essential to this end.

- The fundamental principles of national security, international and regional security, and arms control must be the basis for international agreement. The inevitable economic pressures that will confront individual states should not be allowed to subvert these principles.

- Sustainable, multilateral negotiations over an issue as controversial as arms transfers are best served by beginning with modest objectives that can be expanded over time. The Wassenaar Arrangement represents the most practical and promising forum to date in which to address the dangers of conventional weapons and technology proliferation.

- New international export control policies are needed for a technology market where there are numerous channels of supply and where many advanced technologies relevant to weapons development are commercial in origin. This requires augmenting controls on the supply of a technology, with a greater emphasis on disclosing and monitoring end-use.

- U.S. arms transfer policy can and should be developed and executed separate from policies for maintenance of the defense industrial base. It is not only appropriate but essential that the United States and other nations handle legitimate domestic economic and defense industrial base issues through such separate policies and actions, rather than use them to abrogate or subvert arms control agreements for particular weapons and technologies.

- Arms and weapons technology transfers should take place without the price-distorting mechanism of government subsidies or penalties. The R&D recoupment charge, which is inconsistent with the federal government's treatment of sunk investment costs in any other area of policy or budget expenditure, should be eliminated. Arms exports should not receive subsidized financing; rather, the effort should be to eliminate such distortions internationally.

- There should not be governmental constraints on direct and indirect offsets other than the review, under established standards, of any arms/technology transfer involved. The overall economic and employment impact of foreign trade is highly positive, and any attempt to dictate or curtail pricing, workshare, or "countertrade" agreements between buyer and seller is counterproductive.

- The current fragmentation of U.S. government controls on transfers leads to great inefficiency and uncertain policy implementation, to the detriment of proliferation controls on the one hand and to the disadvantage of legitimate U.S. commerce on the other. Administration, information systems, and routine decisionmaking should be consolidated. An integrated management information system should be developed as soon as possible for use by all agencies involved in the export control process. In the longer run, statutory revisions to integrate the entire process in a single office should be pursued.

- Within the U.S. government, the NSC should give substantially greater priority to leading and improving the interagency arms export control process.

- The Administration should increase the intelligence community's focus and capabilities to understand and monitor conventional weapons and technologies developments and transfers.

Respectfully submitted,

4829

Federal Register

Vol. 60, No. 15

Tuesday, January 24, 1995

Presidential Documents

Title 3—

The President

Executive Order 12946 of January 20, 1995

President's Advisory Board on Arms Proliferation Policy

By the authority vested in me as President by the Constitution and the laws of the United States of America, including section 1601 of the National Defense Authorization Act, Fiscal Year 1994 (Public Law 103–160), and the Federal Advisory Committee Act, as amended (5 U.S.C. App. 2) ("Act"), except that subsections (e) and (f) of section 10 of such Act do not apply, and section 301 of title 3, United States Code, it is hereby ordered as follows:

Section 1. *Establishment.* There is established within the Department of Defense the "President's Advisory Board on Arms Proliferation Policy" ("Board"). The Board shall consist of five members who shall be appointed by the President from among persons in private life who are noted for their stature and expertise regarding the proliferation of strategic and advanced conventional weapons and are from diverse backgrounds. The President shall designate one of the members as Chairperson of the Board.

Sec. 2. *Functions.* The Board shall advise the President on implementation of United States conventional arms transfer policy, other issues related to arms proliferation policy, and on other matters deemed appropriate by the President. The Board shall report to the President through the Assistant to the President for National Security Affairs.

Sec. 3. *Administration.* (a) The heads of executive agencies shall, to the extent permitted by law, provide to the Board such information as it may require for the purpose of carrying out its functions.

(b) Members of the Board shall serve without compensation, but shall be allowed travel expenses, including per diem in lieu of subsistence, as authorized by law, including 5 U.S.C. 5701–5707 and section 7(d) of the Act, for persons serving intermittently in government service.

(c) The Department of Defense or the head of any other Federal department or agency may detail to the Board, upon request of the Chairperson of the Board, any of the personnel of the department or agency to assist the Board in carrying out its duties.

(d) The Secretary of Defense shall designate a federally funded research and development center with expertise in the matters covered by the Board to provide the Board with such support services as the Board may need to carry out its duties.

(e) The Department of Defense shall provide the Board with administrative services, facilities, staff, and other support services necessary for the performance of its functions.

Sec. 4. *General.* (a) The Board shall terminate 30 days after the date on which the President submits the final report of the Board to the Congress.

(b) For reasons of national security or for such other reasons as specified in section 552(b) of title 5, United States Code, the Board shall not provide public notice or access to meetings at which national security information will be discussed. Authority to make such determinations shall reside with the Secretary of Defense or his designee who must be an official required to be appointed by and with the advice and consent of the Senate.

(c) Information made available to the Board shall be given all necessary security protection in accordance with applicable laws and regulations.

4830   Federal Register / Vol. 60, No. 15 / Tuesday, January 24, 1995 / Presidential Documents

(d) Each member of the Board and each member of the Board's staff shall execute an agreement not to reveal any classified information obtained by virtue of his or her service with the Board except as authorized by applicable law and regulations.

William J. Clinton

THE WHITE HOUSE,
January 20, 1995.

[FR Doc. 95-1925
Filed 1-20-95; 5:01pm]
Billing code 3195-01-P

Dr. Janne E. Nolan, Chair. Dr. Nolan is a Senior Fellow at the Brookings Institution and an Adjunct Professor in the National Security Studies Program at Georgetown University. Dr. Nolan served as a national security specialist in the Executive Branch and in the U.S. Senate until 1987, including as a delegate to the U.S.-Soviet conventional arms transfer negotiations during the Carter Administration. She is the author of several books and numerous articles about U.S. security policy, and serves as a member of the Secretary of Defense's Defense Advisory Board.

Edward Randolph Jayne II. Dr. Jayne, of Vienna, Virginia, is a member of Heidrick & Struggles, an international firm providing executive recruiting services. He has held president, chief operating officer, and other executive positions in several aerospace and other high-technology corporations. His prior government service includes the White House staff, National Security Council staff, and the Office of Management and Budget. Dr. Jayne served as a senior advisor to the recent DoD Commission on Roles and Missions of the Armed Forces, and is a member of the Director of Central Intelligence's Military Advisory Panel. He serves in a general officer assignment in the Air National Guard as Assistant to the Commander in Chief, U.S. Space Command.

Ronald F. Lehman. Dr. Lehman is Assistant to the Director of Lawrence Livermore National Laboratory. He was the Director of the U.S. Arms Control and Disarmament Agency under President Bush. He served as Assistant Secretary of Defense for International Security Policy, Ambassador and U.S. Chief Negotiator on Strategic Offensive Arms (START), and Deputy Assistant to the President for National Security Affairs under President Reagan. He served with the U.S. Army in Vietnam.

David E. McGiffert. Mr. McGiffert is a partner in the law firm of Covington & Burling in Washington, D.C. He served as Assistant Secretary of Defense for International Security Affairs from 1977 to 1981, having previously been Under Secretary of the Army from 1965 to 1968 and Assistant to the Secretary of Defense for Legislative Affairs from 1962 to 1965.

Paul C. Warnke. Mr. Warnke is a partner in the law firm of Howrey & Simon in Washington, D.C. He is also a member of the Scientific and Policy Advisory Committee of the U.S. Arms Control and Disarmament Agency, having served as Director of that agency and Chief U.S. Arms Negotiator in 1977–1978. He also served as Assistant Secretary of Defense for International Security Affairs from 1967 to 1969, and as General Counsel for the Department of Defense from 1966 to 1967.